Connecting Continents

This volume draws together richly textured and deeply empirical accounts of rice and how its cultivation in the Carolina low country stitch together a globe that maps colonial economies, displacement, and the creative solutions of enslaved people conscripted to cultivate its grain.

If sugar fueled the economic hegemony of North Europe in the 18th and 19th century, rice fed it. Nowhere has this story been a more integral part of the landscape than Low Country of the coasts of Georgia, South and North Carolina. Rice played a key role in the expansion of slavery in the Carolinas during the 18th century as West African captives were enslaved, in part for their expertise in growing rice. Contributors to this volume explore the varied genealogies of rice cultivation in the Low Country through archaeological, anthropological, and historical research. This multi-sited volume draws on case studies from Guinea, Sierra Leone, and South Carolina, the Caribbean and India to both compare and connect these disparate regions. Through these studies the reader will learn how the rice cultivation knowledge of untold numbers of captive Africans contributed to the development of the Carolinas and by extension, the United States and Europe.

The chapters in this book were originally published as a special issue of *Atlantic Studies*.

Kenneth G. Kelly is Distinguished Professor Emeritus of Anthropology at the University of South Carolina, USA, and Professor of Anthropology by Courtesy Appointment, Syracuse University, USA. He is an archaeologist who explores the Diasporic links between West Africa and the Americas through the lens of plantation slavery and the slave trade and is a pioneer in multi-sited archaeology. He has conducted research in Benin, Guinea, Togo, Jamaica, Guadeloupe, Martinique, and Dominica.

Connecting Continents
Rice Cultivation in South Carolina and the Guinea Coast

Edited by
Kenneth G. Kelly

LONDON AND NEW YORK

First published 2021
by Routledge
2 Park Square, Milton Park, Abingdon, Oxon, OX14 4RN

and by Routledge
52 Vanderbilt Avenue, New York, NY 10017

Routledge is an imprint of the Taylor & Francis Group, an informa business

© 2021 Taylor & Francis

All rights reserved. No part of this book may be reprinted or reproduced or utilised in any form or by any electronic, mechanical, or other means, now known or hereafter invented, including photocopying and recording, or in any information storage or retrieval system, without permission in writing from the publishers.

Trademark notice: Product or corporate names may be trademarks or registered trademarks, and are used only for identification and explanation without intent to infringe.

British Library Cataloguing-in-Publication Data
A catalogue record for this book is available from the British Library

ISBN13: 978-0-367-64412-3

Typeset in Minion Pro
by codeMantra

Publisher's Note
The publisher accepts responsibility for any inconsistencies that may have arisen during the conversion of this book from journal articles to book chapters, namely the inclusion of journal terminology.

Disclaimer
Every effort has been made to contact copyright holders for their permission to reprint material in this book. The publishers would be grateful to hear from any copyright holder who is not here acknowledged and will undertake to rectify any errors or omissions in future editions of this book.

Contents

	Citation Information	vi
	Notes on Contributors	viii
1	Rice and its consequences in the greater "Atlantic" world *Kenneth G. Kelly*	1
2	Atlantic rice and rice farmers: rising from debate, engaging new sources, methods, and modes of inquiry, and asking new questions *Edda L. Fields-Black*	4
3	Sierra Leone in the Atlantic World: concepts, contours, and exchange *Christopher R. DeCorse*	24
4	Employing archaeology to (dis)entangle the nineteenth-century illegal slave trade on the Rio Pongo, Guinea *Kenneth G. Kelly and Elhadj Ibrahima Fall*	45
5	Standing the test of time: embankment investigations, their implications for African technology transfer and effect on African American archaeology in South Carolina *Andrew Agha*	64
6	"This na true story of our history": South Carolina in Sierra Leone's historical memory *Nemata Blyden*	83
7	Risky business: rice and inter-colonial dependencies in the Indian and Atlantic Oceans *Kathleen D. Morrison and Mark W. Hauser*	99
	Index	121

Citation Information

The chapters in this book were originally published in the *Atlantic Studies*, volume 12, issue 3 (2015). When citing this material, please use the original page numbering for each article, as follows:

Chapter 1
Rice and its consequences in the greater "Atlantic" world
Kenneth G. Kelly
Atlantic Studies, volume 12, issue 3 (2015) pp. 273–275

Chapter 2
Atlantic rice and rice farmers: rising from debate, engaging new sources, methods, and modes of inquiry, and asking new questions
Edda L. Fields-Black
Atlantic Studies, volume 12, issue 3 (2015) pp. 276–295

Chapter 3
Sierra Leone in the Atlantic World: concepts, contours, and exchange
Christopher R. DeCorse
Atlantic Studies, volume 12, issue 3 (2015) pp. 296–316

Chapter 4
Employing archaeology to (dis)entangle the nineteenth-century illegal slave trade on the Rio Pongo, Guinea
Kenneth G. Kelly and Elhadj Ibrahima Fall
Atlantic Studies, volume 12, issue 3 (2015) pp. 317–335

Chapter 5
Standing the test of time: embankment investigations, their implications for African technology transfer and effect on African American archaeology in South Carolina
Andrew Agha
Atlantic Studies, volume 12, issue 3 (2015) pp. 336–354

Chapter 6
"This na true story of our history": South Carolina in Sierra Leone's historical memory
Nemata Blyden
Atlantic Studies, volume 12, issue 3 (2015) pp. 355–370

Chapter 7
Risky business: rice and inter-colonial dependencies in the Indian and Atlantic Oceans
Kathleen D. Morrison and Mark W. Hauser
Atlantic Studies, volume 12, issue 3 (2015) pp. 371–392

For any permission-related enquiries please visit:
http://www.tandfonline.com/page/help/permissions

Contributors

Andrew Agha, PhD is an archaeologist with New South and Associates, Inc., USA.

Nemata Blyden is Professor of History and International Affairs at George Washington University, USA.

Christopher R. DeCorse is Professor of Anthropology in the Maxwell School of Citizenship and Public Affairs at Syracuse University, New York, USA.

Elhadj Ibrahima Fall is Rector of the Université Nelson Mandela, Conakry, Guinea.

Edda L. Fields-Black is Associate Professor in the Department of History at Carnegie Mellon University, Pennsylvania, USA.

Mark W. Hauser is Associate Professor of Anthropology at Northwestern University, Illinois, USA.

Kenneth G. Kelly is Distinguished Professor Emeritus of Anthropology at the University of South Carolina, USA, and Professor of Anthropology by Courtesy Appointment, Syracuse University, USA.

Kathleen D. Morrison is the Sally and Alvin V. Shoemaker Professor of Anthropology and department chair at the University of Pennsylvania, USA.

Rice and its consequences in the greater "Atlantic" world

Kenneth G. Kelly

> Plantation slavery and rice agriculture in the Carolina Lowcountry drew upon captive Africans from a wide area of the African continent, but particular note has been made of the contributions of enslaved Africans originating in the Upper Guinea coast region who had sophisticated knowledge of indigenous rice agriculture. The "Black Rice Hypotheses" argues that their knowledge was crucial to the successful plantation regimes. Papers collected in this issue of *Atlantic Studies: Global Currents* explore the consequences of that interaction during the seventeenth, eighteenth, and nineteenth centuries for the societies of the Carolina Lowcountry, as well as for the societies of coastal Guinea and Sierra Leone.

It is a truism that much as "all politics is local," all history is global. It is harder and harder to justify a perspective that focuses too closely on a particular time or place, without acknowledging the links that area of study has to a wide web of people, places, and processes. The articles collected in this special issue of *Atlantic Studies: Global Currents* expressly recognize that they are all addressing aspects of processes (the development of plantation slavery and rice agriculture) that had consequences for people from a wide range of places (Africa, Europe, Asia, the Americas). Scholarship linking the Upper Guinea coast of present day Sierra Leone and Guinea with the rice growing plantation economies of South Carolina has had a profound impact on the way historical trajectories have been conceived of since the early 1980s, if not before. Research by Littlefield and others first pointed to the apparent links between enslaved captives from the Upper Guinea Coast and rice agriculture in the Carolinas.[1] Judith Carney built upon those insights to argue for the foundational and wholesale transfer of rice agriculture technology from the Upper Guinea coast to rice plantations, identified first in the Carolinas, and then elsewhere in the New World, in what became known as the "Black Rice Hypothesis."[2]

While the specifics of the Black Rice Hypothesis have been criticized in various ways,[3] the fundamental notion – that enslaved Africans were more than labor, and exerted their agency in important and transcendent ways – is now widely accepted in a range of mediums, from pottery, to food, to housing, to music.[4] The Black Rice Hypothesis has gone a long way toward forcing scholars to question the role African agency may have played in many different practices. In keeping with the recent trends in microhistory, this has also compelled a recognition that specific histories – of places, of people, of events – matter in the way individuals behaved in novel situations. The articles in this issue of *Atlantic Studies: Global Currents* arose from a two day seminar held at the University of South Carolina and sponsored by the Walker Institute of International and Area Studies that brought together scholars from a variety of disciplines – including history, archaeology, anthropology, and geography – to explore the current range of scholarship that addresses the links between the Upper Guinea Coast and the Carolinas. From the very beginning of our workshop, it became clear that the connections we were seeking between the two regions as they related to slavery and rice were much stronger and longer, with linkages continuing well past the end of the slave trade and into the late nineteenth and early twentieth centuries. In addition to the papers here by Edda Fields-Black, Christopher R. DeCorse, Kenneth G. Kelly and ElHadj Ibrahima Fall, Andrew Agha, and Nemata Blyden, the original workshop had presentations by Judith Carney, Bruce Mouser, Edward Carr, and Leland Ferguson, who were regrettably unable to contribute to the current project. Given the role rice agriculture played either as prime focus of the contributions, or as contributing factor, we felt that bringing a non-Atlantic perspective on rice to the collection would be valuable, particularly as in the Americas, rice is such a dominant narrative through the end of the American Civil War, and then it rapidly disappears, without discussion of what replaced Carolina production. To that end, we added the article by Kathleen Morrison and Mark W. Hauser that discusses exactly what happens to the rice economy in the years following the American Civil War and the collapse of Carolina rice.

    The current collection presents a range of perspectives on the connections between the Upper Guinea Coast and the Carolina Lowcountry. The cultural consequences for Diasporic societies are explored both through the discussion by Fields-Black concerning the impacts of rice cultivation on commercial and subsistence scales for Africans enslaved in the Carolinas, as well as for Africans on the Upper Guinea coast. Two articles discuss the archaeological implications of the slave trade on the Upper Guinea coast, with one exploration of the slave trading establishments in coastal Sierra Leone in the eighteenth and nineteenth centuries (DeCorse), and the other reporting on the first excavations of "illegal" slave trading posts in Guinea that were active during the nineteenth century (Kelly and Fall). These contributions acknowledge the impacts of slave trading in the immediate area of the trading posts through the creation of new Atlantic identities, as well as the consequences to more distant societies. The material traces of the consequences of the Atlantic trade between the Upper Guinea coast and the present day USA is discussed in Agha's contribution which highlights the materialization of the labor of African agents who reshaped the Carolina landscape with the strength of their arms. To remind us that the connections between the Carolinas and the Upper Guinea Coast endured in significant ways following the end of the slave trade and plantation slavery, Blyden describes the personal connections that tied Sierra Leone to the USA, particularly the Southeast, in the decades following the American Civil War. Morrison and Hauser, in their contribution, demonstrate that the Atlantic world that united the Guinea Coast and the Carolinas with Europe extended beyond the Atlantic into the Indian Ocean and Southeast Asia.

    It is our hope that the contributions to this volume will help to reinforce an appreciation of the extensive web of links that have connected these regions over the past four centuries, and that the role of individuals in influencing the direction of history will become apparent. I wish to thank all the participants in the Walker Workshop, whether their papers appear here or not, as all the current contributions have benefited from the exciting discussions we shared over the course of our two days together.

Disclosure statement

No potential conflict of interest was reported by the author.

Notes

1. Littlefield, *Rice and Slaves*; Wood, *Black Majority*.
2. Carney, *Black Rice*.
3. Eltis, Morgan, and Richardson, "Agency and Diaspora,"; Edelson, "Beyond 'Black Rice'," Hawthorne, "From 'Black Rice' to 'Brown'," Eltis, Morgan, and Richardson, "Black, Brown or White."
4. Ferguson, *Uncommon Ground*.

References

Carney, Judith. *Black Rice: The African Origins of Rice Cultivation in the Americas*. Cambridge: Harvard University Press, 2001.
Edelson, S. Max. "Beyond "Black Rice": Reconstructing Material and Cultural Contexts for Early Plantation Agriculture" *The American Historical Review* 115, no. 1 (2010): 125–135.
Eltis, David, Philip Morgan, and David Richardson. "Agency and Diaspora in Atlantic History: Reassessing the African Contribution to Rice Cultivation in the Americas." *The American Historical Review* 112, no. 5 (2007): 1329–1358.
Eltis, David, Philip Morgan, and David Richardson. "Black, Brown or White? Color-Coding American Commercial Rice Cultivation with Slave Labor." *The American Historical Review* 115, no. 1 (2010): 164–171.
Ferguson, Leland. *Uncommon Ground: Archaeology and Early African America, 1650–1800*. Washington, DC: Smithsonian Press, 1992.
Hawthorne, Walter. "From "Black Rice" to "Brown": Rethinking the History of Risiculture in the Seventeenth- and Eighteenth-Century Atlantic." *The American Historical Review* 115, no. 1 (2010): 151–163.
Littlefield, Daniel C. *Rice and Slaves: Ethnicity and the Slave Trade in Colonial South Carolina*. Urbana: University of Illinois Press, 1981.
Wood, Peter H. *Black Majority: Negroes in Colonial South Carolina from 1670 through the Stono Rebellion*. New York: W. W. Norton, 1974.

Atlantic rice and rice farmers: rising from debate, engaging new sources, methods, and modes of inquiry, and asking new questions

Edda L. Fields-Black

> For the past 40 years, scholars of the US South and West Africa have been engaged in a robust debate about the agency of enslaved laborers in the origins and evolution of the commercial rice industry in the colonial South Carolina and Georgia Lowcountry. Though the debate has been contentious at times, scholars studying Atlantic rice farmers have come to agree on a few points: enslaved Africans' provision grounds were probably important in Carolina colonists' experimentation with rice as a staple crop; enslaved Africans continued to practice "heel–toe" sowing techniques until the nineteenth century; African water control and processing techniques served as prototypes for mechanized irrigation and processing machinery. This article suggests the time has come to explore additional questions, particularly in what different ways did subsistence and commercial production shape the lives of African peasants and enslaved Africans? An analysis of the evolution of mangrove rice production in West Africa's Upper Guinea Coast and the South Carolina and Georgia Lowcountry reveals overlap between these two artificial categories. However, the different impacts of intensive mangrove and tidal rice production on the health of African peasants in early modern Upper Guinea Coast and enslaved Africans in the antebellum South Carolina and Georgia Lowcountry are stark indeed.

For the past 40 years, scholars of the US South and West Africa have been engaged in a robust debate about the agency of enslaved laborers in the origins and evolution of the commercial rice industry in the colonial South Carolina and Georgia Lowcountry. At the end of 40 years, the question remains to what degree did enslaved Africans contribute to the development of the commercial rice economies in the Lowcountry? In addition to this important question of agency, new questions should be asked from a circum-Atlantic perspective, such as how did cultivating rice texture the everyday lives of West African peasants and Africans enslaved on rice plantations in West Africa and coastal South Carolina and Georgia?

Peter Wood's *Black Majority* argues enslaved laborers in the Carolina colony provided for their own subsistence by growing a variety of crops, including rice, in their provision grounds in the early colonial period. The earliest British settlers experimented with a variety of crops which grew in temperate and tropical climates, including cotton, indigo, ginger, grapes, olives, and even rice. Once British settlers achieved subsistence in the 1680s, they turned their attention to identifying a staple crop for economic production. Between 1695 and 1720, rice became Carolina's staple crop and remained the backbone of Carolina's economy throughout the eighteenth century. Drawing on demographic data, Wood deduces the percentage of enslaved laborers in colonial South Carolina rose to a majority of the population – surpassing the white population in 1708 – roughly simultaneous to rice becoming the colony's staple crop. Herein lay the beginning of the debate: Wood suggests some West African captives originated from West African sub-regions with long histories of growing, processing, and cooking rice; however, British planters had no experience with the crop, because rice was not grown in Europe's temperate climes. In addition, drawing on advertisements placed in South Carolina newspapers by slave factors, such as Henry Laurens, Woods suggests Carolina planters preferred to purchase captives, such as Gambians, from areas in West Africa where rice was grown.[1] Thus, enslaved laborers were skilled, not simply brute laborers, who made important contributions to South Carolina's commercial rice industry.

Daniel Littlefield's *Rice and Slaves* furthers the discussion by investigating the African background of South Carolina's enslaved labor force and asking whether or not it was a factor in the development of the colony's commercial rice industry. Littlefield documented slave traders' knowledge of the differences among enslaved Africans who originated in Western African sub-regions and preferences for captives from West Africa's rice-growing regions. Building on the work of Peter Wood and Elizabeth Donnan before him and analyzing runaway slave notices, Littlefield argues South Carolina planters actually imported more Angolan captives from a Western African region where rice was not grown, even though they preferred Gambian captives who were familiar with the crop.[2]

Until this point, the literature on the agency of enslaved laborers in the emergence of South Carolina's commercial rice industry was centered on the US side of the Atlantic. Judith Carney's *Black Rice* expands the scope of the investigation to West Africa and West African rice farmers. Carney begins the difficult task of identifying the skills which enslaved laborers originating in the West African Rice Coast region might have possessed if and when they were captured, transported against their wills, and enslaved on Lowcountry rice plantations: Carney makes a careful analysis of the observations recorded by the first Europeans to visit West Africa's rice-growing regions. It reveals the inhabitants of West Africa's Upper Guinea Coast or West African Rice Coast grew rice along a "landscape gradient" in microenvironments ranging from brackish mangrove swamps, to floodplains, inland swamps, and uplands. Carney's "landscape gradient" identifies the underlying principles in both West African and Lowcountry rice-growing systems, showing them to be very much the same. Drawing on her fieldwork research in the Gambia and anthropological work in the Senegambia, the location of which at the nexus of the Sahel and savanna region is prone to drought and famine, Carney argues farmers throughout the West Africa Rice Coast region have created an "indigenous knowledge system" under the constraints of annual fluctuations in the amount and distribution of rainfall.[3] Captives who originated in the West African Rice Coast contributed the "West African rice knowledge system" to South Carolina's commercial rice industry.[4] Carney's work was influenced by literature on "Agroecology," which examines a Western African food production system as a whole knowledge system from production to processing and cooking. These whole knowledge systems consist of complex sets of inputs and outputs with interconnections among component parts.[5]

While some Africanist scholars worked to identify the knowledge possessed by enslaved Africans who were sold in the Upper Guinea Coast and contributed to the Lowcountry's commercial rice industry, some Americanists questioned the validity of the premise on several fronts. David Eltis, Philip Morgan, and David Richardson's "Agency and Diaspora" presents evidence from *The Trans-Atlantic Slave Trade Database* and reveals the number of captives who embarked in Upper Guinea Coast ports disembarked at ports in regions where rice was grown, South Carolina, Georgia, and Maranhao, Brazil, was roughly equivalent to the numbers of Upper Guinea Coast captives who disembarked in the Chesapeake Bay area where rice was not. In addition, Upper Guinea Coast captives did not constitute a majority of the slave imports in South Carolina and Georgia ports before 1750 when the region's commercial rice industry emerged. While they acknowledge the role played by enslaved Africans in introducing rice sowing techniques and processing technology, Eltis, Morgan, and Richardson deny enslaved Africans transferred the indigenous rice knowledge system, "an entire agricultural complex," from the Upper Guinea Coast to South Carolina and Georgia's Lowcountry.[6]

Two studies occupy the middle ground, taking up Eltis Morgan, and Richardson's charge for the literature to become much more "thoroughly Atlantic."[7] Both credit neither planters nor enslaved laborers exclusively for the creation of New World commercial rice industries. In *Plantation Enterprise in Colonial South Carolina*, S. Max Edelson found South Carolina planters synthesizing knowledge from rice-growing in European wastelands and embanking pasturelands with agricultural knowledge from Native Americans and enslaved Africans. British planters used agricultural improvement skills to grow rice as they had grown other foreign crops, like sugar and tobacco. Edelson documents enslaved Africans and British planters infusing rice with separate and distinct meanings, both of which differed from how rice was used in their homelands: enslaved Africans preferred eating rice to guinea corn; planters used rice to make bread whiter and more palatable.[8] Walter Hawthorne's *From Africa to Brazil* argues enslaved people and Native Americans contributed to a creolized agricultural system in which rice was grown as the staple crop in Amazonia, Brazil. European planters contributed knowledge to Amazonia's creolized rice production system and slaveholders also exercised authority over enslaved people's labor. Based on plantation inventories which reveal the geographic origins, a small coastal strip of Guinea-Bissau, and the ethnic origins of the majority of enslaved people, Hawthorne correlates the degree of planter authority and enslaved people's agency in particular areas of their lives. On Amazonia rice plantations, enslaved people also carried and passed down rice cooking techniques from Guinea-Bissau.[9]

Scholars studying Atlantic rice farmers have come to agree on a few points: from the earliest settlement of the Carolina colony, enslaved Africans grew food for their own subsistence in their provision grounds, including but not limited to rice, and sold some of the surplus to local whites. In the late seventeenth century, Carolina planters appropriated the earliest rice-growing and processing technology from enslaved Africans who likely originated in the Upper Guinea Coast and constituted a minority of the relatively small enslaved population of the late seventeenth century. Specifically, heel–toe sowing methods, hollowed-out tree trunks with wooden plugs inserted in both ends to channel and control fresh water flowing into the rice fields, and material culture (mortars, pestles, and fanner baskets) to process rice were modeled after West African prototypes. By the early eighteenth century, however, Carolina planters began modernizing and mechanizing West African antecedents to make them suitable for the demands of commercial production. By 1750, both water control and processing technology were mechanized.[10] Enslaved Africans continued to use "heel–toe" sowing techniques in South Carolina's rice fields up until the early twentieth century.[11]

The debate on the agency of enslaved African laborers in the South Carolina and Georgia Lowcountry and West African rice farmers has occupied center-stage for the past 40 years. It could and probably will go on. It is possible though, the time has come in the Atlantic rice literature to explore additional questions. The time is now to investigate how scholars on both sides of the Atlantic can inform and, yes, challenge one another. At the end of the day, broadening the playing field should provide a more nuanced understanding of Africans and enslaved Africans' experiences in the Old World and the New.

In particular, the literature should use Africans' agency as a starting point for investigating how cultivating rice in a subsistence or commercial economy textured the everyday lives of free West African peasants, enslaved Africans on rice plantations in the Upper Guinea Coast, and people of African descent enslaved in the South Carolina and Georgia Lowcountry. By using African agency in Atlantic rice as a starting point, scholars in a variety of disciplines can begin to deepen our understanding of the connections between the Upper Guinea Coast, from which more than 40% of African captives who disembarked in South Carolina and Georgia ports originated, and the cultures, languages, and societies they and their descendants created in the Lowcountry.

Upper Guinea Coast microenvironments: asking new questions of old fields

Untangling the development of subsistence rice production in the Upper Guinea Coast is a methodological challenge for historians. Its development dates back hundreds, if not thousands of years, before European contact. Thus, it was not recorded in the region's first written sources. Instead, historians must employ interdisciplinary sources to reconstruct its history.

In the Rio Nunez region of present-day Guinea-Conakry, a combination of the comparative method of historical linguistics and biological and botanical studies of mangrove ecosystems reveal the developmental stages of mangrove rice-growing techniques within a coastal land-use system. They provide the earliest tools for reconstructing how the ancestors of coastal dwellers who spoke languages in the Atlantic language family developed an ancient coastal land-use system. For example, "*-*Mer*" or "salt" is one of the most ancient words in Atlantic languages. It both predates Proto-Coastal, an ancestral language common to the Nalu, Mbulunguc, and Mboteni language spoken today. "*-*Mer*" was also spoken ancestral languages in a large swath of the Upper Guinea Coast ranging from present-day Senegal in the north to Sierra Leone in the south, a much broader geographical area than the Rio Nunez region (see Tables 1 and 2). An analysis in five indigenous languages using the comparative method historical linguistics of 5000 vocabulary words related to rice production and the coastal environment in five indigenous languages using the comparative method of historical linguistics reveals a second piece of linguistic evidence in "*-*yop*," *Avicennia africana* and *Laguncularia racemosa*, white mangroves. "*-*Yop*" can be reconstructed to the Proto-Coastal language, but not to other Atlantic languages in the Northern branch, which were spoken in Senegal, Gambia, or Guinea-

Table 1. Inherited forms for "salt" in Northern Branch Atlantic languages (Fields-Black 2008, 64).

	Banyun	Limba	Mbulunguc	Mboteni
Salt	mu-mmer	meci	mbes	ɔ-mbɛl

Bissau (see Table 3). Biological and botanical studies of mangrove ecosystems and coastal land-use delineate the differences between the rooting/oxygenation systems of red and white mangroves and the zones in which they grow. White mangroves grow nearer to land in sandy soils with better drainage, because their spongy horizontal roots, "pneumatophores," can only tolerate limited submersion in brackish water. Patterns in the linguistic evidence and biological and botanical studies reveal Proto-Coastal-speakers became coastal, the common linguistic ancestor of present-day Nalu-, Mbulunguc-, and Mboteni-speakers, became coastal specialists. By c.3000 to 2000 BCE, they acquired knowledge of salt, salinity, and a new ecosystem, the white mangroves located closest to their villages. Dating back to antiquity, this coastal knowledge was much more ancient than the introduction of rice.

After the Nalu, Mbulunguc, and Mboteni languages diverged from Proto-Coastal, their speech communities gained mastery over the coastal environment and its mangrove ecosystems. Their increased knowledge is reflected in the innovation of words such as, "-mak" (*Rhizophora racemosa* or red mangrove), "-bo" (mosquito), "-kuiyoŋ" (rainy season), "-nep" (crab, generic), and "-laŋ" (type of crab) (see Table 4). According to biological and botanical studies of mangrove ecosystems, the tough and tangled aerial roots of red mangroves are designed to flourish submerged in brackish water. Thus, red, as opposed to white, mangroves are located along the mouths of coastal estuaries growing in water-logged soils and submerged up to their aerial roots in brackish waters. By c.1000 CE, Nalu-, Mbulunguc-, and Mboteni-speakers fished, collected shell fish, and began exploiting *Rhizophora racemosa*, red mangroves, bordering the ocean. They continued to develop strategies unique to microenvironments within the Rio Nunez region to exploit the full range of their coastal ecosystem.

After c. 1000 CE, Highlands speech communities whose languages were part of the Southern branch of the Atlantic language group migrated from the interior of present-day Sierra Leone northwest towards the coast. Though their languages were distantly related, Sitem-speakers collaborated with Nalu, Mbulunguc, and Mboteni speech communities which occupied similar microenvironments in the Rio Nunez region. They developed technology uniquely adapted to their local swampy, salty environment. The following linguistic evidence can be traced to the Highlands languages, which originated in the interior of present-day Sierra Leone: "-cap" (to fell, wound,

Table 2. Inherited forms for "salt" in Southern Branch Atlantic languages (Fields-Black 2008, 64).

	Temne	Landuma	Kogoli	Kalum	Sitem
Salt	m-mer	mɛr	mɛɛr	mɛr	mer

Table 3. Inherited forms for *"Avicennia Africana"* in Coastal languages (Fields-Black 2008, 67).

	Nalu	Mbulunguc
A. Africana (white mangroves)	*-yof*	*-yɔp*

chop, and cut down trees or earth), "*-nek*" (mound/ridge), and "*-kofok*" (seed). Words for mounds and ridges and chopping down trees in particular and the agricultural techniques they describe spread areally in Coastal languages of the Rio Nunez region (see Table 5). After the divergence of Proto-Highlands and the migration of Highlands speech communities toward the coast, Sitem-speakers along with Nalu-, Mbulunguc-, and Mboteni-speakers created these words in the coastal Rio Nunez region: "*-cɛɛp*" (to sow and to transplant), "*-foi*" (to fan rice), "*-kobaĺ*" (short wooden fulcrum shovel used to turn the soil and create mounds and ridges), and "*-cɔmp*" (rice flour) (see Table 6). The wooden fulcrum shovel is the key piece of material culture used by rice farmers as far north as present-day Senegal. However, in the Rio Nunez region, coastal specialists adapted its design and the terminology describing it to reflect the amount of weeds and water in their mangrove rice fields.[12] Together, Nalu-, Mbulunguc-, Mboteni-, and Sitem-speakers created technology and material culture which were highly localized and customized to fit microenvironments in the mangrove region.

The migration of a third group of Susu-speakers whose language is part of the unrelated Mande language group facilitated Atlantic farmers' expansion of rice cultivation into the red mangrove region. Nalu, Mbulunguc, Mboteni, and Sitem languages borrowed key terminology related to ironworking, such as "*-xabui*" (blacksmith), "*-fac*" (iron and iron cooking pot), and "*-fanc*" (blade for wooden fulcrum shovel), from Susu (see Table 7). The loanwords are evidence Susu-speakers supplied iron tools, including iron edges for the indigenous wooden fulcrum shovels. Farmers speaking Atlantic languages gained access to iron from commercial interactions with Susu-speakers migrating southwestward to the coast between c.1500 and 1800 CE. Adding iron tips to the end of their wooden fulcrum shovels facilitated Atlantic farmers clearing the red mangroves and intensifying their farming systems in the Rio Nunez region and other parts of the Upper Guinea Coast.[13]

The combination of the linguistic evidence and the biological and botanical studies of mangrove ecosystems paint a different picture than the age-old question in the Atlantic rice literature, the agency of African farmers in the evolution of rice

Table 4. Areal innovations in Coastal Daughter languages (Fields-Black 2008, 72–74).

	Nalu	Mbulunguc	Mboteni
Rhizophora racemosa (red mangroves)	*m-mak*		*e-ma*
Mosquito		*ɔ-bo*	*a-bɔ*
Rainy season			*kuiyoŋ*
End of rainy season	*m-kaak kiyoŋ*		
Crab (generic)	*i-nep*		*a-nep*

Table 5. Inherited forms for cutting down trees in Highlands languages and areal innovations in Highlands and Coastal languages (Fields-Black 2008, 120, 104, 125, 127).

	Nalu	Mbulunguc	Mboteni	Temne	Landuma	Sitem
Mound/ ridge	ma-nɛk	ɛ-nɛk	e-nɛk		ta-nɛk	a-nek
Seed			m-kofok			a-xɔfel
To chop, wound, fell				-cap		
To cut weeds on the bottom before shoveling		a-cappa				
To cut some trees and leave others		e-cappa ɛ-ti				
To cut the earth with a shovel and make a dike		ka-cappa				
To cut trees on the bottom before shoveling (with fulcrum shovel)						ki-cɛpis yika

production technology. Looking back in time and space shifts the emphasis from the agency of enslaved Africans vs. their enslavers in creating a commercial agricultural system. Instead, the interdisciplinary evidence reveals the agency of Africans in the Upper Guinea Coast in developing an innovative, highly localized subsistence agricultural system and customizing it to the fluctuations of coastal microenvironments.[14]

The earliest European traders to encounter the Rio Nunez region in the fifteenth century reported its inhabitants growing rice. Portuguese and Afro-Portuguese traders purchased rice produced by coastal inhabitants. European traders did not have direct contact with some groups of coastal inhabitants who spoke languages from the Northern branch of the Atlantic language family. For example, Andre Alvares d'Almada reported the Portuguese traders "do not have the direct trade with them" – the Nalu who bordered the Beafares on the flank of Bisegue – "we have with other peoples." The Nalu only traded with the Portuguese on the coast via intermediaries, exchanging slaves "by way of the Beaferes of Bisegue and Balola." Almada lamented a "shipload of greenhorns" traders ... "who were ignorant of the customs of these parts" ruined the trade on the river. They traded ivory for a few goods, seized, and

Table 6. Localized areal innovation in Highlands and Coastal languages in Rio Nunez region (Fields-Black 2008, 125–126, 121).

	Nalu	Mbulunguc	Mboteni	Sitem
To sow with finger	ma-cɛɛp			ki-cɛp tecir
To transplant	ma-cɛɛp			ki-cɛp
To transplant rice	-cɛp			pa-cɛɛp
To fan rice in the wind			a-foi malɔ	ki-foi malɔ
Shortest wooden fulcrum shovel	ma-kumbal		faa aŋkumbɛl	toŋ-kumbɛl
Short shovel used to weed soil in the ridges for the second time			porbal aŋkumbɛl	
Rice flour			ku-cɔmp	ki-comp

Table 7. Susu loanwords in Coastal and Highlands Atlantic languages (Fields-Black 2008, 153).

	Susu	Nalu	Mbulunguc	Mboteni	Kalum	Temne	Kogoli	Landuma	Sitem
Blacksmith	xabui	ma-kabinɛ	kabi						
Iron	a-fac	m-fac			kɔ-fac	a-fac	a-fac	a-fac	
Iron cooking pot					kɔ-fac	a-fac			
Wooden fulcrum shovel blade	-fɛnsi		ma-fanc	a-fenc					a-fɛnc

enslaved a dozen people.[15] In present-day Guinea-Bissau, the Balanta did not trade directly with Portuguese traders during the sixteenth century. Almada described Balanta "only [bringing] themselves to see our people reluctantly." Like the Nalu in the Rio Nunez region, the Balanta acquired access to Portuguese goods from Biafada (or Beafare) traders and Buramos in exchange for rice and yams.[16]

The Balanta's relationships with Atlantic trade and traders would change significantly in the seventeenth century, but the Nalu's would largely remain the same. From the mid-seventeenth century, Nalu-, Mboteni-, Mbulunguc-, and Sitem-speaking inhabitants sold rice and salt to Fulbe and Susu caravan traders from the interior in exchange for dyes and cattle.[17] Before the late eighteenth century, they did not directly engage the Atlantic economy unlike the Balanta and other coastal Atlantic groups, most of who lived both north and south of the Rio Nunez. Throughout the Upper Guinea Coast, Portuguese travelers' accounts provide little description of how or where Africans grew rice, primarily because European traders' movements were confined to coastal ports during the dry season.[18]

Across African regions and time periods, intensification, the processes by which cultivators increase yields per acreage, is often part and parcel of the transition from subsistence to commercial production and the emergence of capitalist economies. In the Atlantic literature, irrigation was integral and often the precursor to agricultural intensification. Among rice farmers, building irrigation technology, such as dikes, bunds, dams, and canals, to drain swamps, trap water, and funnel it in or out of desired locations at precise moments during the growing season, was a critical part of intensive agricultural systems and facilitated cultivators using a plot of land for a longer period of time without exhaustion and increasing the yield per acreage. Agricultural intensification occurred in the Rio Nunez region before c. 1000 CE when Atlantic farmers fabricated irrigation systems using dikes and bunds to trap fresh water and desalinate the soils; Atlantic and Mande farmers expanded their coastal land-use system from growing rice in white mangrove areas to red between c.1000 CE and 1500 CE.

Building irrigation technology required increased labor inputs. Coercion and force were often necessary to mobilize the enormous labor inputs required to build and maintain irrigation systems. Coercion and force, however, took different forms in different societies and moments in time.

Oral traditions reveal the coercive nature of the gender- and age-specific division of labor in mangrove rice production among Balanta-speakers in coastal Guinea-Bissau.

Culturally encoded clues in oral traditions which ordinary Balanta farmers related informally in day-to-day interactions reveal the hierarchical social organization of Balanta villages. The Balanta in pre-colonial Guinea-Bissau transformed their social organization to use age-grades to undertake the highly labor-intensive process of cutting down red mangrove trees, building and maintaining the dikes and bunds, and extending the farming system into previously uncultivated and unsettled terrain. The trans-Atlantic slave trade had broad implications for trade and technological innovation among the Balanta. After the mid-seventeenth century, young Balanta men worked for elder men, building and maintaining dikes and bunds in the red mangrove swamps. After many years of service, the young men would be given wives by the senior men and allowed to become heads of their own households. After young men rose to the rank of *b'alante b'ndang*, becoming elders, they controlled the labor of women and young men to establish new rice fields and profited from the fruits of their labor.[19] In the transfer of rice cultivation techniques from West Africa's Upper Guinea Coast where paddy rice production ordered coastal societies to Maranhao, Brazil where upland rice was grown for the commercial market by slaves, enslaved peoples' labor was divorced from the fruits of their labor and the entire intensive rice agricultural system became "de-natured."[20]

Intensification among West African rice farmers included the introduction of new rice species. In the Upper Guinea Coast, Portuguese traders introduced *Oryza sativa*, rice species domesticated in Asia, between the Cacheu and Casamance Rivers in present-day Senegal and the Grand-Bassa River in present-day Liberia. Upper Guinea Coast farmers drew on their experience of and expertise in cultivating *O. glaberrima*, rice varieties domesticated in Africa, to adapt *O. sativa* to grow in the region's microenvironments. They may have realized greater yields as a result of its introduction; however, *O. sativa* is more poorly suited to grow in marginal environments – plagued with too much water and too high percentages of salinity in the soil. *O. glaberrima* yields less, but can grow in the most marginal of microenvironments. That Asian rice species are easier to process, to polish and make "white," became increasingly important with the advent of trans-Atlantic trade in African rice.[21]

European travelers who recorded the first written sources for the Upper Guinea Coast recorded transformations within the region and among its Atlantic inhabitants during the trans-Atlantic slave trade period. They paid some attention to the "thatched huts," houses, and building materials used to construct them, but less to settlement patterns, locations of the rice fields, and their proximity to coastal inhabitants' villages.[22]

South of the Gambia River in present-day Gambia, the entrance of the river was "completely covered with a thick forest of mangroves." They extended away from the river along tidal streams flowing from the Gambia River "(inland) to the tidal limit of salt water." Almada described the mangrove forests as "meadows called *lalas*." During the rainy season from June to November, the Gambia River flooded the *lalas* and thus flooded the mangrove rice nurseries. "From the flooded *lalas*" south of the Gambia River, rice farmers "[recovered] their rice-plants" from rice nurseries. Then, they moved the rice seedlings to higher ground and "[transplanted] them into drier *lalas*, where they soon [gave] their crop."[23] Almada may have confused the order and location of fieldwork.[24] However, the location of *lalas*, along tidal streams flowing from the Gambia River is unmistakable.

Portuguese traders who first encountered the Balanta found them living in dispersed settlements in relatively close proximity to their fields. In the sixteenth century, the Balanta primarily lived in the uplands and grew yams, not rice. By the seventeenth century, the Balanta retreated into isolated areas of the mangrove swamps seeking protection from slaving raids by Mandinga and Fula warriors from the interior. They concentrated their dispersed settlements into *tabancas*, defensive villages. A rise in violence was in part the impetus for coastal Atlantic groups, like the Balanta, to alter their settlement pattern.[25] The violence was a result of raids on coastal groups – sometimes in the case of the Bijago, by coastal groups – which generated captives for the trans-Atlantic slave trade.[26]

In other parts of the Upper Guinea Coast, European travelers provide evidence of inhabitants building "enclosures" around their villages and using defensive architecture for protection.[27] In the Mandinga Kingdom along the Gambia River, any who wanted to get near the king had to "pass through six doors and in front of each door there was a doorman. At the last door, … there were many archers guarding."[28] Among the Floup (Jola) on the Geba-Casamance River, the king's royal compound was surrounded by five concentric circles of "hedges made of stakes." Designed to confuse, disorient, and slow down raiders, each circle had a separate entrance which faced a different direction and caused the king's visitors to "enter in circle and not directly." The heavily fortified central entrance was protected by "an arm of the river," a tidal stream and tributary of the Geba-Casamance River. The king's compound was located in a "fortified area" at the "center of the palisades."[29] Among the Papel on the Mansoa River, the "houses [had] so many doors and rooms that they [were] more like labyrinths than houses." The prevalence of defensive architecture, such as palisades and labyrinths, in coastal villages in the Upper Guinea Coast increased in the seventeenth century to protect coastal inhabitants from raids by slave raiders riding horses and kidnapping children.[30] While the Portuguese accounts paint a picture of coastal villages becoming more dangerous as a result of increased slave raiding, the question remains unanswered, however, were the rice fields located in close proximity to the villages? The travelers' accounts are not focused on coastal inhabitants' agricultural production or intensification. Unlike the plantation sources for the South Carolina and Georgia Lowcountry, they are silent on the location of coastal villages in proximity to the rice fields and the affects agricultural intensification had on coastal inhabitants and communities' health.

By the end of the eighteenth century, plantations in the interior of Guinea's Rio Nunez and Rio Pongo regions and Sierra Leone produced rice for commercial markets in Futa Jallon and Freetown. In the Rio Nunez region, Susu and Fulbe overlords exploited the labor of captives in the lull of trade activity during the rainy season to produce provisions and commodities for trade. The establishment of "The Province of Freedom" in Freetown, the present-day capital of Sierra Leone, created a large market of settlers who depended on the hinterland for foodstuffs. The production of rice with captive labor would transform social institutions in the region's interior.[31] Though Nalu-, Mbulunguc-, Mboteni-, and Sitem-speaking farmers had produced rice for the caravan trade to Futa Jallon, by the end of the eighteenth century, the Rio Nunez became directly integrated into the Atlantic economy.

It seems clear cut; peasants in West Africa using family labor produced rice for subsistence and enslaved laborers in the South Carolina and Georgia Lowcountry produced rice for the commercial economy. But, the lines are clearly blurred. Both subsistence and commercial rice production textured the lives of Upper Guinea Coast inhabitants.

Enslaved Africans' provision grounds: new sources for old questions?

Historians engaged in the Atlantic rice debate agree enslaved Africans' provision grounds and the agricultural experiments enslaved laborers conducted therein were likely precursors to the South Carolina commercial rice industry. The lack of documentation makes it impossible for historians to confirm or deny the link. That enslaved Africans produced rice for subsistence in provision grounds is clear. Unlike West Africa's Upper Guinea Coast, the line between subsistence and commercial rice production was stark. And the difference in how commercial rice production vs. subsistence affected enslaved Africans health was stark as well.

In the US South, the South Carolina and Georgia Lowcountry was unique, because enslaved people grew their food in provision grounds to supplement rations. Throughout the early seventeenth century, the Carolina colonists struggled for subsistence. From the colony's inception, Africans enslaved on Lowcountry plantations provided for the bulk of their own subsistence. Into the nineteenth century, this arrangement required resident absentee planters to provide less for enslaved people. Plantation records provide no descriptions of what enslaved laborers grew in their provision grounds, whether or not they grew rice, and if so, how. In 1700, however, an enslaved man sold small quantities of rice to naturalist John Lawson who recorded the event.[32] Like the Upper Guinea Coast before Samuel Gamble's tour of a Sitem village in 1793, the sources record that the enslaved man sold the rice, but do not describe where or how he produced or processed it.

There are, however, promising leads in the historical sources. Late-eighteenth-century plats of Limerick Plantation show the location of "Negro fields" between Limerick and Kensington plantations in the swamp/lowlands along a creek between the two properties. Documents from Limerick also mention two cases of rice "bought of Negroes" and one case of rice "planted by Negroes."[33] These leads, unfortunately, do not shed light on the critical late seventeenth-century period or the relationship between enslaved Africans' provision fields and the introduction to and evolution of rice-growing technology to the Carolina colony.

Enslaved people throughout the Caribbean grew their own food for subsistence. Anthropologists and archaeologists have studied enslaved Africans' provision grounds on Caribbean plantations. Planters in the Caribbean chose the latter option in the predicament of either importing food to feed enslaved laborers or allowing enslaved laborers to cultivate their own provisions on provision grounds. In the seventeenth century, planters in the British Caribbean were required by law to set aside a specific amount of acreage for enslaved people and indentured laborers to cultivate their own vegetable provisions. Early plots were located on flat plantation lands. Though gangs of enslaved laborers cultivated the plots, they grew one or two crops therein and paid little attention to microenvironments within the fields or the needs of individual crops. Lydia Mihelic Pulsipher suggests "these plantation-managed plots were probably European in conception, location, shape, size and methods used." By the eighteenth century, planters recognized the economic benefits of enslaved laborers cultivating their own provisions and selling the surplus. The custom of allotting Saturday afternoons and Sundays for enslaved people to cultivate for themselves facilitated the planting of larger provision grounds which were located further from the quarters on land unused for commercial production.[34]

Irrigation and agricultural intensification have a profound effect on the health and well-being of rice-growing societies. In the Upper Guinea Coast and the South Carolina and Georgia Lowcountry, cultivators and planters invested time, talent, and labor into intensive agriculture to increase their yields per acreage, to diversify their agricultural systems, and to mitigate risk. In the Lowcountry, enslaved laborers paid the brunt of the price in increased sickness and higher death rates. Enslaved rice-growing societies are powerful examples of the price of intensive agriculture.

Inland rice production, the first stage in South Carolina's commercial rice industry, was extensive instead of intensive. Utilizing the existing landscape, planters used enslaved labor to locate the earliest inland rice fields along small tributaries and floodplains and used the land's natural topography for irrigation. By the mid-1700s, planters had moved into new inland environments where they established large fields with geometric embankments and canal networks.[35]

South Carolina planters used the coastal topography to define irrigation and settlement patterns and field design in three inland locations along the Cooper and Wandoo Rivers. Unlike tidal rice cultivation, inland rice systems required relatively little manipulation of terrain, because planters utilized the topography to provide irrigation for the earliest inland swamp rice fields. Given their limited access to water, inland rice planters and enslaved laborers had to be more creative at manipulating water than tidal rice planters. As demand for rice expanded in the eighteenth century, planters experimented with water control and cleared new inland fields. Though inland swamp cultivation has received precious little attention in the region's literature, by 1739, inland, not tidal, swamp cultivation created the first plantation economy and was the impetus for a surge in the numbers of captives imported directly from Africa, leading to the creation of South Carolina's "Black majority."[36]

Locating their residences on elevated land one tenth of a mile from the rice fields was the typical pattern among inland rice planters along South Carolina's Cooper River in the mid-eighteenth century: "planters built their homes on the 'Edge of Swamps, in a damp moist Situation' because they wanted 'to view from their Rooms, their Negroes at Work in the Rice Fields." Settlement patterns for both planters and enslaved laborers led to high death rates for both; 37% of white men and 45% of white women who survived into adulthood between 1721 and 1760 died before their 50th birthdays.[37] By the 1770s, high death rates among whites prompted planters to relocate their families to higher ground during the deadly flooding season. Rice planters removed their residences to the pinelands and to cities, like Charleston and Savannah, becoming "local absentees."[38]

By the mid-eighteenth century, South Carolina planters began locating their plantations within the tidal influence and experimenting with tidewater rice production. Africans enslaved on plantations along the Cooper, Santee, and Combahee Rivers in South Carolina and Savannah and Altamaha Rivers in Georgia had built "huge hydraulic machines" by the last quarter in the eighteenth century. It became the backbone of the commercial rice industry.[39]

In South Carolina and Georgia, the introduction of floodgates in tidal rice fields in the mid-eighteenth century had the unintended consequence of creating stagnant pools of water. Anopheles mosquitoes bred in the standing water, initially spreading malaria throughout the planter and enslaved communities until planters moved upland and inland.[40] Most rice planters, however, did not alter the settlement patterns of enslaved communities on Lowcountry rice plantations. The slave quarters for the masses of field hands remained in close proximity to the rice fields in which they labored.

The overall death and infant mortality rates on Lowcountry rice plantations were ghastly. Historian William Dusinberre estimates two-thirds of enslaved children born on rice plantations in the nineteenth century died before they were 15 years old; almost 40%, a conservative estimate, of infants expired during their first year of life. In comparison, 38% of children on non-rice plantations in the US South died before they turned 15.

In pockets of the Lowcountry, such as along the Savannah River, the rates were much higher. For example, the enslaved population on the Gowerie plantation suffered a 90% death rate between 1833 and 1864. Gowerie's slave quarters were located on swamp banks to maximize the slaveholders' control over enslaved people's labor, movements, and lives. This deadly location also held enslaved Africans captive to mosquitoes, mosquito-borne illnesses, and stagnant and polluted river water. Diseases such as chronic malaria, respiratory ailments, and cholera also proliferated in the swamps' stagnant water on Savannah River rice plantations. Enslaved infants and children wasted away from tetanus and "puniness." Gastrointestinal and bowel diseases afflicted them with deadly bouts of diarrhea. Settlement patterns imposed on enslaved laborers contributed to immune deficiencies, low infant birth weights, and overall mortality. The addition of miscarriages and stillbirths – which historians have no means of quantifying – to the infant/child mortality rates would have made these ghastly numbers even more horrific. The death rates in the eighteenth century when historical sources are scarcer were likely even more shocking.[41]

The most extreme examples of coercion, force, and "de-natured" intensive agricultural systems can be found in enslaved societies. In South Carolina's coastal plain, coercion and force went hand in hand with the development of commercial rice production. Planters used coercion, brutality, and force to impel enslaved laborers in every stage of rice cultivation and processing, particularly clearing the cypress swamps, laboring in the insalubrious swamps during the cold winter months, and pounding large amounts of rice after their daily tasks were done.[42] The settlement patterns to which planters on Lowcountry rice plantations subjected the enslaved are a prime example of coercion and force that was more often than not used to control labor in intensive and commercial agricultural societies.

Settlement patterns and health effects in the Upper Guinea Coast: new fields to be cleared

There is a pregnant silence in the African literature on rice and rice farmers in reference to whether or not disease rates increased as a result of intensive agriculture, particularly mangrove rice cultivation. On the one hand, the silence in the literature could be a reflection of the larger vacuum of historical sources describing traditional rice cultivation techniques. Historical sources recorded in the Upper Guinea Coast during the early modern period have a "dry season bias." Very few European observers traveled to coastal villages during the rainy season when farmers prepared mangrove rice fields and planted mangrove rice and Anopheles mosquitoes bred in the same swamps and infected coastal villagers. The coastal region was too just deadly.[43]

Ironically, historians' best chance of finding historical sources to shed light on the important question – whether subsistence mangrove rice farming and settlement patterns on the Upper Guinea Coast resulted in the dramatic and deleterious health effects as did commercial tidal rice farming in coastal South Carolina and Georgia – comes from the height of the trans-Atlantic slave trade. It comes from the seventeenth and eighteenth centuries when Atlantic rice farmers who maintained stateless political organizations transformed their settlement patterns, village and housing construction, shrines, and social organizations to protect themselves from being seized as captives and sold first in many cases to African middlemen, then to Europeans on the coast.

Not surprisingly, the evidence comes from oral traditions collected among the descendants of rice farmers, not from European travelers' accounts. Robert Baum drew on oral traditions collected among the Jola in Esulalu. In the eighteenth century, Jola from the north shore of the Casamance River raided Jola who lived on the south shore, seizing people as they worked in the rice fields. The raids occurred primarily in the rainy season when the vegetation grew up and provided lush cover for raiders to ambush their victims. During the rainy season, men and women walked long distances from the villages to their rice fields and spent long hours working in the isolated fields. The isolation of the mangrove rice fields and the paths to them left coastal rice farmers vulnerable: "if they found you in the rice paddies, they seized you." The distance between the rice fields and Jola villages also facilitated slave raiders kidnapping children left in villagers while parents traveled to and worked in rice fields. In the second half of the eighteenth century, Jola on the south shore of the Casamance River instituted a number of defensive measures to protect themselves and their families. They armed themselves with muskets, bows, arrows, and spears. Farmers worked in co-ed or single-sex groups, providing each other with mutual support and protection. Townships did not clear vegetation from surrounding areas. Villagers built their homes with only one outside door, no windows on outside walls, and walled in and covered backyards. Narrow and winding paths and entrances made it more difficult for raiders to get in and flee quickly.[44] Despite the prevalence of compact villages, defensive architecture, iron weapons, and firearms, the isolated rice fields and the paths to them were the places where coastal rice farmers were vulnerable to kidnapping and seizure. When they were working in their rice fields and walking to them, they found it difficult, if not impossible, to protect themselves.

Like the question of the role enslaved Africans' provisions played in the emergence and evolution of rice cultivation technology on coastal South Carolina plantations, there is no "smoking gun" on the West African side of the Atlantic on the impact of commercial rice production on the health of coastal Upper Guinea Coast ricegrowing communities. Lack of evidence to the contrary and circumstantial evidence suggest Upper Guinea Coast rice farmers did not locate their villages in close proximity to their low-lying rice fields. Thus, the rice fields' stagnant water did not cause higher infant mortality or overall death rates. In reference to intensive agriculture and its effects on health and disease, West Africa's rice-growing areas appear to be an exception to the rule. But, historians must also ask different questions of historical sources. Was this the result of the agency Upper Guinea Coast peasant farmers? Or, was it the result of the difference between extensive, subsistence and intensive, commercial agricultural systems? Enslaved laborers on Lowcountry rice plantations were expendable, their supply inexhaustible into the nineteenth century, but family labor in the Upper Guinea Coast was not. Either way, expanding the evidentiary base by incorporating interdisciplinary sources and methods, may shed new light on these important questions and enable historians to examine even more aspects of West African and enslaved rice cultivators' experiences.

In conclusion, though debates among the West African and Atlantic rice literatures have been contentious at times, each has enriched the other, prompted scholars to ask new questions, analyze new sources, and even re-think our methodologies and assumptions. The way forward promises more stimulating collaboration and spirited debate. It might be fruitful to re-frame our analysis and explore how subsistence rice production in West Africa and in enslaved Africans' provision grounds textured rice cultivators' lives differently than commercial rice production textured the lives of enslaved Africans on Lowcountry and Upper Guinea Coast rice plantations. In addition to likely serving as experimental laboratories for rice cultivation technology on Lowcountry rice plantations, did provision grounds provide enslaved people a sense of autonomy, accomplishment, and ownership in the work of their hands and the fruits of their labors when West African rice-growing technology was otherwise "denatured" by the commercial rice-growing industry? Breaking down the binary and examining the gray areas within and between the categories of "subsistence" and "commercial" production is also imperative. If Upper Guinea Coast rice farmers' sustainable and subsistence production and settlement patterns shielded them from the insalubrious effects of stagnant and polluted water where mosquitoes and disease bred, what about conditions for enslaved laborers on Upper Guinea Coast rice plantations? By joining together with archaeologists, anthropologists, and environmental historians, we may find answers to these questions and many more, gaining a better understanding of the lives, skills, and labors of West African rice farmers and enslaved Africans on Lowcountry rice plantations.

Acknowledgements
I sincerely thank the following colleagues for their suggestions at different stages of writing and revising: Andrew Agha, Judith Carney, Leland Ferguson, Hayden Smith, Paul Sutter, and Terry Weik. Any remaining errors or omissions are all mine.

Disclosure statement
No potential conflict of interest was reported by the author.

Notes
1. Wood, *Black Majority*, 27, 35, 36, 131, 144, 155–162.
2. Littlefield, *Rice and Slaves*, 8, 13, 24–28, 109–114, 116, 117–131.
3. Carney, *The Social History*, 1–19; Pélissier, *Les paysans du Sénégal*, 5–17.
4. Carney, *Black Rice*, 1, 2, 28, 43–46, 55–64, 81–106.

5. Email correspondence with Judith Carney, February 2014. Gliessman, *Agroecology: The Ecology of Sustainable*, 23; Gliessman, *Agroecology: Researching the Ecological Basis for Sustainable Agriculture*; Altieri, "Agroecology: The Science of Natural Resource Management"; Carroll, Vandermeer, and Rosset, *Agroecology*; Altieri, *Agroecology: The Scientific*; and Gliessman, Garcia, and Amador, "The Ecological Basis for the Application."
6. Eltis, Morgan, and Richardson, "Agency and Diaspora in Atlantic History," 1335, 1337, 1338, 1340, 1357.
7. Ibid., 1332.
8. Edelson, *Plantation Enterprise*, 47, 48, 68–82.
9. Hawthorne, *From Africa to Brazil*, 8, 12, 19, 20, 139, 173–245.
10. Joyner, *Down by the Riverside*, 48; Edelson, *Plantation Enterprise*, 67, 68, 80–82; Carney, *Black Rice*, 88, 94–97, 110, 113, 136; Morgan, *Slave Counterpoint*, 153, 157, 178 n.49, 183 n.58; Rosengarten, *Social Origins of the African-American*, 4, 14, 45; Carney, "Landscapes of Technology Transfer," 30, 31; and Rosengarten, *Row upon Row*, 18–21, 104–110.
11. Alpern, "Did Enslaved Africans Spark," 50; Edelson, *Plantation Enterprise*, 78; and Eltis, Morgan, and Richardson, "Agency and Diaspora in Atlantic History," 1356.
12. Fields-Black, *Deep Roots*, 55–134.
13. Ibid., 135–160.
14. Ibid., 61–75, 116–132, 146–155.
15. d'Almada, *Brief Treatise on the Rivers*, 13/1, 13/5, 13/3. Portuguese traders did not trade directly with the Falupos and Arriatas south of the Gambia River. Ibid., 13/1, 13/3. The Temne and Bullom in Sierra Leone did not trade with the British or French. Ibid., 18/12. See also Crone, *The Voyages of Cadamosto*, 92. Note: the page numbers in the Hair translation of d'Almada, *Brief Treatise on the Rivers* are inconsistent. Therefore, all references to this text refer to chapter number and section number.
16. d'Almada, *Brief Treatise on the Rivers*, 9/39.
17. Fields-Black, *Deep Roots*, 168–170; Golbéry, *Travels in Africa*, 162, 163; and Rivière, "Le long des côtes de Guinée," 735, 736.
18. Fields-Black, *Deep Roots*, 1–24.
19. Hawthorne, "Nourishing a Stateless Society," 1, 2, 4, 5; Hawthorne, *Planting Rice*, 4–7, 30.
20. Hawthorne, *Planting Rice*, 120, 142; Hawthorne, "The Cultural Meaning of Work," 279–290.
21. Lauer, *Rice in the History*, 37, 38, 45, 46.
22. Pereira, *Esmeraldo de situ orbis*, 94; d'Almada, *Brief Treatise on the Rivers*, 3/6, 5/5, 8/14, 9/1, 9/33, 11/18; and Fernandes, *Description de la Cote Occidentale*, 93, 13.
23. d'Almada, *Brief Treatise on the Rivers*, 6/1, 6/13.
24. Today, mangrove rice farmers in the Upper Guinea Coast sow rice seedlings on higher ground, further from tidal streams and brackish water. After a period of approximately 60 days, they pull up and transplant the seedlings into the mangrove field. Fields-Black, *Deep Roots*, 37–40; Carney, *Black Rice*, 18.
25. Hawthorne, "Nourishing a Stateless Society," 3, 7, 10, 13–16.
26. d'Almada, *Brief Treatise on the Rivers*, 7/2, 9/25, 9/37, 10/3–10/4.
27. d'Almada, *Brief Treatise on the Rivers*, 9/1.
28. Fernandes, *Description de la Cote Occidentale*, 37.
29. Ibid., 61, 63; Mark, *'Portuguese' Style and Luso-African Identity*, 35, 37, 38.
30. d'Almada, *Brief Treatise on the Rivers*, 9/33; Mark, *'Portuguese' Style and Luso-African Identity*, 37, 38, 121–123.
31. Fields-Black, *Deep Roots*, 168–170; Matthews, *A Voyage to the River Sierra-Leone*, 12, 149; Stanley, "Narrative of William Cooper Thompson's," 106–138; Nowak, "The Slave Rebellion in Sierra Leone," 151–169, Barry, *Senegambia and the Atlantic Slave Trade*, 117, 121–123; and Mouser, "Rebellion, Marronage and Jihad," 27–44.
32. Carney and Rosomoff, *In the Shadow of Slavery*, 127–131, 135–138, 159, 221; Stewart, *'What Suffers to Groe'*, 93, 134; Edelson, *Plantation Enterprise*, 67, 68, 77; Lawson, *A New Voyage to Carolina*, 16; Castiglioni et al., *Luigi Castiglioni's Viaggio, 1785-1787*, 171, 172; and Catesby and Edwards, *The Natural History of Carolina*, 1, xvii, xviii.

33. Babson, *The Tanner Road Settlement*, 124 and appendices; email communication with Leland Ferguson (and David W. Babson), June 2014.
34. Pulsipher, "'They Have Saturdays and Sundays'," 28, 29, 31; Mintz and Hall, *The Origins of the Jamaican*, 3, 5, 7, 8, 10, 12, 14, 16–18; Heath and Bennett, "'The Little Spots Allow'd Them'," 38, 40, 43; Wallman, *Negotiating the Plantation Structure*; Bowes, "Provisioned, Produced, Procured," 89–109; Scott and Dawdy, "Colonial and Creole Diets in Eighteenth Century New Orleans," 97–116; Scott, "Who Ate What," 357–374; Franklin, "The Archaeological and Symbolic Dimensions," 88–107; McKee, "Food Supply and Plantation Social Order," 218–239; Pulsipher and Goodwin, "Here Where the Old Time People," 9–37; Pulsipher, "Galways Plantation, Montserrat," 139–159; and McKee, "Delineating Ethnicity from the Garbage," 31, 39. Email communications with Terry Weik and Andrew Agha, June 2014.
35. Smith, "Rich Swamps and Rice Grounds," 35, 36, 39–43, 47–56, 58–61; Smith, "Reserving Water," 193–200, 206.
36. Smith, "Rich Swamps and Rice Grounds," 11, 12, 195–198.
37. Smith, "Reserving Water," 207, 208.
38. Ibid.; Smith, *Slavery and Rice Culture*, 7.
39. Stewart, "Rice, Water, and Power," 47–49.
40. Wood, *Black Majority*, 75, 87; Smith, "Rich Swamps and Rice Grounds," 16, 83, 104–107, 112, 113, 283; Smith, "Reserving Water," 207, 208; McCandless, *Slavery, Disease, and Suffering*, 39–46.
41. Dusinberre, *Them Dark Days*, 7, 13, 50–55, 59, 61–63, 71, 73–75, 77, 80, 102, 236–238, 240–242, 366, 412, 413, 441; Smith, "Rich Swamps and Rice Grounds," 10, 83, 104. Not all historians agree that mortality rates for enslaved Africans were higher and thus conditions were harsher on Lowcountry rice plantations than other kinds of plantations in the US South. See, for example, Smith, *Slavery and Rice Culture*, 207–210.
42. Hilliard, "The Tidewater Rice Plantation," 57–66; Dusinberre, *Them Dark Days*, 28–83, 213–247; and Carney, *Black Rice*, 133–135, 138–141.
43. Fields-Black, *Deep Roots*, 10, 11, 36, 50, 51, 77.
44. Baum, *Shrines of the Slave Trade*, 111, 121.

ORCID

Edda L. Fields-Black http://orcid.org/0000-0001-8621-2204

References

Alpern, Stanley B. "Did Enslaved Africans Spark South Carolina's Eighteenth-Century Rice Boom?" In *African Ethnobotany in the Americas*, edited by Robert A. Voeks and John Rashford, 35–66. New York: Springer, 2013.
Altieri, Miguel A. *Agroecology: The Scientific Basis of Alternative Agriculture*. Berkeley: Division of Biological Control, University of California, 1983.
Altieri, Miguel A. "Agroecology: The Science of Natural Resource Management for Poor Farmers in Marginal Environments." [In English]. *Agriculture, Ecosystems & Environment* 93, nos. 1–3 (2002): 1–24.
Babson, David W. "The Tanner Road Settlement: The Archaeology of Racism on Limerick Plantation." MA thesis., University of South Carolina, 1987.
Barry, Boubacar. *Senegaambia and the Atlantic Slave Trade*. Cambridge: Cambridge University Press, 1998.
Baum, Robert M. *Shrines of the Slave Trade: Diola Religion and Society in Precolonial Senegambia*. New York: Oxford University Press, 1999.
Bowes, Jessica. "Provisioned, Produced, Procured: Slave Subsistence Strategies and Social Relations at Thomas Jefferson's Poplar Forest." *Journal of Ethnobiology* 31, no. 1 (2011): 89–109.
Carney, Judith. "The Social History of Gambian Rice Production: An Analysis of Food Security Strategies." PhD diss., University of California at Berkeley Press, 1986.

Carney, Judith. "Landscapes of Technology Transfer: Rice Cultivation and African Continuities." *Technology and Culture* 37, no. 1 (1996): 5–35.
Carney, Judith. *Black Rice: The African Origins of Rice Cultivation in the Americas*. Cambridge, MA: Harvard University, 2002.
Carney, Judith, and Richard Nicholas Rosomoff. *In the Shadow of Slavery: Africa's Botanical Legacy in the Atlantic World*. Berkeley: University of California, 2011.
Carroll, Carl Ronald, John H. Vandermeer, and Peter M. Rosset. *Agroecology*. New York: McGraw-Hill, 1990.
Castiglioni, Luigi, Antonio Pace, Joseph Ewan, and Nesta Ewan. *Luigi Castiglioni's Viaggio: Travels in the United States of North America, 1785–1787*. Syracuse, NY: Syracuse University Press, 1983.
Catesby, Mark, and George Edwards. *The Natural History of Carolina, Florida, and the Bahamas Islands*, Vols I and II. London: Printed for B. White, 1771.
Crone, G. R. *The Voyages of Cadamosto and Other Documents on Western Africa in the Second Half of the Fifteenth Century*. London: Hakluyt Society, 1937.
d'Almada, Andre Alvares. *Brief Treatise on the Rivers of Guinea (c. 1594)*. Translated by Paul E. H. Hair. Department of History. Liverpool: University of Liverpool Press, 1984.
Dusinberre, William. *Them Dark Days: Slavery in the American Rice Swamps*. New York: Oxford University Press, 1996.
Edelson, S. Max. *Plantation Enterprise in Colonial South Carolina*. Cambridge, MA: Harvard University Press, 2006.
Eltis, David, Philip Morgan, and David Richardson. "Agency and Diaspora in Atlantic History: Reassessing the African Contribution to Rice Cultivation in the Americas." *The American Historical Review* 112, no. 5 (2007): 1329–1358.
Fernandes, Valentim. *Description de la Cote Occidentale D'afrique (Senegal Au Cap De Monte, Archipels)*. Bissau: Centro de Estudos da Guine Portugesa, 1951.
Fields-Black, Edda L. *Deep Roots: Rice Farming in West Africa and the African Diaspora*. Bloomington: Indiana University Press, 2008.
Franklin, M. "The Archaeological and Symbolic Dimensions of Soul Food: Race, Culture, and Afro-Virginian Identity." In *Race and the Archaeology of Identity*, edited by Charles E. Orser, 88–107. Salt Lake City: University of Utah Press, 2001.
Gliessman, Stephen R. *Agroecology: Researching the Ecological Basis for Sustainable Agriculture*. New York: Springer, 1990.
Gliessman, Stephen R. *Agroecology: The Ecology of Sustainable Food Systems*. Boca Raton, FL: CRC Press, 2007.
Gliessman, Stephen R., R. E. Garcia, and M. A. Amador. "The Ecological Basis for the Application of Traditional Agricultural Technology in the Management of Tropical Agro-Ecosystems." *Agro-ecosystems* 7, no. 3 (1981): 173–185.
Golbéry, Sylvain. *Travels in Africa, 1742*. London: Jones and Bumford, 1808.
Hawthorne, Walter. "Nourishing a Stateless Society During the Slave Trade: The Rise of Balanta Paddy-Rice Production in Guinea-Bissau." *Journal of African History* 42, no. 1 (2001): 1–24.
Hawthorne, Walter. *Planting Rice and Harvesting Slaves: Transformations along the Guinea-Bissau Coast, 1400-1900*. Portsmouth, NH: Heinemann, 2003.
Hawthorne, Walter. *From Africa to Brazil: Culture, Identity, and an Atlantic Slave Trade, 1600-1830*. Cambridge: Cambridge University Press, 2010.
Hawthorne, Walter. "The Cultural Meaning of Work: The 'Black Rice Debate' Reconsidered." In *Rice: Global Networks and New Histories*, edited by Francesca Bray, Peter A. Coclanis, Edda L. Fields-Black, and Dagmar Schafer, 279–290. Cambridge: Cambridge University Press, 2015.
Heath, Barbara J., and Amber Bennett. "'The Little Spots Allow'd Them': The Archaeological Study of African-American Yards." *Historical Archaeology* 34, no. 2 (2000): 38–55.
Hilliard, Sam B. "The Tidewater Rice Plantation: An Ingenious Adaptation to Nature." *Geoscience and Man* 12 (1975): 57–66.
Joyner, Charles. *Down by the Riverside: A South Carolina Slave Community*. Urbana-Champaign: University of Illinois Press, 1985.

Lauer, Joseph. "Rice in the History of the Lower Gambia-Geba Area." MA thesis, University of Wisconsin, 1969.

Lawson, John. *A New Voyage to Carolina*. Chapel Hill: University of North Carolina Press, 1967.

Littlefield, Daniel C. *Rice and Slaves: Ethnicity and the Slave Trade in Colonial South Carolina*. Urbana-Champaign: University of Illinois Press, 1991.

Mark, Peter A. *'Portuguese' Style and Luso-African Identity: Precolonial Senegambia, Sixteenth-Nineteenth Centuries*. Bloomington: Indiana University Press, 2002.

Matthews, John. *A Voyage to the River Sierra-Leone on the Coast of Africa, Containing an Account of the Trade and Protection of the Country and of the Civil and Religious Customs and the Manners of the People*. London: Frank Cass, 1996.

McCandless, Peter. *Slavery, Disease, and Suffering in the Southern Lowcountry*. Cambridge: Cambridge University Press, 2011.

McKee, Larry W. "Delineating Ethnicity from the Garbage of Early Virginians: Fauna Remains from the Kingsmill Plantation Slave Quarters." *American Archaeology* 6, no. 1 (1987): 31–39.

McKee, Larry. "Food Supply and Plantation Social Order: An Archaeological Perspective." In *"I, Too, Am America": Archaeological Studies of African-American Life*, edited by Theresa A. Singleton, 218–239. Charlottesville: University of Virginia Press, 1999.

Mintz, Sidney, and Douglas G. Hall. *The Origins of the Jamaican Internal Marketing System*. New Haven, CT: Yale University Publications in Anthropology, 1960.

Morgan, Philip D. *Slave Counterpoint: Black Culture in the Eighteenth-Century Chesapeake and Lowcountry*. Chapel Hill: University of North Carolina Press, 1998.

Mouser, Bruce. "Rebellion, Marronage, and Jihad: Strategies of Resistance to Slavery on the Sierra Leone Coast, c. 1783-1796." *The Journal of African History* 48, no. 1 (2007): 27–44.

Nowak, Bronislaw. "The Slave Rebellion in Sierra Leone in 1785-1786." *Hemispheres* 3 (1986): 151–169.

Pélissier, Paul. *Les Paysans du Sénégal: les civilisations du Cayor á la Casamnce*. Saint-Yrieix, France: Impr. Fabrègue, 1966.

Pereira, Pacheco. *Esmeraldo De Situ Orbis* [in English]. Translated by George H. T. Kimble. London: Kraus Reprint, 1967.

Pulsipher, Lydia Mihelic. "'They Have Saturdays and Sundays to Feed Themselves'." *Expedition* 32, no. 2 (1990): 24–33.

Pulsipher, Lydia M. "Galways Plantation, Montserrat." In *Seeds of Change*, edited by H. J. Viola and C. Margolis, 139–159. Washington, DC: Smithsonian Institution, 1991.

Pulsipher, Lydia Mihelic, and C. M. Goodwin. "Here Where the Old Time People Be: Reconstructing the Landscapes of the Slavery and Post-slavery Era in Montserrat, West Indies." In *African Sites Archaeology in the Caribbean*, edited by Jay Haviser, 9–37. Kingston, Jamaica: Ian Randle, 1999.

Rivière, Claude. "Le long des côtes de Guinée avant la phase coloniale." *Bulletin de l'IFAN, Series B, Dakar* 30, no. 2 (1968): 727–750.

Rosengarten, Dale. *Row upon Row: Sea Grass Baskets of the South Carolina Lowcountry*. Columbia: University of South Carolina Press, 1993.

Rosengarten, Dale. "Social Origins of the African-American Lowcountry Basket." Ph.D. diss, Harvard University, 1997.

Scott, Elizabeth M. "Who Ate What? Archaeological Food Remains and Cultural Diversity." In *Case Studies in Environmental Archaeology*, edited by Elizabeth Reitz, Lee A. Newsom, and Sylvia Scudder, 357–374. New York: Springer, 2008.

Scott, Elizabeth M., and S. L. Dawdy. "Colonial and Creole Diets in Eighteenth Century New Orleans." In *French Colonial Archaeology in the Southeast and Caribbean*, edited by Kenneth G. Kelly and Meredith D. Hardy, 97–116. Gainesville: University Press of Florida Press, 2011.

Smith, Julia Floyd. *Slavery and Rice Culture in Low Country Georgia, 1750-1860*. Knoxville: University of Tennessee, 1991.

Smith, Hayden R. "Reserving Water: Environmental and Technological Relationships with Colonial South Carolina Inland Rice Plantations." In *Rice: Global Networks and New Histories*, edited by Francesca Bray, Peter A. Coclanis, Edda L. Fields-Black, and Dagmar Schafer, 189–211. Cambridge: Cambridge University Press, 2015.

Smith, Hayden R. "Rich Swamps and Rice Grounds: The Specialization of Inland Rice Culture in the South Carolina Lowcountry, 1670-1861." Ph.D. diss, University of Georgia, 2012.

Stanley, Lord. "Narrative of Mr. William Cooper Thomson's Journey from Sierra Leone to Timbo, Capital of Futah Jallo, in Western Africa." *Journal of the Royal Geographical Society of London* 16 (1846): 106–138.

Stewart, Mart. "Rice, Water, and Power: Landscapes of Domination and Resistance in the Lowcountry, 1790-1880." *Environmental History Review* 15, no. 3 (1991): 47–64.

Stewart, Mart. *'What Suffers to Groe': Life, Labor, and Landscape on the Georgia Coast, 1680-1920*. Athens: University of Georgia, 1996.

Wallman, Diane. "Negotiating the Plantation Structure: An Archaeological Investigation of Slavery, Subsistence and Daily Practice at Habitation Creve Coeur, Martinique, Ca. 1760-1890." Ph.D. diss., University of South Carolina, 2014.

Wood, Peter H. *Black Majority: Negroes in Colonial South Carolina from 1670 Through the Stono Rebellion*. New York: Knopf, 1974.

Sierra Leone in the Atlantic World: concepts, contours, and exchange

Christopher R. DeCorse

> Underscoring the unique potential that this region has for the study of the African Diaspora, this article situates the slave trading fort on Bunce Island and the Sierra Leone hinterland in the wider context of Atlantic history. In doing so it underscores the need to view Atlantic exchanges within their specific cultural and historical settings, and to place them within the maritime Atlantic and capitalist world economies. The article further considers the conceptual and methodological challenges faced in tracing African continuities in the Diaspora and in evaluating change in African societies during the period of the Atlantic trade. Bunce Island's history and the trade relations represented present one of the better opportunities to delineate the paths through which enslaved Africans were brought to the Americas. This article examines the specific connections between this portion of Upper Guinea Coast and South Carolina. The importance of an interdisciplinary approach incorporating archaeological data in both the reconstruction of Africa's past and in providing a context for enslaved Africans in the Diaspora is underscored.

Introduction

The exciting aspect of the articles presented in this special issue of *Atlantic Studies* and in the original Walker Institute Workshop at the University of South Carolina, Columbia is their focus on the unique connections between specific areas of the Upper Guinea Coast and the southeastern US, particularly South Carolina. The amount and tempo of work on African Diaspora archaeology and the archaeology of Atlantic Africa signals the potential for a truly transatlantic archaeology.[1] Yet despite the amount of work undertaken, there remain both conceptual and methodological problems in its study, particularly with regard to the examination of African continuities in the Americas. This article underscores the specific historical and economic frameworks within which these social, cultural, and biological exchanges were articulated, and the transformations that they engendered. Ongoing research in the Sierra Leone Estuary and on Atlantic period sites in the Sierra Leone hinterland is used to illustrate both the prospects and problems faced in evaluating Atlantic period transformations in African societies and in tracing specific African connections in the Americas from an archaeological perspective.

Africa and Africans in the Atlantic world

The explanatory value of the Atlantic World as an analytic frame lies in its unique economic history of which Africa was integral.[2] The demands of European economies included a variety of raw materials and resources, including gold. It was, however, the burgeoning plantations of the Americas and their need for slave labor that undergirded the developing Atlantic World.[3] Although the relative economic importance of the slave trade can be debated, there is little question that plantation slavery of the Americas was a fundamental aspect of the Atlantic World's division of labor. The economic worth of the fertile soils of Brazil, the circum-Caribbean, and the Carolinas would have been valueless without labor to exploit them. It was slavery that linked Europe, Africa, and the Americas into the distinctive social, cultural, and economic relations of the Atlantic economy. The modern world would have unfolded quite differently without the forced movement of millions of enslaved Africans.

While Africa's role in the Atlantic World has been underscored by many researchers,[4] tracing the temporal and geographic parameters of the "African" Atlantic, and the transformations it engendered within Africa – especially during the opening centuries of the Atlantic period – are challenging. The nascent Atlantic World began in Africa: Portuguese expansion into the Atlantic islands and along the West African Coast started decades before the discovery of the Americas. Yet, almost from its onset the African trade was integrated into an increasingly global economy that also incorporated Indian Ocean and Asian trade networks spanning a diversity of contact settings. Regional histories unfolded within their distinctive, spatial and temporal positions within the evolving ensemble of relations comprising the world economy.[5] The first slaves from Africa were taken to Cabo Verde almost from the island's initial settlement and a pastoral economy run by slaves had emerged on Santiago by the mid-fifteenth century.[6]

Debate on the impacts of Atlantic maritime economy – particularly the slave trade – has ranged from the perspective that the changes that occurred were negligible, to one of major transformations that had long standing impacts on African economies.[7] Historical and archaeological data have, however, made it increasingly clear that the period coinciding with the emergence of the Atlantic trade was one of dramatic change in African societies, a time marked by changes in settlement and demographic patterns, and the associated sociopolitical structures. Old polities were reformed and new states emerged.[8] In the hinterlands of Sierra Leone, Guinea, and Liberia fortified towns replaced earlier settlement patterns and polities known from later historical accounts and oral traditions emerged.[9] These transformations delineate the frontier of an expanding world economy. The changes that unfolded during the period of the second slavery were equally dramatic, with polities being made and remade.[10] Although these changes were driven by the expanding Atlantic economy, these were nonetheless articulated within local contexts and cultural traditions spanning the *longue duree* of the pre-Atlantic past.[11] Africa did not exist unconnected with other regions prior to the advent of the Atlantic economy. The trans-Saharan trade and the economic and cultural exchanges it engendered – including the spread of Islam – both pre-date the arrival of the Europeans on the West African Coast and they continue to impact the modern world.

Archaeologies of the African Diaspora

Foregrounding Africa's role in shaping the Atlantic World and in understanding the transformations that occurred within it are essential in providing a context for the study of the African Diaspora. The peoples, polities, and cultures from which enslaved Africans were taken were diverse, and varied through time both in terms of the ethnolinguistic groups and regions of Africa represented. The complexities of these historical and cultural settings need to be carefully assessed when evaluating evidence for African antecedents for technologies, social behaviors, and cultural patterns and their material evidence in Diaspora contexts. Contextualizing studies of the Diaspora in terms of the relevant African historical and cultural settings is essential to address the concerns that many Africanists have expressed regarding the lack of engagement with African material that continues to characterize many archaeological studies of the African Diaspora.[12]

The strength of interpretation lies in successfully moving from historically and ethnographically known African populations to peoples in the Diaspora.[13] Unfortunately, making such analogs is challenging; the historical settings and the contexts represented complex.[14] Poor, largely non-existent records, lack of standardization in etymology, and varied histories often make it impossible to trace the ancestries of the enslaved populations represented beyond rather broad geographic or ethnic parameters.[15] Despite increasing work in many areas, historical information, ethnographic data, and archaeological research on African social practices and social organization are lacking for many of the portions of Africa.[16] The areas that today have some of the most developed university and research infrastructures were the locations of colonial research centers, including the *Institut Français de l'Afrique Noire* (now the *Institut Fondamentalde l'Afrique Noire*) in Dakar, the University of Ghana at Legon, and the University of Ibadan. The history of scholarship with regard to the different modern nation states of West Africa remains dramatically different. There are now, for example, dozens of practicing archaeologists in Ghana, Senegal, and Nigeria, in stark contrast to countries such as Guinea, Liberia, and Sierra Leone, which have no local archaeologists and limited institutional infrastructures. Consequently, the component populations of some geographic areas, their histories, and their material cultures are disproportionately represented in the literature.[17] The ethnographic data (whether relating to African-diasporic populations in the Americas or African populations) on which analogs are built are, at times, unconvincing and there is a disjuncture between the evidence presented and the conclusions reached. Various characteristics have sometimes been viewed as "African," despite limited evidence for historical connections between the African and American populations involved; viewed through the static lenses of ethnohistories constructed from limited data dating centuries after the advent of the Atlantic World. African characteristics are consequently left un-positioned in their culture historical contexts, unrecognizing of the sociocultural changes and population movements that have occurred in African populations over the past five centuries.

The studies presented in the Walker Institute Workshop underscore the unique historical connections between the Upper Guinea Coast and the South Carolina Lowcountry. Although the area of what is now Sierra Leone, Liberia, and Guinea provided fewer slaves than some areas of Africa,[18] the region is of special significance in terms of its specific historical intersection with the world economy, and associated cultural continuities with North America. These connections have long been recognized and, indeed, were foundational in African Diaspora studies, including the pioneering works of Lorenzo Dow Turner[19] and Melville Herskovits,[20] both of whom noted cultural continuities between the peoples of the Sierra Leone and the Gullah/

Geechee culture of Georgia and South Carolina. The range of commonalities noted is quite striking in terms of the material culture, culture traits, and linguistic practices represented.[21] These connections have not, however, been substantially explored from an archaeological perspective.[22]

Among the most significant of these continuity studies are of the Gullah language, which includes an African grammar and vocabulary. These features, first compellingly demonstrated by Turner, were subsequently the focus of research by many other scholars.[23] Also of particular significance is the research by Littlefield, Carney, and Fields-Black, which has focused on continuities between African rice agriculture and the Carolina Lowcountry.[24] The later study is especially innovative in terms of the use of African linguistic data in tracing cultivation practices. Also of interest is the study of genetic material from African and North American Diaspora populations, which has indicated a greater number of genetic links to the Upper Guinea Coast, more specifically Sierra Leone, than to other parts of the African continent.[25] On the basis of genetic data, a number of prominent African Americans have traced their ancestry to Sierra Leonean ethnic groups, including actor Isaiah Washington, poet Maya Angelou, and politician Jesse Jackson.[26] The distinctive history and the cultural traditions of the Carolina Lowcountry have led to the 2006 Congressional recognition of the Gullah Geechee Cultural Heritage Corridor, which extends from Wilmington, North Carolina in the north to Jacksonville, Florida.[27]

Europeans on the Guinea Coast

While presenting tantalizing potential for Atlantic history, the African contexts from which enslaved Africans were taken from Sierra Leone to the Americas remains poorly known, lacking historical documentation or oral historical information for many areas until the nineteenth or twentieth centuries. Ongoing, collaborative research by the Syracuse University Archaeological Initiative for the Sierra Leone Estuary (AISLE) is focusing on the cultural and socioeconomic transformations that occurred in coastal Sierra Leone over the past millennium with a particular focus on the period of the Atlantic slave trade.[28] The Sierra Leone Estuary, located at the confluence of the Rokel River and Port Loco Creek, emerged as a major source of slaves during the seventeenth and eighteenth centuries, and slaves continued to be exported from the area well into the nineteenth century. The research undertaken provides both insight into Africa's intersection with the Atlantic World and the region's unique ties to the USA.

Portuguese traders arrived in coastal Sierra Leone in the mid-fifteenth century and subsequently visited the coast regularly, dominating the trade in the region for the following half century. A trade in slaves with Cabo Verde was initiated in the first decades of contact.[29] The Trade was often conducted by Portuguese or Afro-Portuguese creoles who lived on shore and acted as middlemen.[30] The Portuguese also established the first outposts, including what was apparently a briefly occupied royal fort in the Sierra Leone River during the 1480s or 1490s.[31] During the seventeenth century Dutch, French, and English traders increasingly visited coastal Sierra Leone and established a number of smaller factories and outposts in coastal Sierra Leone, including the Sierra Leone Estuary. As one of the largest natural harbors in the world, the Estuary was historically important as both a safe anchorage and as a means of access into the Sierra Leone hinterland: a source of raw materials and slaves. The locations of some of these outposts and the associated African cultural landscapes of which they were part have been surveyed as part of the Syracuse University AISLE.[32]

The most important of the European outposts established in the Sierra Leone Estuary was Bunce Island, located 20 miles from Freetown (Figure 1). The island's fort was Sierra Leone's first declared, national historic site and it is currently the most studied archaeological site in the country.[33] The fort's history and its layout afford unique insight into the organization of the slave trade during its apogee. Bunce Island was established long after the foundation of the first European forts in West Africa.[34] It is possible that the island was the site of an early Portuguese watering station. It was, however, only in the 1670s during the burgeoning slave trade that the initial English trading lodge was established. Many of the other European outposts in West Africa were more impressive than the fort on Bunce, which was dwarfed in size by the larger European headquarters at Christiansborg, Cape Coast, and Elmina in coastal Ghana. Yet the island's fort was the major center of the English, and then British, slave trade on the West African Coast between the Senegambia and coastal Ghana from the 1670s until the abolition of the trade by the British in 1808. During this period, Bunce Island was the place where tens of thousands of enslaved Africans began the Middle Passage to the Americas.

Bunce Island was not particularly significant in terms of the number of enslaved Africans that passed through its walls; many more captive Africans were held in other European outposts that dot the West African Coast. Bunce's particular significance lies in the transport of many of the enslaved Africans that were held within its walls directly to North America.[35] Given Bunce Island's prominence in the British trade on this portion of the West African Coast and the direct links to the USA, it stands as one of the key sites through which many enslaved African destined for the plantations of Florida, Georgia, and the South Carolina Lowcountry likely passed

Figure 1. Photo of the main fortifications on Bunce Island. Photograph by author.

between the late seventeenth and early nineteenth centuries. The island is unique for a number of reasons, including its position on the African coast, its direct ties to the USA, its excellent archaeological preservation, and its layout and organization. Primary and secondary sources dealing with Sierra Leone's past well illustrate Bunce Island's pivotal role in Sierra Leone's intersection with the Atlantic world.[36] Variously known as Bens, Bunce, Bance, or George Island, the site remained British for nearly a century and half, despite attacks by the French, raids by pirates, and destruction by a slave trader. Initially managed by the Company of Gambia Adventurers and then the Royal African Company, the island reached its apogee during the second half of the eighteenth century under the private trading companies of Grant, Oswald & Company between 1748 and 1784, and the Company of John & Alexander Anderson from 1784 to 1808.

Perhaps better than any other enterprise, the activities of Grant, Oswald & Company – spanning across Britain, Africa, and the Americas – illustrate the interconnected entrepreneurship of the Atlantic World; the company's activities representing the ultimate refinement of the slave trade into a unified process that integrated all aspects of production, from the trade in slaves to shipping and agricultural production.[37] The management of Bunce Island was equally characterized by the integration of distinct products, peoples and systems to further trade, along with careful supervision. Acquiring Bunce Island was the company's "single most lucrative shipping and trading opportunity."[38] Located at the farthest point in the Sierra Leone Estuary accessible to ocean going ships, the island's environs offered foodstuffs, timber, ivory, and locations for careening and watering ships. It was also was well positioned to collect slaves coming from the interior. From shortly after the start of their tenure, Grant, Oswald & Company was assured their exclusive rights to the slave trade owing to the African Trade Act of 1750, which the company owners were instrumental in framing.[39] The Bunce Island factors were charged not to kidnap slaves or to wage war on African polities, but to facilitate access to the coast; obtaining slaves through trade with Africans was deemed easier and more efficient than direct capture.[40] As time went on, a network of outposts was established further in the interior to better secure the trade.[41] No other European forts in West Africa employed comparable efficiency in organization, instead primarily relying on African intermediaries. Slaves were gathered at the Bunce Island for sale to European, American, or Afro-European traders, the company charging a premium for collecting the slaves in advance of a ship's arrival and so reducing the amount of time it had to spend on the coast. The company also financed ships that took full cargoes of slaves directly to South Carolina, as well as to Georgia, Florida, Grenada, and St. Christopher (see Figure 2).

Grant, Oswald & Company's direct economic and social ties to the USA set Bunce Island apart from other European outposts in West Africa. The familiarity of the slaves of Sierra Leone and Guinea Coast with rice cultivation made them particularly attractive to the plantation owners of the South Carolina and under the direction of Grant, Oswald & Company, slaves were brought directly to the Lowcountry for sale.[42] The links between Sierra Leone and South Carolina are dramatically illustrated by the story of Priscilla, a 10-year-old girl purchased from African traders in Sierra Leone in 1756. Documentary records were used to trace Priscilla's journey from Bunce Island to Comingtee Plantation in South Carolina, and trace her ancestry through seven generations down to the present (Figure 3).[43] The business and political

Figure 2. A 1760 advertisement for slaves from Sierra Leone arriving on the ship "Bance Island." "Austin, Laurens and Appleby" are listed in the ad: Henry Laurens was Bunce Islands representative in Charleston's and partner in one of the largest slave trading houses in North America. Image courtesy of the Mariners' Museum and Park, Newport News, VA.

connections of the Bunce Island operations spanned the Atlantic. During the Revolutionary War, Bunce Island's Charleston agent, Henry Laurens, became president of the Continental Congress and, after hostilities ended, he was one of the four American diplomats who negotiated independence for the USA under the Treaty of Paris.[44] The British representative at those negotiations was Richard Oswald, Laurens' former business partner and the owner of Bunce Island. A number of other prominent Americans also have ties to Bunce Island, including Presidents George Herbert Walker and George Walker Bush.[45]

Bunce Island is also unique in terms of its archaeological preservation. Although it continued in use after abolition, the island was abandoned in the nineteenth century and has remained uninhabited. This setting is in dramatic contrast to the majority of the European outposts and forts in West Africa, which for the most part were located within or near modern settlements and, in most cases, have been extensively modified or obliterated by development.[46] In other instances, they continued in service as government offices, prisons, lighthouses, and rest houses, and were subsequently modified by reuse and renovation. In contrast, even in light of nineteenth modifications and the ravages of time, Bunce Island remains remarkably intact. It is one of the best preserved slave forts in Africa, and arguably one of the best preserved British overseas sites in Africa.

The current ruins of Bunce Island represent the fort's plan at the end of the eighteenth century when the slave trade with South Carolina well under way. In plan and organization, it is quite distinct from other European forts established in West Africa.[47] At its apogee, Bunce is said to have been well-fortified and considered by one chronicler "the best English fort on the Coast."[48] Yet the defenses were relatively modest and the European garrison small compared to those found at some of the

Figure 3. Ruins of Comingtee Plantation, South Carolina in 2007. Documents indicate that Priscilla, a 10-year-old girl purchased from African traders in Sierra Leone, was taken to Comingtee in 1756. Photograph courtesy of J. Barry Gooch.

other contemporary European outposts in West Africa. Although the Bunce Island fort has a pentagonal shape not uncommon in British military architecture, its construction and the interior arrangements were quite vernacular.[49] Among the most distinct features of the fort were the position and organization of the facilities for holding slaves. In contrast to the dungeons and cells used in other forts, there were separate male and female enclosures that were located at the back of male and female slave yards. Divided by a wall, the slave yards were entered through a double entrance surmounted by a platform that allowed slaves to be monitored from above. The open slave yards are also unusual in their placement immediately behind Bance Island House, a two story, brick and stone building. Windows of the houses ground floor rooms, which looked directly into the slave yards, may have been closed off with ornate iron grates.[50] This is quite different from the arrangements seen other European slave forts where slaves were generally kept well away from the living quarters of the slave traders. Most European outposts also lacked open yard areas specifically for slaves.[51]

In addition to the fort complex, Bunce Island also included a village of *grumetoes* (or *grumetes*); free African laborers employed by the Europeans. The *grumetoes* were crucial to the island's economy, emerging as a distinct population but also a workforce intricately linked to the island's operation. They were the skilled laborers that included carpenters, blacksmiths, and shipwrights. In addition, they also directed the gathering of fresh water, and grew rice, citrus, and other provisions for visiting slave ships on neighboring Tasso Island. During the second half of the eighteenth century, they were increasingly relied on to conduct trade, captain ships, and manage out factories.[52]

Following the enactment of the British prohibition of the Atlantic slave trade for British subjects in 1808 and with the growth of Freetown, a settlement that had been specifically established for liberated Africans, the Company of John & Alexander Anderson shut down their trading operations.[53] As slavery was illegal in the Sierra Leone Colony, slaves could no longer be traded in older established trading areas such as Bunce Island and new outlets were found such as the Mellicourie, Scarcies, and Rio Pongo to the north.[54] Slavery and the trade in slaves also continued in the Sierra Leone Estuary. A series of legislative acts aimed at eliminating slavery were instituted in the Sierra Leone Protectorate during the 1890s and early twentieth centuries. Slavery was finally abolished in Sierra Leone 1928.

The Sierra Leone hinterland in the Atlantic world

While forts such as Bunce are iconic symbols of a trade that brought millions of enslaved Africans to the Americas, they provide neither a beginning nor an end. They are rather points in a journey that took slaves from the African interior to the coastal trade entrepots and then to the Americas. Enslaved Africans were, for the most part, not obtained from the immediate areas of the slave forts or the adjacent coasts but rather the vast hinterlands. Consequently, the histories and the stories that brought most enslaved Africans to Bunce Island and places like it are largely left unknown.[55] In the case of Pricilla, the young girl whose voyage from Bunce Island to South Carolina was noted, we know little more of her origins other than she likely came from the area of Sierra Leone or, possibly, Guinea. There are no records to indicate if she was a Baga or Sherbro from the coast, Mende from the south, or Limba from the far north. Nor are there any hints as to how she came to be a slave. The most tantalizing insights into slave origins include the study of the names of enslaved Africans liberated by the British West Africa Squadron between 1808 and 1860.[56]

The routes by which slaves reached the coast, details of how their enslavement occurred, and the impacts of the trade in the hinterlands from which they were taken are far from clear. The specific routes and details of how slaves were obtained and the specific routes taken by African middlemen to the coast are largely unknown. Direct documentary accounts are scant or non-existent for the vast majority of the West African interior until the late nineteenth or even the twentieth centuries.[57] Accounts of varying quality by African-born slaves provide firsthand stories of their enslavement.[58] Memories of the slave trade are also preserved in a variety of other ways.[59] However, we are left with only hints of the nature of the wider African trade networks of which sites such as Bunce Island were part. Understanding of the transformations in African populations must, therefore, be gleaned through a combination of interdisciplinary resources.

Although Sierra Leone is a relatively small country by African standards – slightly smaller in area than South Carolina – it incorporates tremendous environmental and cultural diversity. Vegetation ranges from coastal swamps and tropical rain forest in the south, to transitional savanna in the north. There are more than a dozen major linguistic groups, which reflect varying degrees of sociocultural cohesion and material expression. Slaves brought to the Sierra Leone Coast may have traveled hundreds of miles from the interior. There is limited evidence that trade connections from the coast and estuary extended as far as the Futa Jallon in the Sierra Leone/Guinea hinterlands by the early sixteenth century.[60] These routes, including those used throughout the slave trade, may have followed trade networks that pre-date the Atlantic period. Specifics and substantive documentary evidence and archaeological evidence does not, however, appear until much later in the nineteenth century. Rivers, such as the Rokel and Port Loko Creek, offered easier transport to and from the interior, a factor that European outposts such as Bunce Island exploited. Yet the majority of travel, by necessity, would have been via foot paths. These routes were controlled by various polities and periodically closed.[61]

The majority of slaves may have been war captives, a supposition based on nineteenth century documentary and oral historical sources.[62] Alexander Gordon Laing's account of his 1821 expedition, which provides one of the first detailed descriptions of the Sierra Leone interior, describes the slave trade as still pervasive throughout the country at that time. Laing detailed Yalunka oral traditions in order "to show by brief narration, the frequency of the wars in which a great interior nation has for many years been engaged, actuated alone by the motive of acquiring riches by the sale of their less powerful neighbours."[63] The accounts recorded by Laing describe the destruction of numerous towns and the sale of the captives to the coast. This pattern of escalating conflict to procure slaves may have emerged almost concurrently with the advent of the Atlantic World.[64] Warfare and raiding, however, were not the only means of enslavement. Slavery was also a way of paying debts or as punishment for crimes. Laing, for example, notes that slaves were divided into "those born in the country, who are not liable to be sold contrary to their inclinations" and "those taken in war, or enslaved on account of debt, or by way of punishment."[65] Despite abolition, the trade in slaves remained important in the Sierra Leone hinterland throughout the nineteenth century, regardless of British abolition or the presence of a settlement specifically established for emancipated slaves.[66] Later nineteenth century sources indicate that larger Yalunka and Fulani polities raided smaller groups such as the Limba for slaves, as well as raiding each other. British expeditions of the 1880s reported many destroyed and deserted settlements, people perhaps having sought shelter in larger fortified towns, fled even further afield, killed or been enslaved.[67] Oral traditions similarly record many episodes of conflicts related to slave raids.[68] The Samori invasions between 1884 and 1892 were partly directed at slave raiding.[69]

Archaeological, ethnographic, and historical data from the Sierra Leone hinterland provides some insight into the sociocultural landscapes from which enslaved Africans were taken. Modern chiefdoms are the result of administrative boundaries imposed by the colonial administration during the late nineteenth and twentieth centuries, and later by the Sierra Leone government.[70] It is, therefore, uncertain the degree to which current or historically known sociopolitical organizations and cultural practices are representative of pre-twentieth century conditions. Ethnographic, historical, and archaeological data indicate that throughout the Atlantic period population was concentrated in small towns of perhaps a few thousand people, which were in turn surrounded by smaller hamlets.[71] Towns and smaller villages banded together in varied alliances under charismatic leaders during periods of war.[72] Trade afforded some rulers and emerging elites avenues to exploit new opportunities, generating new power relations.[73]

New states or incipient states, integrated into the Atlantic economy and, in part, based on the slave trade, emerged. The ability to control agricultural production and distribution through the management of slaves more effectively than neighboring groups may have been a key factor in a polity's expansion. These trajectories of expansion and contraction are comparable to examples from other part of West Africa.

Although the specifics of the sociopolitical organizations represented are uncertain, archaeological data, in combination with oral traditions and limited documentary sources, provide clear indications of dramatic changes in African societies during the Atlantic period (Figure 4). An older pattern of open, dispersed settlements was replaced by settlement pattern consisting of defensive sites. The fortifications employed in these defensive sites were sometimes very elaborate, incorporating systems of walls, defensive ditches, and guard towers. Winding entrances through dense brush were also employed. Fortified towns, hilltop sites, and defensive features dating to the Atlantic period have a wide distribution throughout present day Guinea, Sierra Leone, and Liberia, testament to slave raiding and interethnic conflict (Figure 5).[74] In this respect, their appearance during the seventeenth, eighteenth and nineteenth centuries delineates the frontier an expanding Atlantic economy.[75] Slaves taken from these areas would have moved through interior trade networks, eventually reaching trading enclaves such as Bunce Island, journeys that on foot may have taken weeks.

Figure 4. A Yalunka elder in northern Sierra Leone holds a bow and arrow. Many oral traditions recount episodes of slave raiding. Photograph by author.

Figure 5. Photos of hilltop town of Yagala in northern Sierra Leone. Such inaccessible sites were chosen for defense. Photograph by author.

Conclusion

Our limited view of early Atlantic and pre-Atlantic Sierra Leonean history has important implications for the interpretation of the African past and the history of the African Diaspora. Lacking clear understanding of pre-Atlantic history makes it difficult to fully assess the transformations that have occurred in African societies in the past 500 years and, consequently, the cultural and material artifacts that enslaved Africans may have carried with them to the Americas. Sierra Leone history texts – written by Europeans and Sierra Leoneans alike – out of necessity – largely begin their narratives with the European arrival and primarily focus on later African polities and transformations that occurred centuries after the opening of the Atlantic period.[76] The absence of documentary evidence for early Atlantic history has led some scholars to suggest that Sierra Leone was only occupied by hunter gatherers until the formation of the first settled agricultural communities after the advent of the Atlantic World, between the sixteenth and the nineteenth centuries.[77] "History" only emerges through the lens of the increasing prevalence of documentary source material provided by outsiders and for the most part dating long after the opening of the Atlantic trade. These views of the African past lie in stark contrast to other portions of Africa where archaeological research are testament to African technological, cultural, and sociopolitical complexity long pre-dating European contact.

The documentary accounts and oral traditions of the Sierra Leone hinterland only hint at the conflicts and consequences that resulted from the slave trade and the life histories of the people that were enmeshed in it. They are consequently unsatisfactory in providing substantive grounding for examination of supposed "African" characteristics in Diaspora contexts. Ongoing archival and ethnohistorical research, as well as archaeological fieldwork, promises to provide increasing understanding of Sierra

Leone's past and its wider connections with the Atlantic World. It will, however, likely provide little insight into the individual stories of the millions of captive Africans that came to the Americas. These are, sadly, stories that will be left untold.

Acknowledgements
I thank Ken Kelly for organizing the Walker Institute Workshop at the University of South Carolina and for commenting on initial drafts of this article. I also thank the anonymous reviewers for their useful suggestions.

Disclosure Statement
No potential conflict of interest was reported by the authors.

Notes
1. See Ogundiran and Falola, *Archaeology of Atlantic Africa*. The Atlantic World, the intersection of Africa with it, and the exchanges that these interactions engendered have emerged as key themes in the social sciences. See surveys in Green, *Trans-Atlantic Slave Trade*; Green and Morgan, *Atlantic History*; Mitchell, *African Connections*; Thornton, *Cultural History*; Yelvington, *Afro-Atlantic Dialogues*; and Yerxa, *Recent Themes*.
2. The foci of "Atlantic" history and the conceptual framing of the research undertaken are far from unified in terms of either the geographic and temporal parameters represented, or the conceptual vantages taken. For example, see the varying perspectives of the Atlantic World's margins and concepts discussed in Bailyn, *Atlantic History;* Bailyn and Denault, *Soundings*; Balachandran, "Atlantic Paradigms"; Cañizares-Esguerra and Seeman, *Atlantic in Global History*; DeCorse, *Post-Colonial or Not?*; Fogelman, "Transformation of the Atlantic World"; Gabaccia, "Spatializing Gender"; Kellman, "Beyond Center and Periphery"; and O'Reilly, "Genealogies of Atlantic History."
3. Tomich, "Atlantic History and World Economy," 113–115. See also Solow, *Slavery and the Rise*.
4. For example, see Mitchell, *African Connections*; Thornton, *Cultural History*; and Yelvington, *Afro-Atlantic Dialogues*.
5. As Tomich observes, polities, relations of production, class formation, and ethnicities are not independent of the larger complex of relations of which they were part or of one another, but rather must be seen as constituent relations of the world economy. Tomich, "Atlantic History and World Economy," 105. The need to situate Atlantic transformations in the deeper context of the pre-Atlantic African past is explored in DeCorse, "Post-Colonial or Not?"
6. Duncan, *Atlantic Islands*, 17–24.
7. For example, see Eltis, *Economic Growth*; Fage, "Slavery and the Slave Trade"; Lovejoy, "Impact of the Atlantic Slave Trade"; Morgan, "Africa and the Atlantic"; and Rodney, *How Europe Underdeveloped Africa*.

8. There is documentary evidence for this in areas close to European trading enclaves, but for many areas archaeology is a primary source of information. For example, see DeCorse, *West Africa during the Slave Trade*; DeCorse, *An Archaeology of Elmina*, 31–43; DeCorse, "West African Archaeology"; DeCorse and Spiers, "A Tale of Two Polities"; Green, *Rise of the Atlantic Slave Trade*, 77–84; Kelly, "Archaeology of African-European Interaction"; Monroe, *The Precolonial State*; and Morgan, "Africa and the Atlantic," 232–234.
9. For example, see DeCorse, "Fortified Towns of the Koinadugu Plateau."
10. See DeCorse and Spiers, "A Tale of Two Polities" and compare Eltis, *Economic Growth*, 73–77.
11. DeCorse, *Postcolonial or Not?*; and Kelly, "Using Historically Informed Archaeology".
12. DeCorse, "Oceans Apart"; Fields-Black, *Deep Roots*, 51–53; Hauser and DeCorse, "Low-Fired Earthenwares"; Kelly, "African Diaspora Starts Here"; Posnansky, "Toward an Archaeology"; and Posnansky, "Revelations, Roots, and Reactions."
13. For example, Wilkie and Farnsworth's study of influence of African textile patterns in Afro-Bahamian "aesthetic" choice in European ceramics is strengthened by their consideration of the varied African populations from which they were descended. It should, however, be noted that their consideration could have usefully included reference to the varied textile traditions, as well as other decorative inventories, from across the African regions considered. See Wilkie and Farnsworth, *Sampling*, 35–68.
14. These interpretive challenges are illustrated by the connections between Elmina in coastal Ghana, site of the Dutch headquarters in West Africa from 1637 to 1872, and Curaçao in the southern Caribbean. As these areas were controlled by the same European power throughout much of the slave trade, the study of their contexts and cultures would seem to hold promise for the untangling of the complexities of the Diaspora. Yet the reality of the historical setting makes this challenging. See Haviser and DeCorse, "African-Caribbean Interaction," 329–30; and Kea, "When I Die."
15. Among the most promising of these efforts is the work on names recorded in the Registers of Liberated Africans, which make it possible to at least partially trace the geographic origins of enslaved Africans taken from the Sierra Leone hinterland. See Misevich, "The Origins." This source is, however, only available for the nineteenth century and is a subset of the number or individuals represented.
16. Robertshaw, *A History*; Posnansky, "African Archaeology."
17. DeCorse, *Postcolonial or Not?*; and Holl, "Worldviews."
18. Trans-Atlantic Slave Trade Database; Donnan, *Documents*. Also see brief overview in Rodney, *A History of the Upper Guinea Coast*, 250–252. Edward Ball has suggested that four out of ten African Americans have ancestors who first arrived in the United States via the Charleston coast. Ball, *Slaves in the Family*, 190.
19. Turner, *Africanisms in the Gullah Dialect*; Wade-Lewis, "Impact of the Turner-Herskovits"; Wade-Lewis, *Lorenzo Dow Turner*.
20. Herskovits, "Significance of West Africa"; and Herskovits, *Myth of the Negro Past*.
21. Morgan, *African American Life*; and Sengova, "My Mother Dem Nyus."
22. Barnes and Steen, "Archaeology and Heritage," 2012; and Singleton, "Reclaiming," 2010.
23. Turner, *Africanisms in the Gullah Dialect*; and Sengova, "My Mother Dem Nyus." The 1998 film *Language You Cry In*, traces the origins of a five line Gullah song to a Mende funeral dirge from southern Sierra Leone. The film by Alvaro Topeke and Angel Serrano highlights work by Joseph Opala, Cynthia Schmidt, and Tazieff Koroma. For review of the interpretive problems see Thomas-Houston, "Review."
24. See Littlefield, *Rice and Slaves*; Carney, *Black Rice*; and Fields-Black, *Deep Roots*.
25. Torres, Doura, Keita, and Kittles, "Y Chromosome Lineages."
26. Gondobay Manga Foundation website; McClanahan, "US-funded coalition restores key West African slave-trade 'castle'."
27. "A Unique African American Culture."
28. Amartey and Reid, "Terrestrial and Maritime"; DeCorse, "Bunce Island: A Cultural Resource Assessment"; DeCorse "Archaeological Investigations, Tasso and Bunce Islands"; and DeCorse, "Archaeological Fieldwork."
29. For example, see Hair, "Early Sources"; and Hair, "Sources on Early Sierra Leone (6)".

30. Brooks, *Euroafricans*; and Rodney, *A History*.
31. Pereira, *Esmeraldo*, 96; Hair, "Early Sources"; and Hair, "Sources on Early Sierra Leone (12)."
32. Amartey and Reid, "Terrestrial and Maritime"; and DeCorse, "Archaeological Fieldwork."
33. DeCorse, "Bunce Island: A Cultural Resource Assessment"; DeCorse "Archaeological Investigations, Tasso and Bunce Islands"; and DeCorse, "Archaeological Fieldwork."
34. The first of these was *Castelo São Jorge da Mina* (now known as Elmina Castle) in coastal Ghana, founded in 1482. DeCorse, "Early Trade Posts"; and Hair, *The Founding*; Lawrence, *Trade Castles and Forts*.
35. Hancock, *Citizens of the World*, 198–214.
36. For example, see Fyfe, *A History of Sierra Leone*, 4–5, 7, 9–10, 65–66, 78, 108–110, 118, 152; Hancock, *Citizens of the World*, 172–220; and Kup, *History of Sierra Leone*, 21–22, 26, 48, 55–61, 70–72, 83–96, 100, 107–116.
37. Hancock, *Citizens of the World*, 172–220.
38. Ibid., 172.
39. Ibid., 184–185.
40. Ibid., 199–200. Oral traditions also recount the story of Gumba Smart, who was a slave at Bunce Island who became a trusted agent and then an independent slave trader. See Ball, *Slaves in the Family*, 421–425.
41. Amartey and Reid, "Terrestrial and Maritime."
42. Fields-Black, *Deep Roots*, 52.
43. Ball, *Slaves in the Family*, 194; "Priscilla's Homecoming."
44. Hamer, *The Papers*, 35–36.
45. Akam, "George W. Bush's Great-Grandfather."
46. Cape Coast Castle in Ghana, for example, is far more impressive than Bunce Island in size but it has remained in continuous use over the past three and half centuries, serving as a prison until the 1980s. See Kankpeyeng and DeCorse, "Ghana's Vanishing Past."
47. DeCorse, "Bunce Island: A Cultural Resource Assessment," 16–66.
48. Fyfe, *A History of Sierra Leone*, 7.
49. DeCorse, "Bunce Island: A Cultural Resource Assessment." The only fortifications consist of two semicircular bastions and curtain wall, facing west toward the anchorage. Included in the fort were spaces for the storage of goods, housing for the European garrison, and workshops.
50. DeCorse, "Archaeological Investigations Tasso and Bunce," 8.
51. See discussion of British forts in DeCorse, "Tools of Empire." The view from the back windows of Bance Island House in 1791 was poignantly described by Anna Maria Falconbridge, wife of British abolitionist Alexander Falconbridge, who had dinner with the slave traders on the upper story of Bance Island House. See Falconbridge, *Narrative of Two Voyages*, 32.
52. Hancock, *Citizens of the World*, 193.
53. Bunce Island may have been the first European fort in West Africa to be proposed as a monument to the slave trade. In 1922, J. B. Chinsman suggested that the City Council of Freetown purchase the island from the British Colonial government "so that its caves and tombstones could be preserved as historical monuments of the slave trade." Quoted in Wyse, "*Bankole-Bright and Politics*," 24. Current work under the supervision of the Sierra Leone Monuments and Relics Commission is seeking to preserve and stabilize the island's ruins and provide interpretive facilities.
54. For example, see Deveneaux, *Political and Social Impact*, 178–191; Mouser, *American Colony on the Rio Pongo*; Misevich, "The Origins." Slave trading in the Sierra Leone Estuary continued after British abolition. For example, Laing writing in 1825 attributes the "knavery" and "indisposition to honest labour" among the Timne to their long participation in the slave trade and to the fact that one of the principal markets of the slave trade was at the mouth of a river in their territory. Laing may have been referring to Bunce Island. Laing, *Travels in the Timanee, Kooranko and Soolima*, 106–107. In the 1855, the *HMS Teazer* was dispatched to attack Medina, just northeast of Bunce Island, because the chief was reputed to be dealing in slaves. See Kingston, *Blue Jackets*.
55. Hancock, *Citizens of the World*, 203.

56. See Misevich, "The Origins."
57. For example, see Laing, *Travels in the Timanee, Kooranko and Soolima*; Blyden, "Report on the Expedition to Falaba"; Garrett, "Sierra Leone and the Interior"; Reade, *African Sketch-Book*; Trotter, *The Niger Sources*; Zweifel and Moustier, *Voyage aux Sources du Niger*.
58. See reviews by Fyfe, *Our Children*; and Handler, "Survivors of the Middle Passage."
59. For example, see Shaw, *Memories of the Slave Trade*; Lane and MacDonald, *Slavery in Africa*.
60. For example, see Atherton, "Early Economies of Sierra Leone," 33; Deveneaux, *Political and Social Impact*, 112–114; Hair, "Sources on Early Sierra Leone (12)," 31. However, detailed evidence for specific trade linkages between the coast and hinterland are limited until the late nineteenth century. Archaeological evidence for European trade materials also appears limited until the late nineteenth and twentieth centuries.
61. Evidence for this dates to the nineteenth century. For example, see Deveneaux, *Political and Social Impact*, 112–126; Fyle, *The Solima Yalunka Kingdom*, 93–98; and Laing, *Travels in the Timanee, Kooranko and Soolima*, 25–26.
62. See DeCorse, "Fortified Towns of the Koinadugu Plateau."
63. Laing, *Travels in the Timanee, Kooranko and Soolima*, 381, 399–419. In Temne country, a clamor was purportedly raised against Laing when he was accused of being "one of those white men who prevented the slave-trade, and injured the prosperity of their country." See Laing, *Travels in the Timanee, Kooranko and Soolima*, 106.
64. There is no direct evidence for this in the case of Sierra Leone. However, surveying archival sources for the Senegambia, Green cites evidence for slave raiding and political instability going back to the second half of the fifteenth century. Green, *Rise of the Atlantic Slave Trade*, 78–82.
65. Laing, *Travels in the Timanee, Kooranko and Soolima*, 133, also see 364.
66. Deveneaux, "Political and Social Impact," 112–117; Howard, "Big Men, Traders, and Chiefs," 37–40, 150–160; and Mitchell, "Trade Routes."
67. For example, see Garrett "Sierra Leone and the Interior"; Trotter, *The Niger Sources*, 34. For the history of the Sierra Leone Colony, see Peterson, *Province of Freedom*.
68. For example, see Fyle, *The Solima Yalunka Kingdom*; and DeCorse, "Limba, Yalunka and Kuranko Ethnicity".
69. For example, see Fyle, *The Solima Yalunka Kingdom,* 117–123; and Lipschutz, *Northeast Sierra Leone,* 62–79. In the 1880s and early 1890s, Samori Touré's Islamic state extended across the West African savannah from the Futa Jallon in Guinea eastward through Mali and Burkina Faso to northern Ghana.
70. For example, see Alie, *New History of Sierra Leone*, 152–157; DeCorse, "Fortified Towns of the Koinadugu Plateau"; and Donald, "Changes in Yalunka Social Organization," 128–135.
71. DeCorse, "Fortified Towns of the Koinadugu Plateau." The organization of these settlements is difficult to characterize given the limited information. However, family and kinship ties that were central to the labor needs of a subsistence economy were likely important.
72. Chiefs, who largely functioned as secular leaders, utilized personal ties and charismatic authority to extend their political influence. Other sociopolitical structures such as kinship groups (both maternal and paternal), affines, age grades, and secret societies (evidence for which is all poorly perceived archaeologically) provide cross-cutting forms of more heterarchical social organization.
73. For example, by 1800 the Yalunka settlements in northern Sierra Leone had coalesced into what Fyle refers to as the Solima Yalunka Kingdom. Trade, including slaves, may have been an important factor in the Kingdom's origins and available data suggest that there were a significantly higher proportion of slaves within the Yalunka area. Fyle, *The Solima Yalunka Kingdom,* 49–64; also see Donald, "Changes in Yalunka Social Organization," 9–12, 44–55; and Lipschulz, *Northeast Sierra Leone,*185.
74. For example, see Abraham, "Pattern of Warfare and Settlement," 129–131; Alldridge, *Sherbro and Its Hinterland*, 97, 115, 219, 230, 298–300; Atherton, "Protohistoric Habitation Sites"; Atherton, "Ethnoarchaeology in Africa," 86–90; DeCorse, "Limba, Yalunka and Kuranko Ethnicity"; DeCorse, "Fortified Towns of the Koinadugu Plateau"; Jones, *From Slaves to Palm Kernels*, 169–173; Laing, *Travels in the Timanee, Kooranko and Soolima*, 220–221, 264; Malcolm, "Mende Warfare," 48–49; and Siddle, "War-Towns in Sierra Leone".

75. DeCorse, "Fortified Towns of the Koinadugu Plateau."
76. For example, see Alie, *New History of Sierra Leone*, 31; Fyfe, *A History of Sierra Leone*. Fyle discusses the potential contribution of archaeology, but underscores the limited work undertaken. See Fyle, *History of Sierra Leone*, 7.
77. Siddle, "War-Towns in Sierra Leone" and compare DeCorse, "Fortified Towns of the Koinadugu Plateau."

References

Abraham, Arthur. "The Pattern of Warfare and Settlement among the Mende of Southern Sierra Leone in the Second Half of the Nineteenth Century." *Institute of African Studies, Fourah Bay College Occasional Paper* No. 1, 1975.

Akam, Simon. "George W. Bush's Great-Great-Great-Great-Grandfather Was a Slave Trader." Slate, June 20, 2013, http://www.slate.com/articles/life/history_lesson/2013/06/george_w_bush_and_slavery_the_president_and_his_father_are_descendants_of.html

Alie, Joe A. D. *A New History of Sierra Leone*. Oxford: Macmillan, 1990.

Alldridge, T. J. *The Sherbro and Its Hinterland*. New York: Macmillan, 1901.

Amartey, Samuel Amartey, and Sean H. Reid. "Terrestrial and Maritime Cultural Landscapes of the Atlantic World in the Sierra Leone Estuary." *Nyame Akuma* 82 (2014): 3–11.

Atherton, John H. "Early Economies of Sierra Leone and Liberia: Archaeological and Historical Reflections." In *Essays on the Economic Anthropology of Sierra Leone and Liberia*, edited by V. R. Dorjohn and B. L. Issac, 27–43. Philadelphia, PA: Institute for Liberian Studies, 1979.

Atherton, John H. "Ethnoarchaeology in Africa." *African Archaeological Review* 1 (1983): 75–104.

Atherton, John H. "Protohistoric Habitation Sites in Northeastern Sierra Leone." *Bull. Soc. Roy. Anthrop. Prehist.* 83 (1972): 5–17.

Ball, Edward. *Slaves in the Family*. New York: Ballentine Books, 1999.

Bailyn, Bernard. *Atlantic History: Concept and Contours*. Cambridge: Harvard University Press, 2005.

Bailyn, Bernard, and Patricia L. Denault, eds. *Soundings in Atlantic History: Latent Structures and Intellectual Currents, 1500–1830*. Cambridge, MA: Harvard University Press, 2009.

Balachandran, Gopalan. "Atlantic Paradigms and Aberrant Histories." *Atlantic Studies* 11, no. 1 (2014): 47–63.

Ball, Edward. *Slaves in the Family*. New York: Farrar, Straus and Giroux, 1998.

Barbot, Jean. *Barbot on Guinea: The Writings of Jean Barbot on West Africa*, translated and edited by Paul E. H. Hair, Adam Jones, and Robin Law. London: Hakluyt Society, 1992.

Barnes, Jodi A., and Steen, Carl. "Archaeology and Heritage of the Gullah People." *Journal of African Diaspora Archaeology and Heritage* 1 (2012): 167–224.

Blyden, Edward W. "Report on the Expedition to Falaba, January to March 1872." *Proceedings of the Royal Geographical Society* 17, no. 2 (1873): 117–133.

Brooks, George E. *Euroafricans in Western Africa*. Athens: University of Ohio Press, 2003.

Cañizares-Esguerra, J., and Seeman, E. R., eds. *The Atlantic in Global History*. Upper Saddle River, NJ: Prentice Hall, 2007.

Carney, Judith. *Black Rice: The African Origins of Rice Cultivation in the Americas*. Cambridge, MA: Harvard University Press, 2001.

Corry, Joseph. *Observations Upon the Windward Coast of Africa*. London: W. Nicol, 1807.

Crooks, J. J. *A History of the Colony of Sierra Leone in West Africa*. London: Frank Cass, 1972 [1903].

DeCorse, Christopher R. "Archaeological Fieldwork at Bunce Island: A Slave Trading Entrepôt in Sierra Leone." *Nyame Akuma* 82 (2014): 12–22.

DeCorse, Christopher R. *Archaeological Investigations, Tasso and Bunce Islands, Sierra Leone*. Freetown: Sierra Leone Monuments and Relics Commission, 2011.

DeCorse, Christopher R. *An Archaeology of Elmina: Africans and Europeans on the Gold Coast, 1400–1900*. Washington, DC: Smithsonian Press, 2001.

DeCorse, Christopher R. *Bunce Island: A Cultural Resource Assessment*. Freetown: Sierra Leone Monuments and Relics Commission, 2007.

DeCorse, Christopher R. "Early Trade Posts and Forts of West Africa." In *First Forts: Essays on the Archaeology of Proto-colonial Fortifications*, edited by Eric Klingelhofer, 209–233. Leiden: Brill, 2010.

DeCorse, Christopher R. "Fortified Towns of the Koinadugu Plateau: Northern Sierra Leone in the Atlantic World." In *Landscapes of Power: Regional Perspectives on West African Polities in the Atlantic Era*, edited by Cameron Monroe and Akinwumi Ogundiran, 278–308. New York: Cambridge University Press, 2012.

DeCorse, Christopher R. "Material Aspects of Limba, Yalunka and Kuranko Ethnicity: Archaeological Research in Northeastern Sierra Leone." In *Archaeological Approaches to Cultural Identity*, edited by Stephan Shennan, 125–140. London: Unwin Hyman, 1989.

DeCorse, Christopher R. "Oceans Apart: Africanist Perspectives on Diaspora Archaeology." In *"I, Too, Am America": Archaeological Studies of African-American Life*, edited by Theresa Singleton, 132–155. Charlottesville: University of Virginia Press, 1999.

DeCorse, Christopher R. *Postcolonial or Not? West Africa in the Pre-Atlantic and Atlantic Worlds. Keynote Address, 50th Anniversary of the African Studies Center, University of Ibadan*. Ibadan: African Studies Center, 2014.

DeCorse, Christopher R. "Tools of Empire: Trade, Slaves and the British Forts of West Africa." In *Building the British Atlantic World*, edited by Daniel Maudlin and Bernard L. Herman. Chapel Hill: University of North Carolina Press, in press.

DeCorse, Christopher R. "West African Archaeology and the Atlantic Slave Trade." *Slavery and Abolition* 12, no. 2 (1991): 92–96.

DeCorse, Christopher R., ed. *West Africa during the Atlantic Slave Trade: Archaeological Perspectives*. New York: Leicester University Press, 2001.

DeCorse, Christopher R., and Sam Spiers. "A Tale of Two Polities: Socio-Political Transformation on the Gold Coast in the Atlantic World." *Australian Journal of Historical Archaeology* 27 (2009): 29–42.

Deveneaux, G. K. "The Political and Social Impact of the Colony in Northern Sierra Leone, 1821–1896." Ph.D. diss., Boston University, 1973.

Donald, Leland H. "Changes in Yalunka Social Organization: A Study of Adaptation to a Changing Cultural Environment." Ph.D. diss., University of Oregon, 1968.

Donnan, Elizabeth. *Documents Illustrative of the Slave Trade to America, Vol. 2: The Eighteenth Century*. Washington, DC: Carnegie Institution of Washington, 1930.

Duncan, T. Bentley. *Atlantic Islands: Madiera, the Azores and the Cape Verdes in the Seventeenth Century*. Chicago: University of Chicago Press, 1972.

Eltis, David. *Economic Growth and the Ending of the Atlantic Slave Trade*. New York: Oxford University Press, 1987.

Fage, John D. "Slavery and the Slave Trade in the Context of West African History." *Journal of African History* 10, no. 3 (1969): 393–404.

Falconbridge, Anna Maria. *Narrative of Two Voyages to the River Sierra Leone*. London: Frank Cass, 1967 [1802].

Fields-Black, Edda L. *Deep Roots: Rice Farmers in West Africa and the African Diaspora*. Bloomington: University of Indiana Press, 2008.

Fogleman, Aaron Spencer. "The Transformation of the Atlantic World, 1776–1867." *Atlantic Studies* 6, no. 1 (2009): 5–28.

Fyfe, Christopher. *A History of Sierra Leone*. London: Oxford University Press, 1962.

Fyfe, Christopher. *Our Children Free and Happy: Letters from Black Settlers in Africa in the 1790s*. Edinburgh: Edinburgh University Press, 1992.

Fyle, C. Magbaily. *The History of Sierra Leone: A Concise Introduction*. London: Evans Brothers, 1981.

Fyle, C. Magbaily. *The Solima Yalunka Kingdom*. Freetown, Sierra Leone: Nyakon Publishers, 1979.

Gabaccia, Donna. "Spatializing Gender and Migration: The Periodization of Atlantic Studies, 1500 to the Present." *Atlantic Studies* 11, no. 1 (2014): 7–27.

Garrett, G. H. "Sierra Leone and the Interior, to the Upper Waters of the Niger." *Proceedings of the Royal Geographical Society* 14, no. 7 (1892): 433–455.

Gondobay Manga Foundation Website. Accessed May 26, 2015. http://www.gondobaymangafoundation.org/#/home/

Green, Toby. *The Rise of the Trans-Atlantic Slave Trade in Western Africa, 1300–1589.* New York: Cambridge University Press, 2012.

Greene, Jack P., and Philip D. Morgan, eds. *Atlantic History: A Critical Appraisal.* New York: Oxford University, 2009.

Hair, Paul E. H. "Early Sources on Religion and Social Values in the Sierra Leone Region: (2) Eustache de la Fosse 1480." *Africana Research Bulletin* 4, no. 3 (1973): 49–53.

Hair, Paul E. H. *The Founding of the Castelo de São Jorge da Mina: An Analysis of the Sources.* Madison: University of Wisconsin, 1994.

Hair, Paul E. H. "Sources on Early Sierra Leone: (6) Barreira on Enslavement, 1606." *Africana Research Bulletin* 6, no. 1 (1975): 52–74.

Hair, Paul E. H. "Sources on Early Sierra Leone: (12) The Livro of the 'Santiago' 1526." *Africana Research Bulletin* 8, no. 1 (1977): 28–49.

Hamer, Philip, ed. *The Papers of Henry Laurens*, Vol 3. Columbia: University of South Carolina Press, 1972.

Hancock, David. *Citizens of the World: London Merchants and the Integration of the British Atlantic Community, 1735–1785.* New York: Cambridge University Press, 1999.

Handler, Jerome S. "Survivors of the Middle Passage: Life Histories of Enslaved Africans in British America." *Slavery and Abolition* 23, no. 1 (2002): 25–56.

Hauser, Mark, and Christopher R. DeCorse. "Low-Fired Earthenwares in the African Diaspora: Problems and Prospects." *International Journal of Historical Archaeology* 7, no. 1 (2003): 67–98.

Haviser, Jay, and Christopher R. DeCorse. "African-Caribbean Interaction: A Research Plan for Curaçao Creole Culture." In *Proceedings of the Thirteenth International Congress for Caribbean Archaeology*, edited by E. N. Ayubi and J. B. Haviser, 326–337. Curacao: The Archaeological-Anthropological Institute of the Netherlands Antilles 9, 1999.

Herskovits, Melville J. "The significance of West Africa for Negro Research." *Journal of Negro History* 21, no. 1 (1936): 15–30.

Herskovits, Melville J. *The Myth of the Negro Past.* New York: Harper, 1941.

Holl, Augustin. "Worldviews, Mind-Sets, and Trajectories in West African Archaeology." In *Postcolonial Archaeologies in Africa*, edited by Peter R. Schmidt, 129–148. Sante Fe, NM: School for Advanced Research, 2009.

Jones, Adam. "From Slaves to Palm Kernels: A History of the Galinhas Country (West Africa), 1730–1890." Vol. 68, *Studien zur Kulturkunde.* Wiesbaden: Franz Steiner Verlag, 1983.

Kankpeyeng, Benjamin W., and Christopher R. DeCorse. "Ghana's Vanishing Past: Development, Antiquities and the Destruction of the Archaeological Record." *African Archaeological Review* 21, no. 2 (2004): 89–128.

Kea, Raymond. "When I Die, I Shall Return to My Own Land." In *The Cloth of Many Colored Silks: Papers on History and Society Ghanaian and Islamic in Honor of Ivor Wilks*, edited by John Hunwick and Nancy Lawler, 159–193. Chicago, IL: Northwestern University Press, 2012.

Kellman, Jordan. "Beyond Center and Periphery: New Currents in French and Francophone Atlantic Studies." *Atlantic Studies* 10, no. 1 (2013): 1–11.

Kelly, Kenneth G. "The African Diaspora Starts Here: Historical Archaeology of Coast West Africa." In *African Historical Archaeologies*, edited by Andrew M. Reid and Paul J. Lane, 219–241. New York: Kluwer Academic, 2004.

Kelly, Kenneth G. "The Archaeology of African-European Interaction: Investigating the Social Roles of Trade, Traders, and the Use of Space in the Seventeenth- and Eighteenth-Century Hueda Kingdom, Republic of Bénin." *World Archaeology* 28, no. 3 (1997): 351–369.

Kelly, Kenneth G. "Using Historically Informed Archaeology: Seventeenth and Eighteenth Century Hueda/European Interaction on the Coast of Benin." *Journal of Archaeological Method and Theory* 4, no. 3–4 (1997): 353–366.

Kingston, W. H. G. *Blue Jackets or Chips of the Old Block.* London: Grant and Griffith, 1854.

Kup, A. P. *A History of Sierra Leone, 1400–1787.* New York: Cambridge, 1961.

Laing, A. G. *Travels in the Timanee, Kooranko and Soolima Countries*, Vols. 1 and 2. London: J. Murray, 1825.

Lane, Paul J., and Kevin C. McDonald. *Slavery in Africa: Archaeology and Memory.* New York: Oxford University Press, 2011.

Lawrence, A. W. *Trade Castles and Forts of West Africa*. London: Jonathan Cape, 1963.
Lipschutz, M. R. "Northeast Sierra Leone after 1884: Responses to the Samorian Invasions and British Colonialism." PhD diss., University of California, Los Angeles, 1973.
Littlefield, Daniel. *Rice and Slaves: Ethnicity and the Slave Trade in Colonial South Carolina*. Baton Rouge: Louisiana State University Press, 1981.
Lovejoy, Paul E. "The Impact of the Atlantic Slave Trade on Africa: A Review of the Literature." *Journal of African History* 30, no. 3 (1989): 365–394.
Malcolm, J. M. "Mende Warfare." *Sierra Leone Studies* 21 (1939): 47–52.
McClanahan, Paige.: "US-funded Coalition Restores Key West African Slave-Trade 'Castle'." *The Christian Science Monitor*. Accessed June 26, 2015. http://www.csmonitor.com/World/Africa/2011/0805/US-funded-coalition-restores-key-West-African-slave-trade-castle
Misevich, Philip. "The Origins of Slaves Leaving the Upper Guinea Coast in the Nineteenth Century." In *Extending the Frontiers: Essays on the New Atlantic Slave Database*, edited by David Eltis and David Richardson, 155–175. New Haven, CT: Yale University, 2008.
Mitchell, Peter. *African Connections: Archaeological Perspectives on Africa and the Wider World*. New York: AltaMira Press, 2005.
Mitchell, P. K. "Trade Routes of the Early Sierra Leone Protectorate." *Sierra Leone Studies (new series)* 16 (1962): 204–217.
Monroe, J. Cameron. *The Precolonial State in West Africa: Building Power in Dahomey*. New York: Cambridge University Press, 2014.
Monroe, J. Cameron, and Akinwumi Ogundiran, eds. *Landscapes of Power: Regional Perspectives on West African Polities in the Atlantic Era*. New York: Cambridge University Press, 2012.
Morgan, Philip. "Africa and the Atlantic, c. 1450 to c. 1820." In *Atlantic History a Critical Appraisal*, edited by Jack P. Greene and Philip D. Morgan, 223–248. New York: Oxford University Press, 2009.
Morgan, Philip. *African American Life in the Georgia Lowcountry: The Atlantic World and the Gullah Geechee*. Athens: University of Georgia Press, 2011.
Mouser, Bruce. *American Colony on the Rio Pongo: The War of 1812, the Slave Trade, and the Proposed Settlement of African Americans, 1810–1830*. Trenton, NJ: Africa World Press, 2013.
Ogundiran, Akinwumi O., and Toyin Falola, eds. *Archaeology of Atlantic Africa and the African Diaspora*. Bloomington: Indiana University Press, 2007.
O'Reilly, William. "Genealogies of Atlantic History." *Atlantic Studies* 1, no. 1 (2004): 66–84.
Pereira, Duarte Pacheco. *Esmeraldo de Situ Orbis*, translated by George H. Kimble. Nendeln, Liechtenstein: Kraus Reprint, 1967.
Peterson, John. *Province of Freedom: A History of Sierra Leone, 1787–1870*. Evanston, IL: Northwestern University Press, 1969.
Posnansky, Merrick. "African Archaeology Comes of Age." *World Archaeology* 13, no. 3 (1982): 345–358.
Posnansky, Merrick. "Toward and Archaeology of the Black Diaspora." *Journal of Black Studies* 15, no. 2 (1984): 195–205.
Posnansky, Merrick. "Revelations, Roots, and Reactions – Archaeology and the African Diaspora." *Ufahamu* 29, no. 1 (2002): 45–63.
"Priscilla's Homecoming: A Remarkable Journey." The University of South Florida. Accessed June 26, 2015. http://www.africanaheritage.com/Priscillas_Homecoming.asp
Reade, Winwood. *The African Sketch-Book*, Vols. 1 and 2. London: Smith, Elder, 1873.
Robertshaw, Peter, ed. *A History of African Archaeology*. London: James Currey, 1990.
Rodney, Walter. *A History of the Upper Guinea Coast*. New York: Monthly Review Press, 1970.
Rodney, Walter. *How Europe Underdeveloped Africa*. London: Bogle-L'Ouverture, 1972.
Sengova, Joko. "My Mother Dem Nyus to Plan' Reis." In *Afro-Atlantic Dialogues: Anthropology in the Diaspora*, edited by Kevin A. Yelvington, 211–248. Santa Fe, NM: School of American Research, 2006.
Shaw, Rosalind. *Memories of the Slave Trade: Ritual and Historical Imagination in Sierra Leone*. Chicago: University of Chicago Press, 2002.
Siddle, D. J. "War-Towns in Sierra Leone: A Study in Social Change." *Africa* 38, no. 1 (1968): 47–56.

Singleton, Theresa A. "Reclaiming the Gullah-Geechee Past: Archaeology of Slavery in Coastal Georgia." In *African American Life in the Georgia Lowcountry; The Atlantic World and the Gullah Geechee*, edited by Philip Morgan, 151–187. Athens: The University of Georgia Press, 2010.

Solow, Barbara L. *Slavery and the Rise of the Atlantic System*. New York: Cambridge University Press, 1991.

Thilman, Guy. "Sur l'Existence, fin XVIe, de Comptoirs Neerlandais a Joal et Potudal (Senegal)." *Notes Africaines* 117 (1968): 17–18.

Thomas-Houston, Marilyn M. "Review of the Language You Cry In the Story of a Mende Song, by Alvaro Toepke and Angel Serrano." *American Anthropologist* 101, no. 4 (2000): 826–827.

Thornton, John K. *A Cultural History of the Atlantic World, 1250–1820*. New York: Cambridge University Press, 2012.

Tomich, Dale. "Atlantic History and World Economy: Concepts and Constructions." *Proto Sociology* 20 (2004): 102–121.

Topeke, Alvaro, and Angel Serrano. *Language your Cry In*. San Francisco: California Newsreel, 1998.

Torres, J. B., M. B. Doura, S. O. Y. Keita, and R. A. Kittles. "Y Chromosome Lineages in Men of West African Descent." *PLoS ONE* 7, no. 1 (2012): e29687. doi:10.1371/journal.pone.0029687.

Trans-Atlantic Slave Trade Database. Accessed May 26, 2015. http://www.slavevoyages.org/tast/database/index.faces

Trotter, J. K. *The Niger Sources*. London: Methuen, 1898.

Turner, Lorenzo Dow. *Africanisms in the Gullah Dialect*. Chicago: University of Chicago Press, 1949.

"A Unique African American Culture." National Park Service. Accessed May 26, 2015. http://www.nps.gov/guge/index.htm

Wade-Lewis, Margaret. "The Impact of the Turner-Herskovits Connection on Anthropology and Linguistics." *Dialectical Anthropology* 17 (1992): 391–412.

Wade-Lewis, Margaret. *Lorenzo Dow Turner: Father of Gullah Studies*. Columbia: University of South Carolina Press, 2007.

Wilkie, Laurie A., and Farnsworth, Paul. *Sampling Many Pots: An Archaeology of Memory and Tradition at a Bahamian Plantation*. Gainesville: University of Florida Press, 2005.

Wood, Raymond. "An Archaeological Appraisal of Early European Settlement in the Senegambia." *Journal of African History* 8 (1967): 39–64.

Wyse, A. J. G. *H. C. Bankole-Bright and Politics in Colonial Sierra Leone 1919–1958*. New York: Cambridge University Press, 1990.

Yelvington, Kevin, ed. *Afro-Atlantic Dialogues: Anthropology in the Diaspora*. Sante Fe, NM: School of American Research, 2005.

Yerxa, Donald A. ed. *Recent Themes in the History of the Atlantic World: Historians in Conversation*. Columbia: University of South Carolina Press, 2008.

Zweifel, J., and M. Moustier. *Voyage aux sources du Niger*. Marseille: Barlatier-Feissat, 1880.

Employing archaeology to (dis)entangle the nineteenth-century illegal slave trade on the Rio Pongo, Guinea

Kenneth G. Kelly and Elhadj Ibrahima Fall

> Archaeological research conducted on the Rio Pongo, Guinea, has explored the setting of the nineteenth century "illegal" slave trade and its consequences for the European, American, and African traders engaged in that commerce. Excavated material, coupled with mapping of archaeological features, is employed to investigate the degree to which the trading entities and the local residents were entangled in the Atlantic World that spanned four continents.

Bowing to humanitarian pressures, in 1803 Denmark, followed by Britain and the USA in 1807/1808, made participation in the Atlantic Slave trade an illegal act for their citizens and vessels registered to these nations. This step, arguably the first major and lasting act toward addressing the inhumane practice of slavery, had a significant impact on the slave holding economies, and the societies of West and West Central Africa from where most captives originated. On the African continent, one of the most important consequences was the almost immediate cessation of slave traffic from the most well-known sites of that commerce, particularly the trade ports of the Slave Coast, exemplified by Ouidah, and the ports of the Gold Coast, such as Cape Coast, Accra, and others, as the slave trade shifted to ports south of the equator where the trade continued uninterrupted. However, another consequence, unintended to be sure, and perhaps partly coincidental, was the return of slave trading to the previously marginal areas of the upper Guinea coast, and specifically the region of present-day Guinea. Here, a diverse array of Americans, Europeans, and Africans established a number of slave trading enterprises on the banks of the tidal Rio Pongo and Rio Nunez where their clandestine activities could continue relatively unmolested by the British and later American anti-slave trade patrols that coasted the African shore.

Due to a convergence of geography, politics, and culture, between 1800 and 1860 the Rio Pongo region was a veritable hotbed of interaction, cooperation, and cultural entanglements. Because of a longstanding sociocultural process common to the region, the so-called landlord–stranger relationship,[1] individual "strangers" (in this case, European and American traders) were welcomed into local society, frequently through marriage with the daughters of local elite men, thereby cementing valuable places in the local economy, and equally important, places in existing long distance trade networks. These "Atlantic Creoles" were the most recent iteration of a process that extended back at least to the first arrival of Portuguese traders in the 1600s, and who became significant participants in the intercultural and economic exchanges of the region, consciously signaling their distinct identity through architecture, religion, and daily practice.[2] They served as visible cultural intermediaries, helping to broker exchanges. Geography facilitated the establishment of these trading posts because the Rio Pongo, and to a lesser extent, the Rio Nunez, provided tidewater access some 40 km inland from the coast, bypassing the mangrove swamps and intersecting with long-established trade routes that came from the highlands of the Futa Jallon to the east.[3] Furthermore, these rivers, while passable to ocean-going ships, were generally not suitable for the larger warships such as those employed on the anti-slave trade station. This meant that the slave ships were able to cross the mud- and sandbars at the various river mouths and sail up the still-tidal rivers to the many trading towns where they could acquire their cargos unobserved from the coast. Regional politics played into this equation as well, with the late eighteenth and nineteenth centuries being periods of considerable conflict and warfare in the highlands of the Futa Jallon due to the expansion of the Fouta theocratic state, and that conflict generated captives that were available for sale on the coast.[4] International politics and economics also contributed, as following the Haitian revolution and the collapse of what had been the largest producer of sugar in the world, the Spanish possessions of Cuba and Puerto Rico sought to increase their sugar production, and that required enslaved Africans.[5]

Given this dramatic realignment of the slave trade in the nineteenth century and its significance for Cuban and Puerto Rican slavery, not to mention the on-going trade to Brazil, it is surprising that historical archaeologists have yet to investigate this period, and the impact of this trade on local societies. It is in the spirit of closing this gap that Kenneth Kelly initiated the Rio Pongo Archaeological Project working with project co-director Elhadj Fall, director of the Memoire de Farenya project.[6] Building upon an initial visit to the region by Kelly in 2006, the current (2013–present) project combines the ethnohistoric research of Fall with archaeological investigations at three localities – the present-day villages of Farenya, Sanya Paulia, and Bangalan (Figure 1).[7] All three of these villages were important slave trade destinations in the late eighteenth and nineteenth centuries, and were home to a number of documented traders from Britain, the USA, and elsewhere, and their "Atlantic Creole" families. The trade in slaves and other commodities continued at each of these sites until the late nineteenth century, when "legitimate" trade in peanuts, hides, and other agricultural products was encouraged in the colonial era, and slavery was finally abolished in the Americas.[8] The archaeological work on the Rio Pongo, in essence the first archaeological project to be conducted in the country in over 40 years, consisted of archaeological reconnaissance building on the 2006 visit, archaeological mapping of the visible resources including the extent of abandoned habitation sites, and excavations in a selection of features such as collapsed trade lodges, warehouses, and dwelling areas. We approached the fieldwork with the goal of beginning to understand the degree of cultural entanglement that developed between foreign traders (strangers) and local residents (both "landlords" and others who may have located themselves at the trade centers). We hypothesized that artifacts and features recovered would provide insights to the degree that European traders and their "Atlantic Creole" families had adapted to local circumstances,

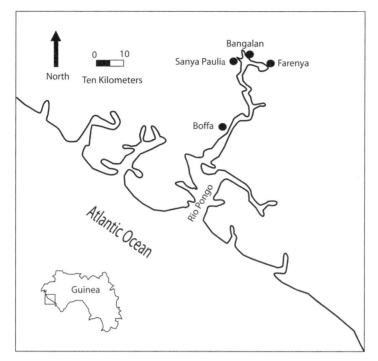

Figure 1. Map of the Rio Pongo region of Guinea showing the project area (villages of Sanya Paulia, Bangalan and Farenya). Maps composed by authors.

and conversely, the ways that local practice was altered or impacted by trade opportunities. Other ways this entanglement might be expressed is through architecture and the use of space in both trading and residential zones. These archaeological research goals were combined with the ongoing ethnohistorical and cultural anthropological investigations led by Fall that were intended to access these and other research questions through consultation with local residents. Beyond archaeological documentation, a key aspect of the project was a training component, providing an introduction to archaeological field and lab methods to a group of Guinean university students and museum employees. This was the first archaeological training opportunity to occur in Guinea in over 40 years, as university training in archaeology is severely constrained.

The research goals of the three month field season (January–April 2013) were to record oral traditions and local histories pertaining to the illegal trade period, and to document archaeological resources relating to the nineteenth-century slave trade at the three sites of Bangalan, Sanya Paulia, and Farenya through surface survey and mapping, and to conduct excavations in selected areas of each site. We began at Bangalan, where local residents, in advance of our arrival, and by their own initiative, had already cleared brush from the remains of an extensive earthen mound complex, said by local residents to have been a trading lodge, and had exposed a massive masonry ramp and causeway that led to a jetty on the river bank.

Bangalan

The modern village of Bangalan corresponds to the location where the nineteenth-century trade center by the same name is indicated on historic maps. Local residents are aware of the archaeological (historic) portions of their landscape, and maintain oral histories that attribute a still-visible complex of earthen mounds and a cannon with a trading center (Figure 2). While Bangalan was an important and active trading post from at the least the beginning of the nineteenth-century, and is documented in the well-known account of Theodore Canot describing events in the late 1820s when he was assistant to John Ormand, Junior, the village was also the residence of other traders.[9] These include John Fraser, well-known Florida-based plantation owner, and South Carolinian Styles Lightbourn, among others.[10] The continued recognition by local residents of the historic component to the village area is one factor that makes Bangalan attractive for archaeological research. Furthermore, it is also important that the current village does not appear to be situated over the historic nineteenth-century occupation, thereby minimizing the mixing of temporal contexts and the challenges modern overburden presents. Fall's oral history project, which was conducted at the same time as excavations, allowed us to stimulate responses to questions to local residents by showing in progress excavations, features, and artifacts. We were surprised when the oral histories associated the still-visible mound complex with a certain "Mungo Paul," an individual who does not correspond to any known historical presence at Bangalan.

Nonetheless, we began our work centered on this collection of mounds. Mapping of the mound complex revealed a quadrangular compound of structures delineating a

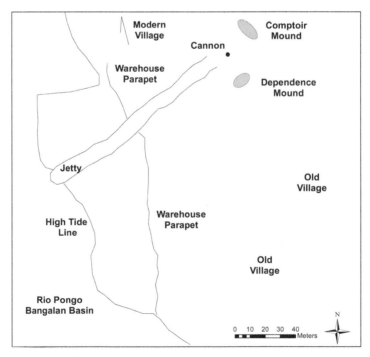

Figure 2.   Map of the site complex at Bangalan. Maps composed by authors.

courtyard in which an eighteenth century cannon was still present. A paved stone ramp led from the courtyard ~160 m to the waters edge where eighteenth and nineteenth-century artifacts still litter the shore. Excavations into the two largest mounds revealed structures that were a blend of local and foreign practices. The mounds were the remains of collapsed structures, built of sun dried mud brick, a practice that continues today, and that our archaeological work showed to be common to other sites in the Bangalan Basin. The structures were also considerably more substantial than present-day residences, in length, width, and height. The thickness of the exterior walls and the accumulation of soil above the interior deposits, deriving from collapsed walls, suggested that these mounds were what remained of two story structures such as is hinted at in the historic accounts of Canot and contemporary illustrations.[11] The construction of two story trading lodges departs from what appears to traditional architectural practice in coastal Guinea although it is possible that this is a residual Afro-Portuguese practice as well.[12] Excavation revealed that beneath more than 1 m of unconsolidated soil derived from wall melt, the two structures each had multiple lenses of compacted floor deposits overlaid with continuous dense charcoal layers indicating repeated burning episodes, likely related again to the documented, and undocumented, conflagrations that continually threatened thatch roofed structures (Canot 1854, Mouser 1972, 2011).[13] Artifacts recovered from the two structures were limited to small items and fragments of broken pottery, both imported and local. These artifacts are consistent with structures that were intensively used, frequently swept or cleared out, and may well have been habitation rooms rather than storage. In addition to identifying multiple levels of occupation in the structures, an unexpected find from one structure was that beneath repeated occupation levels, at a point ~135 cm below the current ground surface, evidence came to light of an earlier building, also rectangular (based on straight walls) that was oriented on a different bearing than the later structure. This earlier occupation was sealed beneath intact compact floor layers, and also included a post and post-hole feature. The superimposed structures were the first indication that the lodge area had undergone significant reorganization at some point, probably near the beginning of the nineteenth century, to reflect its current form. It is possible that this reorganization is associated with the transitions between traders, such as between Ormond, Senior and Junior.

Other components of this commercial complex included the ramp, quayside, and associated other structures at a parapet or platform half way along the 160 m long ramp. Archaeological survey of the level area at the top of this parapet indicated the remains of at least one masonry structure and a masonry wall. Local residents spoke of this area having been the location of the warehouses or storerooms used to shelter the trade goods arriving from abroad, as well as the African products stockpiled for export, although not including captive Africans. The size and scope of the ramp and ruins was much greater than Diallo's reference to them in 1970 led one to expect. Excavations at this location showed a deeply stratified set of deposits, of which the earliest included white salt glazed stoneware (produced between ca. 1740 and 1765), thereby suggesting a time depth to the occupation at Bangalan that might be longer than expected and possibly predate traders such as John Ormond, Senior.

The causeway was clearly associated with the port/quay for the trading lodge up the slope to which it led directly, and the labor invested in its construction was considerable, creating a gently sloping ramp rising as much as seven meters above the surrounding terrain, from the water's edge. The foreshore adjacent to the quayside was largely obscured by dense mangrove growth and mud accumulation, so artifacts were not visible in this area. However, a pedestrian survey along the shore in areas to the east and west that were accessible revealed the presence of European made ceramics and considerable quantities of glass wine and liquor bottles. These ceramics and bottles dated throughout the nineteenth century, demonstrating the scale of continued trade occurring at this location in Bangalan. The pedestrian survey of the accessible sectors of the foreshore also revealed the presence of another quay or improved port area. This port, nearly 40 m west of the ramp, was visible at low tide, when the receding water exposed a stone-paved rectangular area that served as a loading/unloading area and/or an area for careening or building small boats. The likelihood of boat building or maintenance activities in the area is strengthened by the widespread recovery of copper nails at Bangalan, as well as at other sites.[14] There were extensive surface deposits of early to mid-nineteenth-century bottles adjacent to and near this feature, along with more limited imported ceramics. We presume that this feature predated the more substantial ramp and quay because there was no clearly defined access from the waterside feature to the ramp, as one would expect if it was used concurrently or after the construction of the ramp. It is likely, given its location on the river's edge, and the nearby warehouse construction on the parapet, that this waterside pavement was used before the parapet was raised and filled. Clearly, trade activities here were substantial, given the investment in infrastructure. Archaeological recovery of imported ceramics and bottles provide a tangible link to the extensive trade that occurred here, much of it in goods that leave little in the way of archaeological trace.

Accounts by Canot and others show that the trading lodges were not isolated complexes, but were surrounded by villages or towns where local Africans, *grumetes* (hired Africans working in the trade), visiting traders, and likely captives, resided.[15] We sought to characterize these occupations via pedestrian survey, coupled with limited excavation, to identify and delimit the associated settlement to the west and east of the lodge at Bangalan. The artifact scatter in this area was very clearly visible because the land has recently been used for dryland agriculture (we were present in the dry season when the crops had been harvested and little vegetation remained). The former village extended from the shore of the Bangalan basin on the south, and was located on the extensive natural terrace that overlooked the tidal river. Little in the way of topography provided clues to locations of structures, but we judgementally placed several small test excavations in the area to test for subsurface integrity of archaeological deposits, and for any variations in the kinds of material culture present. One location exposed an intact trash deposit feature with bottle glass, imported and local ceramics, and preserved animal bone. Based on the bottle glass and imported ceramics in this feature, the trash pit dates to the early nineteenth century. Animal species present included sheep/goat, cattle, and unidentified, but medium-sized mammal. The presence of imported materials, principally bottle glass, ceramics, and beads throughout the site of Bangalan demonstrated that trade materials were penetrating to all segments of the settlement, and thus likely to all sectors of society. In spite of the presence of imports, locally manufactured materials remained widespread, showing that imported materials augmented, and did not replace, local production. Although it is not possible to definitively determine bottle contents, the fact that most bottles recovered were originally produced for alcoholic beverages suggests that wine and/or spirits were common in the trade village as well as in the lodge. Interestingly, tobacco pipe, while present, was not very common in either location.

The overall results for the archaeological work at Bangalan were to identify a key trading lodge and its associated storage areas, ramp, and quayside, and to locate and delimit the extent of the nineteenth-century village. Despite extensive pedestrian survey and interviews with local residents, the only archaeological features that were clearly identifiable due to their topography or associated significant artifacts, such as cannon, were in the area we identified as the trading lodge. This posed the question of which trader or traders were associated with this complex, which should be the location of the greatest "Atlantic Creole" entanglement. Local oral traditions associated it with a "Mungo Paul," who does not, to the best of our understanding, correspond with any trader known to have been resident at Bangalan, and in particular, does not seem to correspond to either John Ormond, Senior or Junior, who were the best known residents of Bangalan in the first decades of the nineteenth century. The artifacts present on the living floors and in the structures at the lodge complex date to the period during which both Ormonds, Canot, Lightbourn, and the successors to Ormond should have been present. Curiously, neither the name Ormond nor Canot, or any permutation thereof (Mungo John, Mungo Teodoro, etc.) elicited any recognition from local residents (a pattern that was to repeat itself at Gambia/Bakoro). This lack of local memory of some of these historical figures may well be associated with the more recent founding of the modern village, after the heyday of the slave trade, or conversely, due to the rise to prominence of other actors in local memory.

The archaeological data identified through survey and excavation directly informs the research questions surrounding the issues of entanglement. Artifacts recovered from the village area surrounding the trading lodge complex demonstrated that while the majority of material culture, primarily ceramics, was of local origin there was also evidence of the incorporation of imported ceramic vessels into the daily practice of the residents. Other imported materials recovered from this area included bottle glass, suggesting that the use of (presumably) alcoholic beverages was widely practiced here. As the village area yielded no evidence of architecture it is likely that houses in this area were lightly built, and whatever ruins may have remained following abandonment were destroyed by subsequent cultivation in the area. This suggests that the architectural signaling of Atlantic Creole identity through two story structures was limited to the trading establishments, and not widely practiced at Bangalan. The materials recovered from the village, however, show that some imported materials found their way to nearly all corners of village that were occupied, and therefore the presence of imported materials itself does not clearly indicate an Atlantic Creole identity. It was unfortunate to not recover ordinary houses, as that would provide evidence for comparison with the more substantial trading lodges. In contrast, the trading lodge complex architecture demonstrates the use of indigenous construction techniques, but applied to significantly more substantial structures. This conforms to the model of Atlantic Creole identity put forth by Mark.[16] Artifacts associated with the trading lodge complex, while limited, show a greater reliance on imported materials, tempered by the use of local materials, particularly ceramics, thus it may be that the relative quantities of imported goods may play a role in signaling identity.

Farenya

Whereas Bangalan was host to a number of traders, Farenya is primarily associated with a single Atlantic Creole lineage, that of Lightbourn/Nyara Beli. Farenya is the most well-known of the three villages we studied, in large part due to the association that village had with Henrietta Conté, second wife of former President Lansana Conté (ruled 1984–2008). She claimed descent from the local trader Elizabeth Baily Gomez Lightbourn, or Nyara Beli, who had been the wife of South Carolinian Stiles Lightbourn, a trader active in the area between approximately 1800 and the late 1820s.[17] Nyara Beli, who was the daughter of a regional chief on a tributary of the lower Pongo, and could trace her lineage to earlier Afro-Portuguese in the area, continued her involvement in the slave trade until at least the 1850s, and was a considerable economic presence up to her death in the 1880s.[18] She also is popularly associated with a variety of extraordinary powers, and was said to have been a sorceress. This association with the former national leadership has led to Farenya having a popular impact out of scale with its historical importance, as is seen in popular novels,[19] a range of Guinean theses and field research from the 1960s to the present,[20] and the political influence formerly wielded by Conakry residents from Farenya.[21] Nonetheless, Farenya was an important site for Rio Pongo trade from the early 1800s to the early 1900s, and warranted investigation and documentation. This need for documentation was all the more apparent following Kelly's visit in 2006 when he witnessed the ill-advised attempts to "restore" the site of Nyara Beli's "palace" by destroying over two-thirds of the earthen mound, and building an as-yet uncompleted concrete block structure on top of what is left of the mound. Further damage to the historic and archaeological core of the trading village was wrought when, in the early 2000s, a series of bungalows were constructed in anticipation of a tourist boom that never happened. This tourist *campement* was constructed on the site where several nineteenth-century trade buildings had previously existed, and despite extensive earthmoving in the bungalow construction, trash deposits, ceramics, bottles, and other artifacts occasionally surface in the area. Further afield of the palace district other nineteenth century remains had been identified, and local residents showed us yet others.[22] Therefore, our goals were to (1) check the archaeological integrity of the "palace" site in light of the adverse impacts of the "renovation," (2) develop an accurate map of the "port" area adjacent to the "palace" to record the resources in danger in the center of the village, (3) map and conduct test excavations at the site of the early church, claimed to be the first Anglican church on the Rio Pongo, (4) record the sites of Betia and Yenia, attributed to daughters of Nyara Beli, and (5) record the associated features along the south bank of the Rio Pongo (Figure 3).

Initial excavations at the palace showed it to be highly disturbed from the "renovation," but the artifacts present in the construction fill suggest that what remains of the mound does correspond to an occupation in the late nineteenth century, if not earlier. The renovation construction, which included excavating a "basement" and foundations, building concrete block walls, and pouring concrete slabs, has destroyed perhaps two-thirds of the mound. Little in the way of archaeological data confirm the attribution of the mound to Nyara Beli or any elite occupation, but the scale of the mound and the imported materials draw comparison to the lodge at Bangalan. Thus it is likely that the mound is what remains of a two story Atlantic Creole

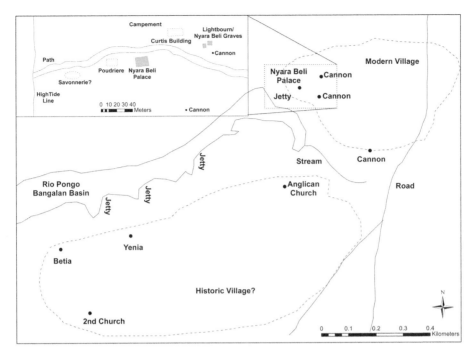

Figure 3. Map of the site complex at Farenya. Maps composed by authors.

structure. There remains the possibility that construction may have capped potentially undisturbed contexts below the cement floors.

The mapping of the core historic area of Farenya was less discouraging, as we were able to record a number of historic features, some of which may be contemporary with the "palace." We worked with local residents to determine their identification of the features, although it is apparent that there has been some selective recall of the histories of some locations. For example, one structure, likely a warehouse or storage structure, is popularly referred to as the *poudrière*, or powder magazine. However, this building is immediately adjacent to the palace, and lies between the palace and the river's edge, so if the palace was to be shelled from the river, which it was, the powder magazine would have taken the brunt of the shelling. Therefore it is highly unlikely that the building in question served for storage of gunpowder. Between the poudrière and the port is an area called the *savonnerie* where it is said that Nyara Beli had a soap "factory." A surface search of this forested area failed to reveal any archaeological deposits. Another building facing the palace, which is generally unnamed by locals, was, according to data collected by Baldé in early 2000s, the trading lodge owned by the Curtis family, rivals to the Lightbourn/Nyara Beli family.[23] Indeed, it was part of this complex that was destroyed to make way for the construction of the tourist bungalows in 2004, and the Curtis family was unable to protest, as the development was undertaken with the support of the president's household. Although we documented the resources present in the vicinity of the "palace" that are arguably related to some of the earliest activities at Farenya such as cemetery graves, cannon, paths, etc., the archaeological remains in this area have been significantly compromised by continued inhabitation, the use of parts of the area as a boat construction yard, and neglect and/or misguided attempts at preservation. An example of the latter can be found with the cemetery site, where tombs alleged to correspond to some of the members of the Lightbourn clan (Nyara Beli, Stiles, and Stiles, Junior) are present. Notwithstanding the historically problematic identification of one of the tombs with Stiles Lightbourn (who is believed to have died not in Farenya, but elsewhere), any existing structures or features of the tombs have been obscured by recent coatings of cement.

Despite the rather disappointing condition of the palace area of Farenya, work in other areas was much more successful. Based upon archaeological surface evidence, it appears that much of Farenya's nineteenth-century occupation was located south and west of the present-day village site, in areas where extensive surface scatters of nineteenth-century artifacts such as ceramics, glass, gunflints, etc. are found.[24] The core concentration of artifacts extends from a point above the high tide mark in the small stream that marks the current southwest boundary of Farenya, west and south several hundred meters in each direction. Based upon the density and dispersion of these artifacts, it appears that much of the nineteenth-century village site of Farenya was not adjacent to the palace of Nyara Beli, but occupied the southern slopes above the uppermost extent of the Rio Pongo. The importance of this part of the site is reinforced by the presence of archaeological remains of a church, said to be the first Anglican Church (St Peter and St Paul) on the Rio Pongo, established in 1881.[25] Further evidence of its significance are the several stone jetties or wharfs on the river bank. Inspection of these features at low tide revealed the presence of nineteenth-century bottle glass and imported ceramics adjacent to them, but not elsewhere on the river bank, demonstrating that the jetties were used for loading or unloading small craft. West of the church site, on promontories overlooking the river, are the sites of two imposing dwellings – Yenia (~700 m to west) and Betia (~1050 m to west) – associated with the daughters Jennifer and Elizabeth of Nyara Beli and Lightbourn. We chose to conduct excavations at the church site, Betia, and Yenia.

The ruins of the church of St Peter and St Paul lies in a clearing approximately 500 m due south of the palace site.[26] The ruin is presently visible and demarcated by a rectangular alignment of stones apparently associated with the exterior walls of the structure. The site was relatively unchanged since Kelly's visit in 2006. We transit mapped the area, recording several graves in the trees to the east of the ruin. With the approval of the elders of Farenya, we established excavations in locations to cross-cut the exterior wall in three locations: on the west end, east end, and south side, and also conducted test excavations in the cleared areas to the north and south of the visible foundation. Results of the excavations on the church walls showed that the alignments of 15–20 cm diameter laterite cobbles on the surface correspond to the dimensions of the church, but they are not associated with the original construction. Beneath the cobbles, there was approximately 10–15 cm of sterile sand, and below that was the base of a wall constructed with large rectangular laterite stones. These well-shaped stones constituted the wall base, to a depth of at least two courses, and in some places as much as three courses deep. Therefore it appears that the surface cobbles were placed more recently to demarcate the extent of the church, but do not relate to its building or occupation. Given that one of the graves east of the church ruins has a now quite degraded coating of cement, it may be that the outline corresponds to a pilgrimage or visit to the site. This hypothesis remains to be confirmed. Excavations at the church also demonstrated that at least on the east (altar?) end of the structure, the stone wall post-dates an earlier mud brick wall which lay approximately 1 m to the west of the east wall. While the mud brick wall may be associated with an interior feature, it is more likely that the structure was enlarged when the stone wall was placed, and that the original construction of the church used the locally traditional mud brick construction. In fact, the church is known to have burned in the late 1880s, so the mud brick wall may relate to an earlier incarnation of the building. Excavations outside the church were largely sterile, suggesting that the area immediately surrounding the church was an unoccupied space.

Excavations in the areas of Betia and Yenia were also undertaken, both to characterize the occupations of the area, and to better understand the nature of Farenya's disposition on the south bank of the Pongo. We exposed the house site at Yenia, so named for its association with Lightbourn/Beli daughter Jennifer or Mamie Yenie, as well as a stone-paved pathway that led from the house site at the top of the hill down 25 m of elevation to terminate at the water's edge over 100 m distant where a stone jetty provided access to the river. As with the scale of the paved causeway at Bangalan, the sheer size and length of the paved river access at Yenia was entirely unexpected. The hillslope that the causeway descended was very overgrown with dense woodland brush approximately 5 m high, obscuring surface visibility except in the areas where it was removed. It is highly likely that were the slope to be completely cleared, additional architectural evidence would be visible here. At Yenia the structural remains consisted of a single platform approximately 6 by 12 m, and raised about one meter above the surrounding surface. Test excavations of a 1×12 m trench bisecting the mound revealed evidence of its construction. The platform had been created by constructing a mud brick retaining wall, and filling the interior with soil. As the fill was largely sterile of artifacts, it suggests that this structure was built before the area was inhabited to a significant degree. Artifacts present on the surface surrounding the structure date primarily from the mid-nineteenth century or later, thus fitting within the time frame expected by a dwelling belonging to a daughter of Lightbourn/Nyara Beli. Given the imposing size of the mound, its position to visually dominate the upper Pongo, and the density of artifacts in the immediate area, it is likely that the house here was two story, as is typical of the Atlantic Creoles. However, specific architectural evidence of any structure built on top of this platform remained elusive.

We also mapped and conducted test excavations at the site of Betia, associated with another of the Lightbourn/Nyara Beli daughters, Elizabeth. This site was much more overgrown, and we were able to get the main mound cleared for mapping and testing, but any associated features remained obscured by dense undergrowth. In contrast to Yenia, the main mound at Betia is not as large in surface area, but substantially taller. Excavations here of a 1×6 m transect showed it to be a more complex structure, having undergone substantial renovation and enlargement. This was clearly demonstrated by the shaped stone retaining wall that was later obscured by a second retaining wall that expanded its footprint. Furthermore, the height of the structure was achieved with a shaped stone retaining wall built up in a step fashion to produce a much higher platform on the mound's surface. As at Yenia, archaeological work exposed the construction of the platform mound that presumably supported a structure, but direct evidence of that building was not recovered in our excavations. Although local residents states that it was the site of a residence, the massive nature of the structure does suggest that it may have served another purpose, such as a lookout or gun platform.

According to our local resident colleagues, at various places along the south shore of the upper Rio Pongo there are other remains of fairly large or massive structures, but no others associated with the Lightbourn/Nyara Beli family. Our pedestrian surveys, both formal and informal, revealed the presence of a non-continuous distribution of mid- to late nineteenth-century ceramics and glass along with local materials. These artifacts were visible on the surface in areas where vegetation was sparse, principally along the upper reaches of the hillsides. The slopes, such as where Betia was located, tended to be heavily obscured by dense vegetation. Local residents were able to point out some additional archaeological features on the landscape, including a concentration of stones that was claimed to be associated with an early church, and a nearby grave said to be that of a European. The early church remains were not tested due to a lack of time, and the surface indications were inconclusive as there were no obvious structural remains. The appearance of the grave site was consistent with an isolated burial, as it consisted of a rock pile similar to European graves elsewhere in the Pongo basin, however it was not archaeologically investigated. Associated with the church site, and approximately 100 m west, was a grove of trees, none of which were apparently very old, that was said by our local colleagues to have been a cemetery for Africans. This cemetery did not have any visible grave markers, but present-day tradition for local funerary practice is to mark graves with one or more saplings that grow into trees. Thus, the grove may be associated with a cemetery.

The density and continuity of nineteenth-century artifact distribution along the areas we surveyed of the south bank of the upper Rio Pongo was unexpected. These artifact concentrations, along with the presence of several stone jetties between Betia and the head of the river, are strong indications that a significant population was present along this stretch, and that Farenya may not have been as uniquely important as it is alleged. Clearly there were more zones of embarkation and debarkation than the "palace" of Nyara Beli, and there were associated settlements. While we did not conduct any excavations in the extensive area of surface deposits, surface indications showed that the overwhelming majority of imported ceramics present dated to the nineteenth century. This evidence suggests that regardless of whether trader lodges were concentrated in present-day Farenya near the "palace" site, or more dispersed, the growth of Farenya along the south bank of the Rio Pongo appears to be a nineteenth-century phenomenon. It is worth noting that the entire south bank is almost completely devoid of the large trees that characterize present-day Farenya, Sanya, and Bangalan. Given the exposed and very hot nature of most of the south bank, it seems likely that when the area was occupied, there must have been more trees, and a few relict trees remain in the vicinity of Betia and more so, at Yenia. This suggests that there may have been some significant changes in the local ecology associated with deforestation and clearing for agriculture that may have impacted the accumulation of mud and silt along the upper Rio Pongo. This in turn may have meant that some of the upper reaches may have been more readily accessible at low tide than at present.

Sanya Paulia

Whereas Farenya is situated at the head of the Rio Pongo, and Bangalan on the north edge of the Bangalan Basin closer to where the trade paths extending from Timbo and the Futa came to an end, Sanya Paulia, the locus of our third area of work, lies closer to the entrance to the Bangalan Basin. Aerial images of Sanya show that the modern village is concentrated on what is in essence an "island" of deeper soils (indicated by large trees and other vegetation) in a surrounding area of sparser vegetation and exposed bedrock. Sanya has a well-known trading presence that dates at least to the beginning of the nineteenth century, if not earlier. The family founded by Paul Faber (the source of the Paulia portion of the place name) were the traders of greatest renown at Sanya.[27] According to local traditions, in addition to the Faber family, other trading families, most notably that of Curtis, also played a significant role at Sanya. Archaeological features remaining at Sanya include a jetty at the port, two large structural mounds, two cannon batteries (of four that were known to be present in oral histories), and mounds and artifact scatters associated with the nineteenth-century village at Sanya. Just outside of the modern village of Sanya there lie also the ruins of two early churches, a presbytery/schoolroom, and a small graveyard (Figure 4).

The research at Sanya concentrated on testing the two mounds, both of which were said to be associated with the Faber concession, mapping the extent of the nineteenth-century materials, testing in the former village area, and recording the adjacent historic sites, such as the church complex. Testing of the two mounds involved excavating a trench into each mound to (1) determine the construction sequence, (2) determine chronology, and (3) attempt to determine the function of each mound. The mound closest to the port, which local residents asserted had been the house of Paul Faber, stands approximately 2–4 m above the surrounding ground surface. On the side facing the port, there is evidence of a raised and paved forecourt two meters high,

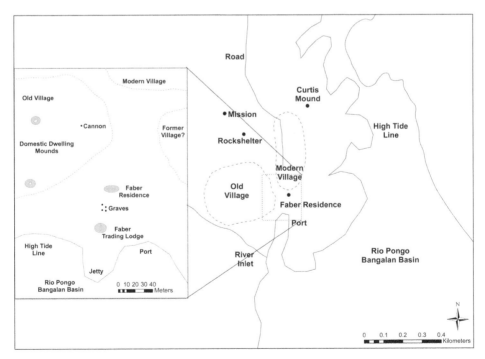

Figure 4. Map of the site complex at Sanya Pauila. Maps composed by authors.

perhaps where trading activities occurred, such as described by Canot elsewhere. Our excavation revealed evidence of the mound's construction, showing that there had been mud brick walls retaining fill to build up the structure, and the top had been improved with a mud surface. Although no evidence of structural walls was identified on the platform, it seems likely that the mound served to elevate a structure, perhaps the trading lodge, above the surrounding ground surface to better see approaching traffic on the water, and to take advantage of breezes from this height. Little in the way of artifact data was recovered from this excavation, posing challenges for identifying the function of the structure, although what was recovered confirmed an early–mid-nineteenth-century association.

Excavations at the second structure revealed a more complex construction sequence, including the building of mud brick retaining walls to create an elevated platform, but also some destruction, with evidence of collapsed or fallen walls in the form of wall sections and scattered mud bricks in the fill making up the slopes. Excavations of the uppermost section of the mound showed it to constitute a mud brick structure that was placed on the platform at the summit of the mound. According to local histories, this structure was the residence of the wife of Paul Faber, and the archaeological remains were consistent with a residential structure. It is possible that the mound closer to the port was the trading lodge, given the lack of residential materials recovered there. As with the first structure, the elevation was probably to facilitate views and ventilation.

Additional excavations were conducted in the open area west of the two main mounds, where surface indications suggested the remains of warehouses, and in the old mango grove further west, where a series of small elevations appeared to correspond to village housing. The excavations in the open area were inconclusive, revealing undifferentiated sandy deposits with nineteenth-century artifacts. Local residents informed us that there had been larger mounds present in this area, but they had been "mined" for soil for brickmaking. Much more promising were the excavations in the western section of the village area, where two mounds were excavated, each of which revealed architectural remains associated with mud brick houses. In one house, a 3 × 4 m excavation exposed portions of at least three rooms, including interior partitions, along with evidence of multiple floor layers. The other structure, located at the far western edge of the village, was less complex, although evidence of both an exterior wall and retaining wall for a platform were identified. Artifacts associated with these structures demonstrated long-term occupations, from at least the early/mid-nineteenth century, through the late nineteenth/early twentieth centuries.

We also completed extensive surface pedestrian survey at Sanya to record features such as the cannon batteries, the jetty and port artifact distributions, and the artifact distributions to the east of the principle mounds and present-day village. This area, extending several hundred meters north–south, and approximately 100 m to the east, is currently open and exposed sand. However, the area has a high density of nineteenth-century artifacts such as would be associated with village life. The area had little indication of any structural features, and it is cross-cut with elevated ridges of bedrock. Careful inspection of the elevated ridges showed that crevices and hollows in the ridges as much as 2 m above the current surface retained nineteenth-century artifacts. Thus, it is highly likely that the present-day ground surface has deflated considerably due to erosion. This, coupled with cultivation in this area of the site, strongly suggests that some portions of the historic site of Sanya have been adversely affected by environmental degradation, echoing the theme at Betia and Yenia.

Additional pedestrian survey in conjunction with village elders and a representative of the Curtis family revealed the location of the Curtis concession, which belongs to another of the important trading lineages of the Rio Pongo area. This concession, characterized by several low earth mounds and an artifact distribution at the waters edge, is located at the northern end of the present-day village. Due to time constraints, were unable to conduct any excavations here. That the archaeological indications suggest a larger settlement than today is not surprising as in the 1880s, the population of Sanya was estimated at 1500.[28]

We also mapped the Catholic Church and presbytery ruins that lie outside of the village and were established in the 1880s.[29] Our local colleagues led us to this site, and showed us the very visible remains of the masonry church, but also showed us a stone ring adjacent that was said to be the remains of the first church here. The presbytery structure was also masonry, and appeared to be a double-pen design, and based upon the quantity of fallen stone, may well have had two stories. Further to the west of the presbytery was a small graveyard with five visible tombs, one of which is said to be that of Paul Faber, although probably the Atlantic Creole son of the founder.

While we were based at Sanya, our local colleagues showed us some additional historic resources in the area, including the complex of trading structures at Bakoro and a large stone jetty at Gambia. Bakoro was a very important trade center in the twentieth century, eclipsing the trade at Bangalan, Sanya, and possibly Farenya. Several of the major French West African trade companies maintained outposts at Bakoro, where they traded local agricultural products for imported goods. Today, the historic center of the village is home to a mosque and a former trading lodge/house, with the rest of the trading establishments having fallen into ruin. Several muzzle loading cannon remain in the vicinity, but as with the other cannon in the area, they are at considerable risk of theft for sale as antiques or scrap. Bakoro lies at the tidal head of one branch of the Bangalan Basin, and would have been accessible by small boats only at high tide, as was the case at Farenya, thus limiting its usefulness. However, Bakoro does lie at the juncture of several land-based routes to the west, north, and to the interior.

Roughly equidistant between Sanya Paulia and Bakoro is the site of Gambia. Little in the way of archaeological material is easily visible here, although there is a very well-constructed and substantial wharf that extends into the Bakoro branch, which would have about 3 m of draught at high tide, enabling fairly large vessels to shuttle cargo to and from the shore. There is also a dense deposit of nineteenth-century bottle glass and ceramics along the shore. Gambia was the location of the trading establishment run by Theodore Canot, who worked for Edward Joseph, in the late 1820s, after he left the employ of John Ormond at Bangalan.[30] Interestingly, our local colleagues had no recollection of the name Gambia being associated with Canot – instead they attributed the name to the presence of Wolof fishermen from The Gambia who had camped there. This is another example of the challenges faced in conducting research here, where the question of the veracity of oral traditions is very real. Based upon pedestrian survey and GPS mapping of mounds, stone alignments, and other features, this location was home to a much more substantial occupation than would be expected by temporary lodgings for itinerant fishermen. Artifacts visible on the ground surface in open spaces (of which there were very few) were consistent with an occupation beginning in the middle third of the nineteenth century. While we were unable to conduct any test excavations at Gambia due to a lack of time, we were able to record close to a dozen archaeological features that likely correspond to individual buildings in the trade settlement of Gambia, demonstrating the importance of this locality. This site will be the focus of future work.

Conclusions

The results of this first significant archaeological work on the Rio Pongo were highly successful. We demonstrated that archaeological sites in the Bangalan Basin are much more numerous, varied, and extensive than earlier accounts have suggested.[31] It is also encouraging that the archaeological resources remain, with a few notable exceptions, in relatively good states of preservation. Our interactions with local resident colleagues also demonstrated that with the investment of time spent living and talking with local people, additional historical accounts and locations will be shared. Archaeological data, primarily glass and ceramics, confirm the degree to which residents of the local villages as well as the Atlantic Creole traders were entangled in a web of materials, some of which were incorporated in keeping with tradition, and other that were given new meanings. The ubiquitous distribution of imported trade goods speak to the way virtually all residents of these sites were touched by the transformations wrought by the "illegal" trade in the region. Since the early nineteenth century, life for the majority along the Rio Pongo has undergone a series of transformation, as new ideas and people entered the region in large part due to the importance of trade in slaves and other commodities. Traditional religious practices attested to in early accounts were transformed with the introduction of Christianity, and more recently, Islam. Large populations have come and gone, as is seen by the former extent of Sanya and Farenya. It is also likely that the population growth in the region led to significant environmental changes, with accelerated erosion and concomitant river silting. Extensive infrastructure for trade, in the form of jetties and warehouses, hummed with activity, and are now silent. Imposing Atlantic Creole houses once dominated the landscape at Bangalan, Sanya and Fareny, and have now vanished, leaving only archaeological traces.

While we recognize that the work reported here is largely preliminary, the great potential of this region is ready to be tapped. Additional projects planned for Gambia will focus on a detailed recording of the layout of a single trading outpost used for a relatively short period of time. The analysis of the archaeological and ethnohistorical data collected during the fieldwork reported here is ongoing, and will continue to contribute to a more nuanced perspective on the range of interactions between traders, local elites, and local residents. Some of our survey work identified areas said to have been used as "baracoons" or places to hold captives awaiting transport and the artifacts collected from these areas may proved to be distinct, lending credence to that interpretation.

Acknowledgements

This article is dedicated to the memory of Ahmed Tidjane Cissé, former Minister of Culture and Historical Patrimony of Guinea. Minister Cissé was unflagging in his support of this project, and was a tremendous advocate for the preservation of Guinean heritage in all forms. His guidance and advocacy will be missed. We wish to acknowledge the cooperation and support of the residents of Bangalan, Sanya Paulia and Farenya for their welcome and assistance. We gratefully thank Encore-Dubai for their generous donation of metal detecting equipment.

Disclosure statement

No potential conflict of interest was reported by the authors.

Funding

The financial support essential for this project came from a variety of sources, including a Wenner-Gren Foundation for Anthropological Research International Collaborative Grant, The American Philosophical Society Franklin Research Grant, and the University of South Carolina ASPIRE research grant program. Their support is gratefully acknowledged. Logistical support in Guinea was provided by the US Embassy and Ms Nancy Estes, USAID.

Notes

1. Brooks, *Landlords and Strangers*, 135–137, 168–169; Mouser, "Landlords-Strangers," 429.
2. Kelly, "(African) Atlantic Creoles," 1. See also Berlin, "Atlantic Creoles." On material practice, see Mark, *"Portuguese" Style*.
3. Fields-Black, *Deep Roots*, 168; Kelly, "Preliminary Archaeological Reconnaissance," 24; Kelly, "Archaeological Perspectives," 136–137; Mouser, *American Colony*, 4.
4. Hawthorne, *Planting Rice*, 80; Levtzion, *Islam*, VII:29; Mouser, "Landlords-Strangers," 431, 433; Mouser, *American Colony*, 7.
5. Blackburn, *Overthrow of Colonial Slavery*, 394–395; Misevich, "Origins," 162; Moráguez, "African Origins," 188.
6. Ministère de la Culture et Patrimoine Historique, *Memoire de Farenya*.
7. Kelly, "Preliminary Archaeological Reconnaissance," 24–31.
8. Law, *From Slave Trade*, 1; Mouser, "Continuing British Interest," 774.
9. Mayer, *Captain Canot*, 73.
10. Diallo, "Implantation Coloniale," 15; Mouser, *American Colony*, 47–49; Schafer, "Family Ties," 2.
11. Mouser, *American Colony*, 5; Mouser, *Voyage*, cover illustration.
12. Mark, *Portuguese Style*, 77–78.

13. Mayer, *Captain Canot*, 233; Mouser, "Trade and Politics," 107.
14. See Fields-Black, *Deep Roots*, 182.
15. Fields-Black, *Deep Roots*, 168.
16. Mark, *"Portuguese" Style*.
17. Mouser, *American Colony*, 50.
18. Mouser, *American Colony*, 50.
19. Sidibé, *Ecumes*.
20. Baldé, "Rio Pongo"; Diallo, "Implantation Coloniale"; Sorry, "Monograph Historique".
21. Montgomery, "Lightbourns of Farenya," 19.
22. Kelly, "Preliminary Archaeological Reconnaissance," 24–29.
23. Baldé, "Rio Pongo," 13.
24. Baldé, "Rio Pongo," 12.
25. Barrow, *Fifty Years*, 154.
26. Sorry, "Monograph Historique," 34.
27. Mouser, "Trade and Politics," 91.
28. Barrow, *Fifty Years*, 132.
29. Diallo, "Implantation Coloniale," 58.
30. Mayer, *Captain Canot*, 97. In Canot's text Gambia is spelled Kambia.
31. Diallo, "Implantation Coloniale".

References

Baldé, Maladho Siddy. "Le Rio Pongo du XVème au XIXème siècle: Une Histoire à travers des Photos de Première Main." Draft document, 2013.

Barrow, A. H. *Fifty Years in Western Africa: Being a Record of the Works of the West Indian Church on the Banks of the Rio Pongo*. London: Society for Promoting Christian Knowledge, 1900.

Berlin, Ira. "From Creole to African: Atlantic Creoles and the Origins of African – American Society in Mainland North America." *William and Mary Quarterly* LLIII, no. 2 (1996): 251–288.

Blackburn, Robin. *The Overthrow of Colonial Slavery, 1776–1848*. London: Verso, 1988.

Brooks, George E. *Landlords and Strangers: Ecology, Society, and Trade in Western Africa, 1000–1630*. Boulder, CO: Westview, 1993.

Diallo, Mamadou. "Implantation Coloniale à Travers les Vestiges au Rio Pongo." Memoire D'histoire. Institut Polytechnique Gamal Abdel Nasser, Conakry, 1970.

Fields-Black, Edda L. *Deep Roots: Rice Farmers in West Africa and the African Diaspora*. Bloomington: Indiana University Press, 2008.

Hawthorne, Walter. *Planting Rice and Harvesting Slaves: Transformations along the Guinea-Bissau Coast, 1400–1900*. Portsmouth, NH: Heinemann, 2003.

Kelly, Kenneth G. "Preliminary Archaeological Reconnaissance of Sites Related to the Slave Trade Era along the Upper Rio Pongo, Guinea." *Nyame Akuma* 65 (2006): 24–32.

Kelly, Kenneth G. "Archaeological Perspectives on the Atlantic Slave Trade: Contrasts in Time and Space in Benin and Guinea." In *Slavery in Africa: Archaeology and Memory*, edited by Paul J. Lane and Kevin C. MacDonald, 127–146. London: British Academy, 2011.

Kelly, Kenneth G. "(African) Atlantic Creoles." In *Preserving African Cultural Heritage*, Dakar, edited by Ibrahima Thiaw and Hamady Bocoum. Dakar, IFAN-Cheikh Anta Diop and Université Cheikh Anta Diop de Dakar, in press.

Law, Robin. "Introduction." In *From Slave Trade to "Legitimate" Commerce: The Commercial Transition in Nineteenth-century West Africa*, edited by Robin Law, 1–31. Cambridge: Cambridge University Press, 1995.

Levtzion, Nehemia. *Islam in West Africa: Religion, Society and Politics to 1800*. Aldershot: Variorum, 1994.

Mark, Peter. *"Portuguese" Style and Luso-African Identity: Precolonial Senegambia, Sixteenth-Nineteenth Centuries*. Bloomington: Indiana University Press, 2002.

Mayer, Brantz. *Captain Canot; or Twenty Years of an African Slaver*. New York: D. Appleton, 1854.

Ministère de la Culture et Patrimoine Historique. *Mémoire de Farinya: Projet d'étude, de sauvegarde et de valorisation du patrimoine culturel et historique issu de la traite des esclaves sur le littoral guinéen.* Conakry: Ministère de la Culture et du Patrimoine Historique, 2011.

Misevich, Philip. "The Origins of Slaves Leaving the Upper Guinea Coast in the Nineteenth Century." In *Extending the Frontiers: Essays on the New Transatlantic Slave Trade Database*, edited by David Eltis and David Richardson, 155–175. New Haven, CT: Yale University Press, 2008.

Montgomery, Warner M. "The Lightbourns of Farenya and Charleston." Paper presented in Conakry, Guinea, November 23–24, 1999.

Moráguez, Oscar Grandío. "The African Origins of Slaves Arriving in Cuba, 1789–1865." In *Extending the Frontiers: Essays on the New Transatlantic Slave Trade Database*, edited by David Eltis and David Richardson, 176–201. New Haven, CT: Yale University Press, 2008.

Mouser, Bruce L. "Trade and Politics in the Nunez and Pongo Rivers, 1790–1865." PhD diss., University of Indiana Press, 1972.

Mouser, Bruce L. "Landlords-Strangers: A Process of Accommodation and Assimilation." *International Journal of African Historical Studies* 8, no. 3, (1975): 425–440.

Mouser, Bruce L., ed. *A Slaving Voyage to Africa and Jamaica: The Log of the Sandown, 1793–1794.* Bloomington, IN: Indiana University Press, 2002.

Mouser, Bruce L. "Continuing British Interest in Coastal Guinea-Conakry and Fuuta Jaloo Highlands (1790–1850)." *Cahiers d'Etudes Africaines* XLIII, no. 4 (2003): 761–790.

Mouser, Bruce L. *American Colony on the Rio Pongo: The War of 1812, the Slave Trade, and the Proposed Settlement of African Americans, 1810–1830.* Trenton, NJ: Africa World Press, 2013.

Schafer, Daniel L. "Family Ties that Bind: Anglo-African Slave Traders in Africa and Florida, John Fraser and his Descendants." *Slavery and Abolition* 20, no 3 (1999): 1–21.

Sidibé, Yamoussa. *Les Ecumes de la Rancoeur.* Paris: Publibook, 2010.

Sorry, Charles E. "Monographie Historique du Rio Pongo du XVème à la fin du XIXème siecle." Memoire d'Histoire. Institut Polytechnique Gamal Abdel Nasser, Conakry, 1975.

Standing the test of time: embankment investigations, their implications for African technology transfer and effect on African American archaeology in South Carolina

Andrew Agha

> Thousands of Africans were taken from their homelands, enslaved in South Carolina, and put to work for the purpose of making their plantation owning masters large profits. Rice was the crop that was responsible for this massive importation of people. Research of the last 30 years has attempted to find direct links between African technology transfer, European involvement and the relic rice fields around Charleston. This article describes the author's 17 years of historical archaeology on the embankments, ditches and fields of eighteenth and nineteenth century inland rice plantations. Regardless of who was responsible for rice in South Carolina, African hands transformed the natural environment and local geography into a hydrological network of cultivated plantations.

Introduction

Despite decades of research and inquiry into the cultivation of rice along South Carolina's coast,[1] we still do not have concrete evidence of the specific processes that converted the inland fresh water swamps near Charleston into rice fields. Early colonial letters from the 1690s through the 1720s give only minimal descriptions and passing accounts about where rice was being grown, where the first rice seed came from, and how and who was growing the crop.[2] While this information is valuable, rice itself is given more attention than the rice *fields*; descriptions of the procedure involved in land selection, water drainage, ditch location, soil types, construction techniques, native vegetation and the labor required to introduce rice are absent from these narratives. To date, research has focused primarily on the origins of rice, rice seed and the ethnic background and knowledge of the workers transported to Carolina.[3] Scholars have not focused on the mechanics behind rice field creation: the ways the wilderness was turned into a built environment through water control and agriculture. Researchers are busy searching archives and libraries for the answer to "who" introduced and grew rice, but the material record of rice growing standing up tall in the dark swamps all around Charleston is waiting to be utilized as a fresh data source.

When I started studying rice cultivation in 1998, I became obsessed with finding the origins of rice. I was a sure student of the "black rice" school: Wood, Carney, Littlefield, Ferguson, Porcher, Stewart, and Joyner were my textbooks. This school of thought enticed me to look towards West Africa as the chief source of rice knowledge, as the premise of the time was that West Africans played more than a passive role in the adoption, adaptation and production of viable rice crops in Carolina.[4] At the same time historical archaeologists were hunting for African cultural markers at the plantation sites and settlements of the enslaved.[5] My training was in plantation archaeology and I took the search for Africanisms into the remaining intact colonial inland swamp rice fields that surround Charleston. I believed that if the old rice fields were treated like archaeological sites, they might yield evidence to support the transfer of West African technology to the Carolina Lowcountry.[6]

Years of study passed and I felt I was losing sight of what really mattered. Recording information, conducting excavations and mapping vast rice landscapes may eventually disclose patterns that can be attributed to a region of Africa or a people of origin, and I knew that this work was important and would be beneficial to the overall understanding of Africans in American history. However, my archaeological investigations were not detailing just the engineering aspects of how the earthen components were constructed: I was documenting the actual labor exerted by the enslaved Africans themselves. This is something that cannot be discovered at the dwellings of these captive workers. Witnessing the products of their labor first hand by walking on the embankments and digging through the soil and clay they piled, molded and shaped with their hands and tools, now forever memorialized within the modified soil, yields evidence that cannot be obtained by uncovering the architecture of slave villages and the refuse of daily life that are more commonly examined by archaeologists.

Questioning embankments

During what years were enslaved Africans performing the most labor? I asked this question in 1998 while working on the James Stobo plantation site. Stobo was a planter of indigo and inland rice at Willtown, SC. Settlers established Willtown 25 miles southwest of Charles Towne in the last quarter of the seventeenth century, making it the second oldest community in the Carolina colony. The Charleston Museum led two years of excavation at James Stobo's settlement (c.1740–1800), revealing the complete floor plan of the manor house and evidence of outbuildings.[7] While I was a student learning the techniques and ideas of historical archaeology, we were tasked by our teachers to query the archaeological record and surrounding plantation landscape. My question required data. But where was I to find it?

Historical archaeologists have been studying the homes and yards of enslaved Africans for only 40 years.[8] These studies led to discoveries of architecture, foodways and other elements of culture and social relationships on colonial and antebellum plantations that provided the basis for later questions focused on contact with Native Americans, religious practices, slave accommodation and resistance, creolization, and other essential inquiries into the lives of people who were living within the sphere of domination, power and control of their owners, the planters. Almost all of these Africans and their descendants resided on plantations; agriculture was the primary reason they were in America. Strangely, no archaeological investigations had focused on the relationships the enslaved had with the land and the specific crops they raised.

Excavating the settlements that housed enslaved Africans on plantations has shown what kinds of foods they ate, what crafts they produced, how they organized space both inside the house and in the surrounding yards, and what kinds of labor was performed within the settlement. Knowing this, I wondered if data from the

Stobo settlement could provide an answer to my research question. As I dug at Stobo's settlement, I continued to stare off into the distance, south from the manor house and into the swamp where earthen embankments subdivided the lowland into giant squares. What could these features reveal? When and why were they built? Who built them? It struck me that the majority of the enslaved spent most of their waking hours in the rice fields and not in the settlement. Would the fields, then, be the "artifacts" I needed to answer my question?

To quantify the Africans' labor and when it was exerted the most during Stobo's tenure I read all available sources on colonial rice production, looking for historical accounts that described embankment construction. I found nothing. I then read dozens of archaeological investigations for excavations in rice fields and asked several Southeastern archaeologists if they had ever dug on an embankment. I again found no information. Thus, necessity drove me to devise methods to systematically excavate the embankments that caught my attention and distracted me on a daily basis.

Soil is an artifact

The first embankment I investigated sits 200 feet south of the Stobo manor and settlement. Figure 1 displays a photo of this berm. It has a shallow ditch on both sides and lies in a perfectly straight line for almost a half of a mile on an east/west orientation. The causeway road, or road that connected the settlement to the furthest extent of the rice fields, crosses the embankment perpendicularly. I picked the causeway and bank

Figure 1. Photo showing intact upland embankment at the Stobo Plantation (image by author).

juncture as the starting point for excavations, hoping that human traffic up and down the causeway to and from work every day had generated trash as people passed by the bank. Also, trash from the settlement might have been thrown out in this area. I hypothesized that these items may have been turned up in the soil as it was dug to make the ditch and piled to create the embankment. They would be locked in place and date the bank's creation and repairs. Friends, colleagues from The Charleston Museum, and I dug small, 1-foot round shovel test holes on top of the embankment and in the adjacent ditch. By the end of the first day, after almost 15 of these test pits, we had enough artifacts to interpret a date.[9]

After this first phase of work, I started to dig in the space directly north of the embankment. This area was higher in elevation than the swampland to the south. These additional tests yielded nails, brick rubble, European ceramics, tobacco pipe fragments, bottle glass and slave-made colonoware pottery. I found more artifacts than expected, and since this locale lies 200 feet from the main settlement, I thought it possible that in the past buildings may have been located next to the embankment. Perhaps refuse from the area had been displaced during ditch clean-out and rebuilding/repairing required for embankment maintenance. Artifacts inadvertently moved from the ground and into the embankment would give me better dates for the earthwork.

One small shovel test in the embankment uncovered a burned soil lens. To see more of this soil type I dug two seven- by three-foot excavation units end to end. A 14-foot long profile revealed both the modified and unaltered soils from the center of the bank, through the ditch, and well into the intact ground to its north side. Figure 2 displays a profile drawing and photograph of this trench profile. As excavation progressed, it became clear that the burned soil lens was actually the original ground surface underneath the embankment. I recorded the shape and depth of the ditch. The sterile soil from below the old humus was piled high above the burned soil lens, and ditch

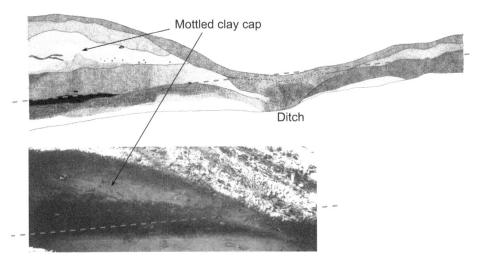

Figure 2. Profile drawing and photo of trench excavation in the embankment at Stobo Plantation. Dotted red line denotes old ground surface at the time of bank construction (images by author).

clean-out soils were piled on top. Artifacts from the period prior to Stobo sat both in the burned soil lens and the intact humus below, which indicated that Stobo was the planter who directed his labor force to build this embankment sometime after 1740. I was able to discern that the ditch was cleaned out periodically and that the soil from this labor was used to rebuild the bank. This finding came from cross-mending a ceramic sherd from the very top of the bank to a sherd from the bottom of the old humus soil north of the ditch. When laborers cleaned out the ditch, they must have cut into intact soil, displaced one of these ceramics and deposited it at the top of the bank.

A second 14- by three-foot cross section was dug between the first cut and the causeway. Similar artifacts were found, but not the burned soil lens. Also, the soil in the top half of the bank was different from the first cut. Artifacts from the mid-eighteenth century were found lying at the bottom of the soil layer in the second cut, as well as in the middle of the first cut between sterile fill deposited at different times. These artifacts in relation to the soil suggested that this bank was repaired sometime after the 1760s, maybe even after a hurricane that struck the Charleston area in the late 1750s.[10]

After learning these details, I conducted more research on inland rice fields to determine how the embankment I was studying related to rice cultivation. Inland fields were technologically similar to the more commonly known tidal rice fields, but distinct in important ways. Tidal fields line the major rivers of South Carolina and utilized the rise and fall of the tide for field flooding. Embankments bordered the floodplain to create fields and wooden sluice boxes called "gates" opened and closed mechanically to let water on the fields and off again. Inland swamp rice worked differently.[11]

Interior swamps eventually drain into rivers. They vary between narrow 100-foot wide or less micro-floodplains with a seasonal creek as a drain to larger watersheds that stretch over 1000-feet wide with major waterways cutting through them. Colonists erected large embankments called "dams" at the foot of these swamps to stop water from flowing through them and at the head to prevent water backing up into the fields during downstream floods. Embankments on the linear sides called "facing banks" were built along with "facing ditches" that channeled the water backing up against the head dam. These two dams and facing embankments created an interior space that was then subdivided into "squares" demarcated by ditches, embankments and "quarter ditches." Water controls called "trunks" were placed in the facing embankment and head dam. When the trunk was opened, water flowed into the facing ditches and open trunks on the facing banks allowed water to flood the fields inside. Water backed up against the head dam created a "reservoir." As the crop required water, the trunks were opened, and the crop was flooded for support and strength. The lower trunks were opened to drain off the water when needed.[12] This was the basic hydrological principle and technology that governed how every inland swamp rice field operated. It was a system based on the knowledge of gravity, water, soils and on immense human labor.

Why, then, did the bank I dug at Stobo's plantation fail to fit this description? Here, there is no clear reservoir upslope and the embankment ditch was too shallow to provide any major water transport. Other known inland fields I had seen were smaller, the banks closer together, and the ditches deeper. Based on comparative data and historical examples, I concluded that the bank I dug was built to keep the activity area and buildings to its north dry and well drained. This area may have served a particular plantation function and thus needed protection from encroaching flood water rising up from the river and swamplands to the south. I identified a reservoir some distance to the south lying above a small set of inland swamp rice fields, and I followed a shallow ditch from this reservoir across the high ground, along the causeway road, and back to the ditch on the south side of the bank. The embankment, although not a critical component of an inland rice field, apparently functioned as part of a larger drainage system that supplied water to the reservoir far away.

Standing in the excavation cut, looking at the lensing of soil that mark the unique loads of earth piled one upon another, I realized that I was staring at the results of the enslaved Africans' actual labor, and that the layers themselves are artifacts: material culture created through the alteration of the earth.

Did enslaved African labor practices involved in rice cultivation affect how cultural, ancestral memories were materialized in the plantation settlements across the Lowcountry? Were choices based on cultural preferences embedded in the archaeological record? Little attention had been given to the locations where the enslaved spent the majority of the day – the fields of their labor. If we rely only on one spatial component of their lives – their homes – then we miss opportunities to understand the major forms of self-expression.

Archaeology of agriculture

Besides digging this earthwork, I created a detailed map of every identifiable embankment and ditch associated with Stobo's plantation. This landscape study shows the vast network of ditches and banks and how they relate to each other. A few years after my initial work at Willtown I had the fortune to continue mapping other inland rice fields from the eighteenth century. My employment at Brockington and Associates, a cultural resource consulting firm in Charleston, took me to several different inland rice systems. Housing and commercial development construction prompts archaeological, historical and architectural projects required by State and Federal permitting agencies. As a result, Brockington historian Charlie Philips and I had explored a number of intact inland rice systems within a 30-mile radius of Charleston.

During one routine survey, at the settlement of the Glaze-Poppenheim Plantation, we identified a mid-eighteenth-century settlement on high ground, and inland rice embankments in the swamp below. We drew a detailed map using sub-meter Global Positioning System (GPS).[13] Shortly after this project, Philips and I mapped another inland field system on pre-1740s Woodstock Plantation.[14] This system was different from Stobo and Glaze-Poppenheim. Each plantation landscape exhibited unique responses to the characteristics of the geography, slope of the land, flow of water, as well as to the planter's background and knowledge of agriculture, the cultural particularities of the enslaved Africans and their agricultural knowledge. Our mapping efforts reinforced the need to document these various rice landscapes, especially since modern development was encroaching on them more each year. Through our work, the Glaze-Poppenheim Plantation rice fields was recognized as a stand-alone archaeological site: the first inland rice field ever to be recorded as such in South Carolina.[15]

A particular compliance project gave me another opportunity to excavate an embankment. The late eighteenth-century Bolton-on-the-Stono Plantation, owned by Thomas Middleton, was an inland plantation that did not grow rice.[16] However, embankments near the settlement, primarily along both sides of a major causeway road, gave access from the landing on the Stono River deep into the interior of the plantation. We used a backhoe to cut a profile through one of the embankments that provided a complete profile of its composition. This embankment was similar to the Stobo bank in construction but had a heavy clay "cap" that made up the top third of the earthwork.[17] The clay was solid and very thick. The Stobo bank exhibits some clay mottled with the sterile fill in the top third as well, but nothing like the Bolton example. Since the embankments facing this Bolton road were still intact and sturdy, I hypothesized that the use of clay was a technological innovation for adding strength against erosion and damage. This would have required extensive labor on top of the task of embankment construction. In return, the labor needed for upkeep, repair and maintenance was likely reduced. This use of clay may appear to be "common sense;" I see it as a difficult negotiation between the planter and his work force. Did the enslaved Africans know that using clay in this way would save them labor in the future? Was the clay the planter's idea? Was this a standard, already-known technique borrowed from road construction? Was the clay harvested because the ground in this particular spot has natural clay as subsoil? The Bolton project shows that embankment construction involved not simply piling up fill created from the ditch. Instead, the soil and clay was strategically deposited to build an earthwork that would last for centuries.

In 2007 I excavated an upland embankment at Dean Hall, a rice plantation founded by Alexander Nesbitt in 1725.[18] In 1820 it changed hands to Charleston merchant William Carson. The Carson family grew rice at Dean Hall until 1909, when a hurricane ended almost 200 years of continuous rice cultivation. Tidal fields at Dean Hall were developed sometime in the 1790s, but that did not mean the inland fields were abandoned. By 1800 most planters had switched from inland to tidal production, and new rice planters planted only along the riverside. Some planters managed their labor so that both tidal and inland rice were worked at the same time.[19] Both Nesbitt and Carson managed their labor in this way. I wondered: Did embankment construction and technology differ between the two types of fields? What ideas, if any, transferred from the older, inland rice technology to the later tidal techniques? Did tidal rice encourage new ways to build embankments?

When William Carson purchased Dean Hall, he acquired the entire enslaved population of almost 200 people. These people and their ancestors and predecessors had been growing rice for almost 100 years at this location. Carson had no personal knowledge or experience in rice cultivation. Matthew Myrick, Nesbitt's overseer, admitted that he learned everything he knew about growing rice from Old Joe, the driver who was already in charge of the inland and tidal fields prior to Carson's tenure.[20] Based on the circumstances, it is plausible that the inland swamp rice technology at Dean Hall since the 1720s was adapted and modified to create and maintain the tidal fields near the end of the century. The drainage systems implemented at Dean Hall were so effective that Captain George W. Cullum, the engineer who planned Civil War era Fort Sumter in the Charleston harbor, visited Dean Hall to observe how Carson's drainage systems improved hygiene and sanitation.[21] Cullum may have been viewing the handiwork of Africans – technology that came from the rice fields.

An interesting and rare drainage system was in place around the slave village. This village was built sometime in the 1790s by the last Nesbitt planter. Carson rebuilt everything in 1820, replacing the single room cabins with two-family houses that were raised off the ground on brick piers. Sometime after 1843 he had an embankment

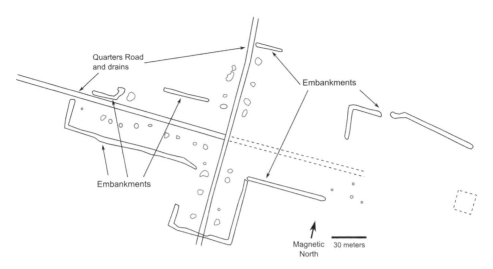

Figure 3. Embankment and brick features identified at the slave settlement for Dean Hall Plantation (image by author).

and ditch built to surround the village. Figure 3 shows a plan view of the embankment as it encircled the settlement. The archaeology I conducted at this site identified many above ground brick foundations, wells and other landscape features but this embankment was by far the most impressive feature of all. The Quarters Road still traversed the village with ditches to either side and embankments on the outside to prevent the road from flooding. This road/ditch system also drained the settlement with the water flowing south to meet the reservoir for the inland swamp rice fields. The encircling embankment tied into the road ditches, further improving the drainage of the living quarters and yards.

I cut this perimeter bank in two locations: one cut was on higher ground near the center of the village, the other cut was in the lowest elevation west of the first cut. Both excavations were conducted with a backhoe to expose a full profile of the embankment. Figure 4 displays a photo and profile drawing of one of these cuts. A large

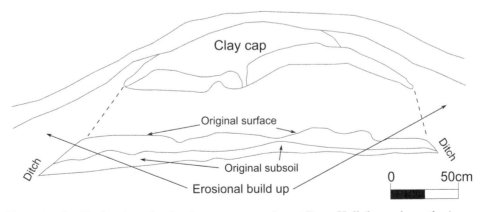

Figure 4. Profile drawing of embankment cross section at Dean Hall (image by author).

clay cap was revealed in both cuts, identical to that seen in the Bolton example. Again, I interpret the use of clay here as a technological soil adaptation that assured strength and longevity.

The presence of clay caps demonstrates the enslaved Africans' knowledge of soil and clay. My work argues that embankment design and implementation was not a random, unconsidered act of labor. We tend to think of "ditch digging" as an activity that does not require much thought. The three upland embankments that I have studied show, instead, an act that required planning, foresight and highly skilled manual labor. The Dean Hall village embankment stood strong against erosion and flooding for over 150 years and the archaeology shows that the clay cap withstood the ravages of the natural elements.

A deep knowledge of dirt

After my investigations at Dean Hall, I was involved in a major road project for Charleston County.[22] A new road was needed to connect two major thoroughfares. The space between: inland swamp filled with miles of intact embankments and ditches. The swamp to be crossed was the Bluehouse Swamp, portions of which I had already mapped at the Woodstock Plantation inland rice system with my colleague Charlie Philips. The proposed road corridor was going to pass through 11 well preserved banks and their adjacent ditches and canals. Historical research paired with our previous mapping efforts demonstrated that archaeology could help road builders mitigate the destruction of portions of these essential rice field elements. Besides excavations, we had a chance to map the inland rice systems of several plantations and incorporate previous work into a planning document that the State of South Carolina would be able to use to assess inland rice landscape features for inclusion into the National Register of Historic Places (NRHP).[23]

Philips' historical work showed that the inland fields associated with Woodlands Plantation were built before 1740.[24] Extensive mapping of upland and swamp embankments and their ditches allowed us to say where we thought rice once grew. We picked two embankments in the heart of the swamp that we felt were directly associated with water management for rice fields. Bank 1 had a ditch to only one side while Bank 2 had a small ditch on one side and a larger ditch or canal on the other. Bank 2 had a matching embankment on the other side of the ditch/canal, so that these two banks worked together to control the large ditch between them.

A backhoe with a smooth blade was employed to cut a trench through Banks 1 and 2, in order to expose the soil profile that would tell us how each earthwork was constructed, and how the two related to their associated ditches. Bank 1 revealed a soil profile similar to that found at the Stobo Plantation. Where I had seen clay caps in the upland banks, here the topmost layer was a mix of gray sticky clay and loam. Figure 5 displays a photo and profile drawing of Bank 1. This mixed soil cap had been purposefully prepared in an almost perfect marriage of the two soil types. The side of the bank closest to the ditch appeared to have been taller and was reinforced with additional soil layers to protect it against water that passed through the ditch and alongside the bank. Had the bank been made of only sand and/or loam, water action would have washed the wall away in a short time. This bank provides evidence for the use of specific soils to manage and control water; something I had not seen before.

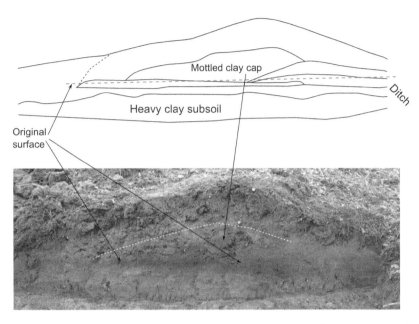

Figure 5. Profile drawing and photo of Bank 1 from Woodlands Plantation. Dotted red line denotes old ground surface at the time of bank construction (images by author).

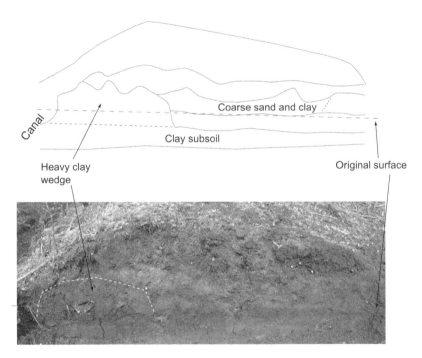

Figure 6. Profile drawing and photo of Bank 2 from Woodlands Plantation. Dotted red line denotes old ground surface at the time of bank construction (images by author).

Bank 2 was cut next. This double-bank with center ditch made me think that the internal composition would be different from Bank1, but I had no idea the difference would be so radical. The ditch between Bank 2 and the neighboring bank was roughly five feet wide, and water flowed freely through it the day we conducted this field work. The moving water proved one important thing: these two banks were constructed to withstand running water, and had done so for many, many years. Figure 6 displays a photo and profile drawing of Bank 2. Africans and African Americans who built this did so by first stripping off all topsoil where the banks and ditch were to be built. They went down to parent subsoil clay. The clay is gray, thick and very sticky, totally unlike the dry, blocky and partly friable clay incorporated into the caps of upland banks. Next, the clay was quarried along the line of the intended ditch. This loose clay was then piled and packed on both sides of the ditch to form two linear ridges. The clay walls and floor of the ditch would not erode as water passed by. When the workers created the clay ridges they mixed the loose clay fill with the clay subsoil so perfectly that I was unable to see a line between the two. The process was similar to what potters would do when joining two clay slabs together to make a vessel: they do not show their work, only the perfect, finished form. Once the clay ridge in Bank 2 was set, the workers then mounded a thick lens of very coarse sand and large clay lumps on the clay floor next to the ridge until both the ridge and this mound were level. On top of the clay ridge and soil mix is the cap: a rich mix of subsoil clay and sandy loam that mirrors that seen in Bank 1.

Banks 1 and 2 in this swamp have reinforced sides against their ditches. Both banks were components of an inland rice field and they managed the flow of water so that rice could grow. The attention given to Bank 2, however, shows a technological skill unlike anything I have seen in the seven embankments I have excavated since 1998. Did African agriculturalists bring to America the knowledge of managing how water flows through ditches? What specific memories concerning soil and hydrology crossed the Atlantic with them? How quickly did they learn to master the Carolina environment? My fieldwork and review of the Charleston County Soil Survey[25] proved that the coarse sand was not naturally occurring in the Bluehouse Swamp. Where did this sand come from? Did the enslaved find an upland source for this specific sand and bring it into the swamp? I had never seen this kind of sand used in any embankment other than Bank 2. My excavations at Woodlands Plantation raised new questions about labor management, ancestral African technology and the origin of hydrological engineering in South Carolina.

As a second component of the road project, we attempted to recover rice seed from the Bluehouse Swamp.[26] Small holes were dug in four discrete locations to collect soil for analysis in the hope of finding preserved rice grains. The presence of rice grains in the soils would designate the fields that grew rice. Some enclosed spaces within the swamp might have served purposes other than rice growing. This information would be critical for interpreting inland rice fields and for better understanding the labor of the enslaved. Unfortunately all four soil samples yielded no rice grains. This may be due to the aerobic environment of the derelict field. Or, it could be that the sections of embanked space I chose never did grow rice. More soil sampling is needed from any and all inland rice field settings around the Charleston area. If grains are found, we may discover the varieties that early colonists observed and we may be able to tell when white rice varieties were adapted to the swamps.

After completing these excavations, Philips and I mapped other portions of Bluehouse Swamp along with several other inland rice plantations. We compiled our GPS coordinate data from our on-the-ground mapping efforts with aerial photographs, contour maps, soil maps and historic plats. All of these resources were integrated in a geographic information system.[27] We could see how the plats differ from our field observations. We recorded fields in the swamps that were never drawn on historic plats. We learned how old property lines – embankments themselves – were incorporated into the inland rice systems. Settlements, from both the plats and archaeological investigations, could be placed in context with the earthworks and ditches. The years of operation and eventual abandonment were derived. Lastly, two major mapping efforts from the 1980s – Leland Ferguson and David Babson's "Great Map" of the East Branch of the Cooper River and Dan Elliott's extensive map of eighteenth-century Crowfield Plantation[28] – were incorporated into our surveys to see how modern development and erosion has affected the resources they recorded. Our map project is a foundation for future inland rice researchers to use when attempting to identify field systems that can be included in the NRHP. The road project in the Bluehouse Swamp has identified resources that researchers have overlooked since the start of African American archeology in the late 1960s.

The detailed mapping of embankments in the field, when combined with available historic map information, creates a new data set that points to new questions about Lowcountry South Carolina rice plantations. Visualizing the enslaved at work, we can think about their lives in more comprehensive ways. Rice was the crop responsible for the importation of thousands of Africans to South Carolina. The information we have gleaned from the inland swamp rice fields can be paired with what archaeology has taught us about upland settlements to illuminate the origins and development of rice cultivation in the Charleston area.

The future of the past

For the past 17 years I have been walking the swamps looking for new rice fields and their landscape features, and doing archaeology on plantation sites that were home to the enslaved Africans who made up the majority of people in South Carolina. Understanding labor and plantation production continues to be the driving force behind my work. Integrating agricultural fields with living quarters allows us to broaden our interpretations of South Carolina's past. While a great deal has been accomplished, many more things are left to try.

The detailed mapping of inland rice plantations should continue. I have mapped only 11 plantations that lie within a 30-mile radius of Charleston. Rice was grown near all major population centers along the South Carolina and Georgia coasts. This crop was perfected first near Charleston in the early eighteenth century and spread north and south for 100 years. Does the complexity of inland rice fields change as the distance from Charleston increases? How does the size of the swamp influence the kinds of water controls, ditches and embankments in settings near to and far from Charleston? How uniform is embankment technology along the coast? Were embankments constructed in new inland settings after 1800, and are they similar to tidal bank composition?

Some inland settings stayed in cultivation after tidal rice became the dominant mode of rice production. Were inland fields improved in the nineteenth century as a result of tidal technology? Knowing the layout of inland fields reveals the "layout" of the labor regime implemented by the planters. How did the time requirements needed for embankment management, repair and ditch clean-out work, vary from place to place and decade to decade? The inland embankments, then, dictate the labor needs of the plantation, which affected the amount of time the enslaved Africans had away from the fields, back at their homes.

As I map new inland fields, I may see patterns emerge that are dependent on geography, soil type, soil permeability, distance from salt water and period of plantation operation. These data can be compared to historical embankment configurations in different countries. For example, the land "improvers" in Great Britain drained and dried out their swamps, or fens, by embanking and ditching the fenland so that they could plant crops there.[29] West Africans have been growing rice for over 1500 years and have utilized environments different from those they encountered in America.[30] Historians who work on Carolina rice origins may find similarities between these foreign agricultural landscapes and sites in America. Embankment innovations could have roots in West Africa, and further study may reveal tangible evidence of African technology transfer. Rice researchers, then, may find the "sources" they have searched for far away from home.

I have witnessed and recorded a few unique features in inland rice fields that are unexplainable. One such feature is a juncture of three embankments that come together to create a small triangle. When I stand inside this triangular enclosure, the embankments appear to be walls and the ground surface is higher than the fields that surround them. I believe some of the fill from the ditches was mounded in the triangle's center. These enclosures are sometimes in the middle of large field systems, or near the edge. They may have served specific functions associated with rice labor. Maybe they were locations where the freshly cut rice stalks were stacked for drying before being transported to the settlement for processing? Or, perhaps they served as a dry refuge for laborers to eat meals, store tools and take shelter from storms. Archaeologist Leland Ferguson visited an active rice field in Sierra Leone in 1991 and recorded what he referred to as a "field kitchen."[31] He observed open fire cooking, a shed that housed supplies and tools, stools and other effects needed for the day's work. Did these "field kitchens" once exist in South Carolina's inland rice fields? I call these potential sites "field stations" as they may have served functions beyond kitchen chores during different parts of the rice year. I plan to excavate at these enclosures in the future.

The years I have spent in inland rice fields have accustomed me to their components, such as the trunks built for water control. Of the many jobs performed by enslaved Africans, one worker called the "trunk minder" was employed to manage water flow, both onto and off of the rice crop. Rice was flooded to destroy weeds and pests, to irrigate, and to support the crop from falling over as the seed heads enlarged. I wonder what the trunk minder ate and drank all day? What else did he do while waiting on water to move? How many hours were required, and from that time, how much trash was generated that became artifacts for archaeologists to find centuries later? Excavations in these places can reveal the details of a specific enslaved African's life that could never be found at the houses in a slave village. The remains of trunks today appearing as scars in the embankments occur at specific intervals in relation with dams and reservoirs. During a recent field assessment at Hampton Plantation, located on the Santee River near McClellanville, South Carolina, I recorded the positions of over 10 trunks that had been obliterated by time but whose locations are still visible. These are the kinds of places I hope to excavate in the future.

Lastly, my research may contribute to a new hypothesis for the most enigmatic artifact found in association with Africans in America: colonoware. Colonoware is a ceramic that was manufactured by enslaved people on plantations throughout the coastal zone of South Carolina.[32] This low fired earthenware is most likely the product of interactions between Africans, Europeans and Native Americans. The frequency and intimacy of interactions among these three groups has been the subject of decades-long debate. However, one fact cannot be disputed: colonoware pottery is found in its greatest quantities on the slave settlements of rice plantations. Between 1820 and 1857, some 200–250 enslaved Africans – by this time African Americans – lived and worked at Dean Hall rice plantation. My excavations at their settlement recovered the largest colonoware assemblage ever found on a single site before.[33] These 59,020 sherds of pottery are eloquent evidence of the lives of those enslaved individuals.

The enslaved needed clay to make this pottery. But not just any kind of clay, it had to be of a quality that met specific criteria.[34] The clay they found probably had plant roots and organic matter in it, as well iron concretions, coarse sand and other impurities. Sometimes on sites we find colonoware sherds that exhibit entirely clean, smooth and grit-free clay mixtures. At Dean Hall, we identified sherds with entire oak leaves embedded within the clay of the vessel, as well as large cinders that show evidence of wood chips that burned within the pottery as it was fired.[35] If the rice clays were good enough to make functional vessels, did they forego cleaning the organics out of the clay to save time that could be spent on other things?

Archaeologists who first began to identify and interpret this pottery in the late 1970s and early 1980s believed that large pits dug near the houses in slave villages were clay quarries that produced the raw material for colonoware pottery production.[36] When comparing the clay characteristics to the qualities generally required by a potter (plasticity, cleanliness, porosity, moisture, etc.), some of the clay types met a few of these qualifications. However, the researchers utilized testing strategies that created inconclusive[37] and slightly subjective[38] results.

From a close reading of the Dean Hall landscape, I have hypothesized that suitable colonoware clay sources were derived from the inland rice fields, not the settlement. While clay found at the settlement roughly conforms to the composition needed to make a vessel, the more desirable clays underlay the fields the workers frequented daily. Archaeology shows that embankments were made of clay – soils with a clay mix and caps of clay. Bank 2 in the Bluehouse Swamp shows an advanced use of clay – an understanding we might expect from an experienced sculptor or potter. In West Africa, pottery has been made for centuries and is still made today. Studies have demonstrated links between clay-walled house builders and potters working together in architectural labor.[39] Besides walls for houses, large walls were and are made of stone and sometimes clay for defensive needs in towns and house compounds.[40] In the South Carolina environment, were colonoware potters involved in the construction of embankments? Did West Africans and their ancient knowledge of pottery and clay architecture make a difference between successful field impoundments and those that failed? Did Africans known as potters command a premium at American slave markets? As I continue to excavate rice plantations and their settlements, I aim to conduct elemental analyses of the pottery and inland rice field clays to look for correlations.

South Carolina's enslaved past began with seventeenth-century Guinea trade, where tropical cultivars, like sugarcane, and a labor force was derived for first the English colonies of the Caribbean, and a few decades later, Carolina.[41] West Africans were brought into the colony with strained but intact minds. Historical and archaeological evidence shows crafts like basketwork, pottery, wood carving and architecture were employed on plantations up and down the Carolina coast.[42] If the technological capacity for pottery production transferred partly or completely intact from West Africa, then did African rice technology transfer as well? Can we link South Carolina's enslaved roots in the Guinea trade, which partly formed the origin of Carolina agriculture, to the roots of rice cultivation? If historians have shown rice connections between South Carolina and the Guinea coast, then further studies of early inland rice fields could reveal evidence of technological transfer.

My work in rice fields began as a quest to understand slave labor; rice fields are slave labor materialized. I have conducted excavations in and mapped many miles of embankments across the South Carolina Lowcountry. After 17 years doing this research, I have come to believe, to paraphrase Charles Joyner, that we are closer to the beginning rather than the end of what there is to learn about lives of the enslaved. Archaeology gives us a promising path for reaching the starting line.

Acknowledgements

I would like to thank Dr Kenneth Kelly for allowing me the opportunity to publish this work. Special thanks to Dr Theodore Rosengarten and Dr Max Edelson for comments on earlier versions of this article. I also thank the Lane Family of Willtown Bluff, The Charleston Museum, Brockington and Associates, Beazer Homes, E.I. Nemours DuPont Corporation, South Carolina Department of Transportation, Charleston County, and the Archaeological Research Collective, Inc. Lastly, I thank Dr Hayden Smith and Charlie Philips for their love of rice history and Carolina swamps.

Disclosure statement

No potential conflict of interest was reported by the author.

Notes

1. Wood, *Black Majority*; Littlefield, *Rice and Slaves*; Chaplin, *An Anxious Pursuit*; Carney and Porcher, *Geographies of the Past*; Stewart, *What Nature Suffers to Groe*; Carney, *Black Rice*; Edelson, *Plantation Enterprise*; Fields-Black, *Deep Roots*.
2. Agha, Philips, and Fletcher, *Inland Swamp Rice Context*, E3–E4; Heyward, *Seed From Madagascar*; Doar, *Rice and Rice Planting*; Porcher, "Rice Culture"; Carney, *Black Rice*, 83–84.

3. Alpern, "Eighteenth-Century Rice Boom"; Eltis, Morgan, and Richardson, "Agency and Diaspora."
4. Littlefield, *Rice and Slaves*; Carney, "Landscapes of Technology Transfer"; Carney, *Black Rice*.
5. Ascher and Fairbanks, "Excavations of a Slave Cabin"; Wheaton, Friedlander, and Garrow, *Yaughan and Curriboo*; Singleton, "The Archaeology of Slavery"; Singleton, *I, Too, Am America*; Adams, "Early African-American Domestic Architecture"; Adams, "South Carolina Slave Houses"; Ferguson, *Uncommon Ground*; Agha, "Searching for Cabins."
6. Agha, "Rice Dike Construction," 275–282.
7. Zierden, Linder, and Anthony, *Willtown*.
8. Ferguson, *Uncommon Ground*; Singleton, "The Archaeology of Slavery"; Singleton, *I, Too, Am America*; Joseph et al. "Historical Archaeology"; Orser, "Archaeology of the African Diaspora"; Ogundiran and Falola, *Archaeology of Atlantic Africa*.
9. Agha, "Rice Dike Construction," 279–282.
10. Agha, "Inland Swamp Rice Embankment."
Agha and Philips, "Landscapes of Cultivation," 20–22.
11. Carney, *Black Rice*.
12. Heyward, *Seed from Madagascar*, 12–13; Agha, Philips, and Fletcher, *Inland Swamp Rice Context*, F41–48.
13. Chambliss and Bailey, *Palmetto Commerce Park Tract*.
14. Lansdell, Philips, and Bailey, *Weber Research Tract*.
15. Chambliss and Bailey, *Palmetto Commerce Park Tract*.
16. Franz, Agha, and Philips, *Bolton on the Stono*, 29–30.
17. Ibid., 258.
18. Agha, Philips, and Isenbarger, *Traditions in Rice and Clay*.
19. Smith, "Rich Swamps and Rice Ground," 95–104.
20. Agha, Philips, and Isenbarger, *Traditions in Rice and Clay*, 48.
21. Ibid., 55.
22. Agha et al., *Palmetto Commerce Parkway Extension*.
23. Agha, Philips, and Fletcher, *Inland Swamp Rice Context*.
24. Ibid., E25.
25. Miller, *Soil Survey of Charleston*.
26. Agha, Philips, and Fletcher, *Inland Swamp Rice Context*, E30.
27. Ibid., A-1–A-39.
28. Garrow and Elliot, *Crowfield Archaeological Survey*, 65.
29. Wood, *Locke and Agrarian Capitalism*, 60–64.
30. Fields-Black, *Deep Roots*; Fall, Elhadj Ibrahima, personal communication, September 2013.
31. Ferguson, *Sierra Leone Field Notes*.
32. Anthony, "Colono wares"; Anthony, "Tangible Interaction"; Ferguson, *Uncommon Ground*.
Isenbarger, "Potters, Hucksters and Consumers"; Agha, *St. Giles Kussoe*, 71.
33. Agha, Philips, and Isenbarger, *Traditions in Rice and Clay*, 3–6.
34. Ibid., 618–620.
35. Ibid.
36. Wheaton, Friedlander, and Garrow, *Yaughan and Curriboo*; Drucker and Anthony, *Spiers Landing Site*, 125–127.
37. Drucker and Anthony, *Spiers Landing Site*, 125–127.
38. Wheaton, Friedlander, and Garrow, *Yaughan and Curriboo*.
39. Denyer, *African Traditional Architecture*.
40. Ibid., 35, 71, 167.
41. Agha, *St. Giles Kussoe*, 12, 24.
42. Ferguson, *Uncommon Ground*; Morgan, *Slave Counterpoint*; Genovese, *Roll Jordan Roll*; Pollitzer, *The Gullah People*.

References

Adams, Natalie P. "Early African-American Domestic Architecture from Berkeley County, South Carolina." Master's thesis, University of South Carolina, 1990.

Adams, Natalie P. "'In the Style of an English Cottage:' Influences on the Design, Construction, and Use of South Carolina Slave Houses." Paper presented at the annual meeting for the Archaeological Society for South Carolina, Columbia, SC, February 23, 2002.

Agha, Andrew. "African American Slaves and Rice Dike Construction." In *Willtown: An Archaeological and Historical Perspective*, edited by Martha Zierden, Ronald Anthony, and Suzanne Linder, 275–282. Columbia: South Carolina Department of Archives and History, 1999.

Agha, Andrew. "An Analysis of the Cultural Material and Deposits in an Eighteenth Century Inland Swamp Rice Embankment, Willtown Bluff, Charleston County, South Carolina." On file, The Charleston Museum, 2001.

Agha, Andrew. "St. Giles Kussoe and 'The Character of a Loyal States-Man': Historical Archaeology at Lord Anthony Ashley Cooper's Carolina Plantation." Report prepared for Historic Charleston Foundation, 2012.

Agha, Andrew, and Joshua N. Fletcher. "Addendum Report Regarding Additional Inland Rice Fields within the Supplemental Study Area of the Palmetto Commerce Parkway Extension Project, Charleston County, South Carolina." Prepared for THE LPA GROUP INCORPORATED, Columbia, SC. Report prepared by Brockington and Associates, Inc., Charleston, SC, 2007.

Agha, Andrew, and Charles F. Philips, Jr. "Landscapes of Cultivation: Inland Rice Fields as Landscapes and Archaeological Sites." *African Diaspora Archaeology Newsletter*, September 2009. http://www.diaspora.illinois.edu/news0909/news0909.html#1

Agha, Andrew, Charles F. Philips, Jr., and Joshua Fletcher. "Inland Swamp Rice Context, c. 1690–1783." National Register of Historic Places Multiple Property Documentation Form. Prepared by Brockington and Associates, Inc., Charleston, SC, 2010.

Agha, Andrew, Charles F. Philips, Jr., and Nicole M. Isenbarger. "Traditions in Rice and Clay: Understanding an Eighteenth-Nineteenth Century Rice Plantation, Berkeley County, South Carolina (38BK2132)." Prepared for E.I. Nemours DuPont Corporation. Report prepared by Brockington and Associates, Inc., Charleston, SC, 2012.

Agha, Andrew, Charles F. Philips, Jr., Edward Salo, Jason Ellerbee, and Joshua N. Fletcher. "Cultural Resources Survey of the Palmetto Commerce Parkway Extension Project, Charleston County, South Carolina." Prepared for LPA Group, LLC. Report prepared by Brockington and Associates, Inc., Charleston, SC, 2007.

Alpern, Stanley B. "Did Enslaved Africans Spark South Carolina's Eighteenth-Century Rice Boom?" In *African Ethnobotany in the Americas*, edited by Robert Voeks and John Rashford, 35–66. New York: Springer, 2013.

Anthony, Ronald. "Colono Wares." In *Home Upriver: Rural Life on Daniel's Island*, edited by Martha Zierden, Leslie Drucker, and Jeanne Calhoun, 7-22–7-55. Ms. on file, Columbia: South Carolina Department of Highways and Public Transportation, 1986.

Anthony, Ronald. "Tangible Interaction: Evidence from Stobo Plantation." In *Another's Country: Archaeological and Historical Perspectives on Cultural Interactions in the Southern Colonies*, edited by Martha Zierden and Joseph W. Joseph, 45–64. Tuscaloosa: University of Alabama, 2002.

Ascher, Robert, and Charles H. Fairbanks. "Excavation of a Slave Cabin: Georgia, U.S.A." *Historical Archaeology* 5 (1971): 3–17.

Carney, Judith. "Landscapes of Technology Transfer: Rice Cultivation and African Continuities." *Technology and Culture* 37 (Spring 1996): 5–35.

Carney, Judith. "The Role of African Rice and Slaves in the History of Rice Cultivation in the Americas." *Human Ecology: An Interdisciplinary Study* 26 (December 1998): 525–545.

Carney, Judith. *Black Rice: The African Origins of Rice Cultivation in the Americas*. Cambridge: Harvard University Press, 2001.

Carney, Judith, and Richard Porcher. "Geographies of the Past: Rice, Slaves, and Technological Transfer in South Carolina." *Southeastern Geographer* 33 (November 1993): 127–147.

Chambliss, Mallory L. Jr. and Ralph Bailey, Jr. "Cultural Resources Survey of the Palmetto Commerce Park Tract, Charleston, South Carolina." Prepared for Spring Grove

Associates, Charleston, SC. Report prepared by Brockington and Associates, Inc., Charleston, SC, 2005.

Chaplin, Joyce E. *An Anxious Pursuit. Agricultural Innovation & Modernity in the Lower South, 1730–1815*. Chapel Hill: University of North Carolina Press, 1993.

Denyer, Susan. *African Traditional Architecture: An Historical and Geographical Perspective*. New York: Africana Publishing Company, 1978.

Doar, David. *Rice and Rice Planting in the South Carolina Lowcountry*. Charleston, SC: Charleston Museum, 1936. Reprint, 1970.

Drucker, Leslie, and Ronald W. Anthony. "The Spiers Landing Site: Archaeological Investigations in Berkeley County, South Carolina." Prepared for the United States Department of the Interior Heritage Conservation and Recreation Service Interagency Archaeological Services-Atlanta. Report prepared by Carolina Archaeological Services, Columbia, SC, 1979.

Edelson, S. Max. *Plantation Enterprise in Colonial South Carolina*. Cambridge, MA: Harvard University Press, 2006.

Eltis, David, Philip Morgan, and David Richardson. "Agency and Diaspora in Atlantic History: Reassessing the African Contribution to Rice Cultivation in the Americas." *The American Historical Review* 112 (December 2007): 1329–1358.

Eubanks, Elsie I., Christopher T. Espenshade, Linda Kennedy, and Marian Roberts. "Data Recovery of the 38BU791 Bonny Shore Slave Row, Spring Island, Beaufort County, South Carolina." Prepared by Brockington and Associates, Atlanta, 1994.

Ferguson, Leland. *Uncommon Ground: Archaeology and Early African America, 1650–1800*. Washington, DC: Smithsonian Press, 1992.

Ferguson, Leland. "Privately Held Sierra Leone Field Notes." October 13, 1993.

Fields-Black, Edda L. *Deep Roots: Rice Farmers in West Africa and the African Diaspora*. Bloomington: Indiana University Press, 2008.

Franz, David M., Andrew Agha, and Charles F. Philips, Jr. "Bolton on the Stono: Data Recovery Excavations at 38CH2017." Prepared for Beazer Homes, Charleston, SC. Prepared by Brockington and Associates, Inc., Charleston, SC, 2012.

Genovese, Eugene D. *Roll, Jordan, Roll: The World the Slaves Made*. New York: Vintage Books, 1976.

Heyward, Duncan Clinch. *Seed from Madagascar*. Chapel Hill: University of North Carolina, 1937. Columbia: University of South Carolina, reprinted in 1993.

Isenbarger, Nicole M. "Potters, Hucksters, and Consumers: Placing Colonoware within the Internal Slave Economy Framework." Master's diss., University of South Carolina, 2006.

Joesph, Joseph W., ed. Forum "Crosses to Bear: Cross Marks as African Symbols in Southern Pottery." *Historical Archaeology* 45, no. 2 (2011): 132–188.

Lansdell, Brent, Charles F. Philips, Jr., and Ralph Bailey, Jr. "Cultural Resources Survey and Testing of the Weber Research Tract, Charleston County, South Carolina." Prepared for Weber USA Corporation, Summerville, SC. Prepared by Brockington and Associates, Inc., Charleston, SC, 2006.

Littlefield, Daniel C. *Rice and Slaves, Ethnicity and the Slave Trade in Colonial South Carolina*. Urbana: University of Illinois Press, 1981.

Miller, E. N. *Soil Survey of Charleston County, South Carolina*. Washington, DC: United States Department of Agriculture, 1971.

Morgan, Philip D. *Slave Counterpoint*. Chapel Hill: University of North Carolina Press, 1998.

Ogundiran, Akinwumi, and Toyin Falola, eds. *Archaeology of Atlantic Africa and the African Diaspora*. Bloomington: Indiana University Press, 2007.

Orser, Charles E. Jr. "The Archaeology of the African Diaspora." *Annual Review of Anthropology* 27 (1998): 63–82.

Pollitzer, William S. *The Gullah People and Their African Heritage*. Athens: University of Georgia Press, 1999.

Porcher, Richard D. "Rice Culture in South Carolina: A Brief History, the Role of the Huguenots, and the Preservation of its Legacy." *Transactions of the Huguenot Society of South Carolina* 92 (1987): 1–22.

Singleton, Theresa A. "The Archaeology of Slavery in North America." *Annual Review of Anthropology* 24 (1995): 119–140.

Singleton, Theresa A., ed. *I, Too, Am America*. Charlottesville: The University of Virginia Press, 1999.

Smith, Hayden Ros. "Rich Swamps and Rice Grounds: The Specialization of Inland Rice Culture in the South Carolina Lowcountry, 1670–1861." PhD diss., University of Georgia, 2012.

Stewart, Mart A. *"What Nature Suffers to Groe:" Life, Labor, and Landscape on the Georgia Coast, 1680–1920*. Athens: University of Georgia Press, 1996.

Wheaton, Thomas R., Amy Friedlander, and Patrick H. Garrow. "Yaughan and Curriboo Plantations: Studies in Afro-American Archaeology." Submitted to National Park Service, Southeast Regional Office. Soil Systems, Inc., Marietta, Georgia, 1983.

Wood, Peter H. *Black Majority, Negroes in Colonial South Carolina from 1670 through the Stono Rebellion*. New York: W. W. Norton, 1974.

Wood, Neal. *John Locke and Agrarian Capitalism*. Berkeley: University of California Press, 1984.

Zierden, Martha, Suzanne Linder, and Ronald Anthony. *Willtown: An Archaeological and Historical Perspective*. Archaeological Contributions 27. Charleston, SC: The Charleston Museum, 1999.

"This na true story of our history": South Carolina in Sierra Leone's historical memory

Nemata Blyden

> Sierra Leone and South Carolina have had strong ties since the era of the slave trade. Throughout the nineteenth and twentieth centuries that connection was maintained. This article explores the ties between the two regions, arguing that in recent years Sierra Leone's historical memory has focused on the Low Country region, as its citizens in Diaspora seek to connect themselves to aspects of American history.

In 1756 a 10-year-old girl was enslaved in Africa. Transported to South Carolina, she was sold by prominent slave trader Henry Laurens to Elias Ball, a South Carolina planter, who noted the purchase in his diary in June of that year.[1] Henry Laurens had strong business and personal ties with Richard Oswald, an Englishman and major partner in the London-based firm that operated the Bunce Island slave factory in Sierra Leone, West Africa. Bunce agents regularly sent ships with enslaved Africans and other goods to Charleston. Consequently, "the profitable slave trade connection between Oswald and Laurens – between Sierra Leone and South Carolina – was significant enough to affect the course of American history."[2] The little girl, named Priscilla, may well have been enslaved at Bunce. She was captured along the Guinea Coast of West Africa, in the area that is now Sierra Leone.[3] By the time she was taken, Europeans and Africans had been trading along this coast for more than 200 years, and there was a heavy concentration of women and men from the region that is today Guinea, Sierra Leone and Liberia in the Low Country region of the USA.[4]

This essay explores the links that began with the enslavement of Africans, produced African centered communities such as the Gullah in the USA, and continues as Sierra Leoneans seek to (re) establish their relationship with African-Americans, (re)connecting with the American side of their history. I examine the long-standing connection between South Carolina and Sierra Leone, exploring the many ties that have linked the two spaces for centuries, as well as the growing interest among Sierra Leoneans in claiming (reclaiming?) ties with the Low Country. While it was indeed the slave trade that first linked the two regions, the connection between Sierra Leone and South Carolina, in particular, continued in the centuries following the slave trade and its abolition. We now know of the very direct links between African-Americans in South Carolina and the Guinea coast. This relationship has often been explored in terms of the historical and cultural relationship with rice cultivation and slavery, given that the people in this region of Africa were known for their indigenous knowledge of agriculture and rice growing techniques. South Carolina planters desired Africans in the area that became known as the Rice Coast for these skills. We are now well aware of the consequences of importing such large numbers of Africans from this region both for Africa and for the development of African-American culture in the Low Country. The rice growing practices brought by Africans to South Carolina have been well documented by scholars, as have the cultural influences left by the large population of Africans involuntarily transported to the region.[5] The Gullah communities, in particular, have been studied in depth as scholars recognize their African antecedents in the rice growing areas of West Africa. Many of their belief systems, food ways, cultural retentions, technology, among other practices, can be traced back to West Africa. Less well known are later connections between this region of North America and the small country of Sierra Leone.

The relationship between African-Americans and Africa has typically been examined by looking at black Americans' desire to connect with their African heritage rather than the other way around. Indeed from the moment they left its shores African men and women longed to reconnect with their homeland. In the centuries following their enslavement, African-Americans pursued ties with Africa in a variety of ways. Early scholarship looking at contacts between Africa and its American descendants highlighted the influences enslaved Africans brought to the Americas. Later studies looked at the contributions black Americans made to the continent – including the settlement of Liberia, black missionary movement and Pan Africanism.[6] While much is known about Sierra Leone's historical connection to the USA, its early ties to that nation have not been recognized until recently. This recognition has come, in large part, because Sierra Leoneans are increasingly highlighting their ties to African-American history. The growing numbers of Sierra Leoneans currently living in the USA are keen to establish their connection to the USA, prompting greater interest in African-American influences in their country, and a longing to understand that past.[7] Sierra Leoneans on the continent have also drawn attention to those links, encouraging meaningful engagement with a certain slice of America's past. More and more Sierra Leoneans are claiming part of African-American history. But why this sudden interest in engaging with their American past? A look into the nation's history might help clarify.

"Back" to Africa

The beginnings of the small settlement known as Freetown, established in 1787, is itself intensely bound up with that of the Americas. A British humanitarian effort to settle free blacks from Britain and North America, Freetown's origins were integrally connected to the antislavery movement in Britain, as abolitionists searched for a place to settle the many African-Americans who cast their lot with them in the American War of Independence. In 1787 spearheaded by Granville Sharp, a small settlement was established on the peninsula of Sierra Leone.[8] The Province of Freedom, as the early community came to be known, was to be a shining example of humanitarianism and Christian civilization in West Africa. Early settlers included black loyalists who had fought in the American War of Independence. Evacuated from North America, many ended up in Britain where, along with other unfortunate blacks, they were labeled The Black Poor. In 1787 a small group sailed from England, becoming pioneers of the Freetown settlement. They were joined in 1792 by loyalist blacks transported to Nova Scotia in the wake of the war, who, dissatisfied with their circumstances in Canada petitioned to leave for Africa. Initially governed by the Sierra Leone Company, Sierra Leone became a British Crown colony in 1808.

Over the course of the nineteenth century, other blacks from the USA made their way to Sierra Leone. By the middle of the nineteenth century the descendants of the Black Poor and Nova Scotians, along with Jamaican Maroons and Liberated Africans gradually merged into a society with a culturally distinct population. Because the colony's genesis was closely associated with the antislavery movement in Britain it was attractive to diasporan blacks "returning" to the home of their ancestors. African-American emigration movements in the nineteenth century have been well documented.[9] Seeking freedom from oppression and equality, waves of African-Americans, beginning in the eighteenth century left the USA to build new lives in Africa, motivated by a host of reasons. African-Americans came to Sierra Leone as entrepreneurs, missionaries, teachers, and even as exiles.

The first "American" settlers in Sierra Leone, the Nova Scotians, quickly put to flight British humanitarians ideas regarding their place in their new homeland. These men and women had escaped the tyranny of American slaveholders, fought alongside white loyalists, and rejected marginalization in Canada. For those who chose to cast their lot with the British during the war of independence, "liberty, democracy, and Africa were the goals of this profound revolutionary force."[10] Though their claims to citizenship in the USA had been rejected, they nevertheless came as "Americans," with clear political ideals influenced by the revolutionary spirit of their former masters. The Nova Scotian reaction to attempts to circumscribe their position was born out of their experience in the USA. Fleeing the tyranny of post-revolutionary America they came loyal to what they thought were the egalitarian ideals of the British humanitarians who had established the settlement. They chose Britain over America because the rhetoric of democracy expressed in white America excluded them. In Sierra Leone, however, the two ideals of democracy and loyalist sentiment clashed, resulting in confrontations between African-Americans and their British benefactors. Believing in their own agency these black Americans were sure to conflict with authorities, contemptuous of the ideas they stood for.[11]

The Nova Scotians quickly became the bane of British administrators who soon discovered the former slaves' reluctance to abdicate the freedom they had fought so hard to gain.[12] They had fought in the American War of Independence for the very freedom they assumed they had found in Sierra Leone. Company officials found these sentiments abhorrent. In 1800 the Nova Scotians rebelled against the constituted authorities in response to perceived injustices in the colony. The rebellion was crushed, but the black loyalists continued to press for their rights. In 1808 a British governor in Sierra Leone, frustrated with this streak of independence, blamed their American experience for these ideas about liberty and equality:

> It is evidently nothing but the fear of the guns of a British man of war that keeps the Colonists in their allegiance & unless this treasonable spirit be completely checked in the rising generation the sooner the British Government evacuates the Colony the better, as to keep it would only be to nurse a race of traitors ready to imitate the example of their former lords and masters.[13]

Ironically, these settlers had sought to escape their "former lord and master."

There were several South Carolinians among the black loyalists who sailed from Nova Scotia to Sierra Leone. In fact, one scholar has argued that a large percentage of loyalists who ended up in Nova Scotia and Sierra Leone came from South Carolina and Virginia.[14] David George, John Kizell and Boston King all had experiences in the Low Country state before arriving in Sierra Leone. Evacuated to Nova Scotia at the end of the war, they eventually joined the group petitioning for settlement in the newly established West African colony. Born on a Virginia plantation around 1742, George was born to parents enslaved in Africa. He ran away to South Carolina, where he lived among the Creek and Natchez nations. Sold by a Natchez chief to a plantation in Silver Bluff, South Carolina, he converted to Christianity and was baptized by a Baptist minister. He became a preacher, and in 1775 founded one of the earliest black churches in the USA, the Silver Bluff Baptist church.[15] In 1778 George fled to British lines and gained his freedom. He would, in 1782, be among the black loyalists evacuated to Halifax, Nova Scotia. In Sierra Leone George ministered to a Baptist congregation in his own chapel until his death in 1810.[16] George realized a dream that eluded many African-Americans – he saw his parents' homeland. In an account of his life published in 1793, George remembers his feelings at seeing the shores of Africa for the first time: "There was a great joy to see the land the high mountain, at some distance from Freetown, where we now live, appeared like a cloud to us."[17] George brought the religious fervor he had adopted in South Carolina to his new home, influencing not only his fellow Americans, but the Africans he encountered as well.[18] Several other loyalist blacks arriving in Sierra Leone via Nova Scotia had South Carolina ties.

Boston King born on a Charleston plantation around 1760, fled to British troops in 1780, and was evacuated to Nova Scotia in 1783. Baptized in the Methodist church, like George he became a preacher.[19] King decided to emigrate to Sierra Leone despite his relatively comfortable circumstances in Canada because of "a desire that had long possessed my mind, of contributing to the best of my poor ability, in spreading the knowledge of Christianity in that country."[20] In Sierra Leone King became one of the earliest Methodist preachers, and sought to convert indigenous Africans. In 1794 he was sent as a missionary to Africans on the Bulom shore, and later became a teacher, no doubt fulfilling his dream of spreading Christian knowledge.[21] Others came with more practical objectives to improve their mother country.

When John Kizell sailed from Nova Scotia in 1792 he was returning home, not in the figurative sense the others did, but to the place from which he had been taken. Kidnaped as a teenager in Sierra Leone, Kizell was probably of Sherbro origin, born in the region to which he returned. Enslaved in 1773/1774 the teenager was brought to Charleston where he soon took flight to British lines. Like George and King he was evacuated to Canada, later sailing to Africa. In Sierra Leone he became an entrepreneur, shuttling between his home region and the newly established colony. One scholar has described him as a "proponent of African commerce."[22] Having once been enslaved Kizell pointed out the evils of the slave trade to local chiefs, conveying to Sherbro chiefs the evils of slave trading.[23] While negotiating with them on the part of the British Kizell

> took this opportunity of talking to the chiefs on the Slave Trade. I told them that the blood of their people cried against them, and that God heard it. They had killed the poor of the land; the people that should work the land; and had sold them to fill their bellies.[24]

He worked with colony officials, pushing for greater African economic independence.

Kizell was instrumental in the negotiations that resulted in Paul Cuffe, a New England businessman, bringing African-American settlers to Freetown in 1811.[25] Kizell was also part of the discussion with the American Colonization Society's (ACS) first colonists who made a stop in Sierra Leone before settling Liberia.[26] In 1820, the year Liberia was founded, Kizell wrote in support of the Society's bid to send free people of color to Africa. "You must strive to send my brethren home" he wrote to a representative of the ACS,

> let them come and sit down in our valleys, and on our hills, and near our rivers, and all the country will soon break forth into a song. The Sherbro country is full of meat, and fish, and bread, and oil, and honey. Send us people to eat them.

Having been back in his homeland for almost 30 years by then, he believed "God has sent me here and set me down to make a place for my brethren."[27] Like George and King he saw the benefits he could bring to Africa, and indeed was highly regarded by the colony's British administration for the work he did. In 1812 the local governor commended Kizell, observing "he is an intelligent man; has always presented an excellent character; and has the welfare of his native country sincerely at heart."[28]

While King, Kizell, and George would settle under British authority in Freetown Isaac Anderson, another Charlestonian, did not live his days out peacefully, dying in the cause of the freedom he had pursued while a slave in South Carolina. The African-born Anderson was enslaved in Charleston where he worked as a carpenter. Like the others he ran to British lines, making his way to Sierra Leone via Nova Scotia. However, his search for freedom was short lived. When the settlers arrived in Sierra Leone a string of broken promises frustrated men like Anderson who in 1793 wrote to the directors of the Sierra Leone Company that

> we expected to have had some more attention paid to our complaints, but the manner you have treated us, has been just the same as if were slaves, come to tell our masters, of the cruelties and severe behavior of an *Overseer.*[29]

In 1800 Nova Scotian settlers, dissatisfied with the limitations placed on them, hostile to taxation, and resentful of broken promises, rebelled against British authorities. Anderson was at the forefront of the rebellion against perceived injustices in the colony, and was eventually hanged for his role as a leader.[30] The freedom he had sought when he ran to British lines eluded him.

The South Carolinian black loyalists were led in their quest for freedom by a former slave from North Carolina, Thomas Peters. Peters' story, in many ways, mirrors that of the South Carolinians. African born, he was brought as a slave to the USA. On the eve of the American Revolution, Peters was enslaved on the plantation of one William Campbell.[31] Like David George and Boston King, he escaped to British lines, and was evacuated to Nova Scotia. There Peters led the petition to England, resulting in the Nova Scotian migration to Sierra Leone. African-Americans continued to settle in the colony throughout the nineteenth century, and black South Carolinians were among the many who sought to create new lives for themselves. In 1827 the Church Missionary Paper for the Use of Weekly and Monthly Contributors, reported the story of a former slave in Charleston. Nearly 70 years old, James Creighton bought a schooner and sailed to Sierra Leone. Creighton, enslaved in Africa as a boy of nine, was taken to South Carolina where he became a barber by trade. He saved the money he was paid from this trade and, according to the report, "resolved to revisit his native country, for the purpose of imparting the knowledge of Christianity to the people." Reverend John Raban, a missionary in Sierra Leone who recounted Creighton's story confirmed "that he was indeed in that colony and speaks of him as a very religious and upright man," who had "found hereby the knowledge of a Savior in a strange land, he returned to his native shores, in order to impart that knowledge to his own Nation." Not much else is known about Creighton, but for his contributions to the cause of Christianity in Sierra Leone the paper believed that "the name of James Creighton ought to be had in remembrance, and his example should stir us all up to greater zeal for the Salvation of the perishing World."[32]

Perhaps the most well known South Carolinian in Sierra Leone during the nineteenth century was Edward Jones. In background and life experience he was extremely different from the black loyalists King, George and Kizell, and from James Creighton, the former slave. Unlike the four men Jones was never enslaved. Born into a free black family, Edward was the son of Jehu Jones, an affluent hotelier in Charleston. Jehu was born to a slave woman, Margaret Matthews, who likely bore the children of her owner. Margaret owned property, which she probably passed on to her children. Jehu began his career as a tailor with a shop on Charleston's Broad Street, and went on to run a boarding house on the same street a few years later.[33] A member of the Brown Fellowship society, an elite self-help organization established by the mulatto population of Charleston, he would have been highly regarded in the free black community. By the time his son Edward set off for Amherst College in 1822, Jones was the proprietor of a hotel on Broad Street near St Michaels Episcopal Church. Catering exclusively to white clients, many prominent Americans were his guests while he owned it. Jehu Jones was said to socialize with whites seldom keeping "the company of even light-complexioned free blacks, and never of slaves," but his son would seek to be a champion for his race. Jehu's affluence allowed him to educate his children and Edward benefited from a higher education, becoming the first black graduate of a predominantly white institution when he graduated from Amherst in 1827.[34] He went on to study theology and was ordained a priest in the Episcopal Church.

By 1831 Edward Jones was in Sierra Leone where he assumed his first job as schoolmaster in the Liberated African village of Kent.[35] Settling into colony life he married the daughter of a German Missionary and a Nova Scotian woman.[36] An active educator, journalist, and missionary he worked tirelessly for the benefit of the colony's indigenous population. Jones became the first black principal of the Christian institution that would become Fourah Bay College, influencing many in the colony to pursue higher education.[37] However, like the Nova Scotians before him Jones ran afoul of British administrators who believed African-Americans were a bad influence on the African population. Jones, too, was charged with using his American ideals to cause trouble. In 1836 when the local governor accused another African-American, Daniel Coker, of being the primary instigator of a petition circulated in the colony, Jones was also implicated.

Coker, long resident in the colony was part of the first group of settlers sent out by the American Colonization Society that resulted in the settlement of Liberia. A co-founder with Richard Allen of the African Methodist Episcopal church,

Coker had fled oppressive conditions in the USA. Remaining in Sierra Leone he became an active member of the community. In 1847 the governor again accused Coker of stirring up trouble by allowing political meetings to be held at the hotel he owned. Governor Campbell labeled the participants treasonous, characterizing them as foreigners who fomented discontent in the colony. Coker, described as "an American by birth," was labeled the ringleader while Edward Jones, then chaplain in the colony, was cited for "his total disregard for all authority, indolent example, and the democratic doctrines, he was instilling."[38] The Charleston born Jones had not fled racism in the USA to tolerate it in Africa.

With long residence in the colony Jones became more active politically, and was embroiled in several controversial cases. The most significant involved the colony's Trinidadian Queens Advocate, Alexander Fitzjames, in his power struggle with the governor, Stephen Hill, in 1862. Supported by other diasporan blacks the case polarized the elite in the colony along racial lines. Hill with his European supporters stood against the Trinidadian, supported by men of color – the few black West Indians in the colony, Edward Jones, and the white Bishop of the Church Missionary Society. In his complaint to the Colonial Office Hill argued that race was at the center of the controversy, observing that all the men against him, with the exception of Jones, were of mixed race and West Indians. Jones he described as "an American, one degree removed from a negro."[39] In spite of his struggles with the colonial administration Jones continued to work tirelessly for the colony and its black population. His privileged background notwithstanding he did not distance himself from native Africans. Jones made Sierra Leone his home, becoming its first naturalized citizen in 1845. Edward Jones died in 1865.

"Back" to America

The ties between Sierra Leone and South Carolina persisted throughout the nineteenth, and into the twentieth century. When Sierra Leoneans traveled to the USA, they often visited the southern state. This was the case of Jacob Hazeley, frequently billed as the "African lecturer." Hazeley toured the USA at the end of the nineteenth century, giving lectures on Africa and its cultures. In the late 1870s he visited the nation's capital and Richmond, Virginia. One news report, heralding his arrival, claimed he had "traveled extensively in the interior of Africa in the gold regions of that country and visited the gold mines."[40] In 1883 the Cleveland Gazette reported Hazeley's talk at the Zion Baptist Church in Cleveland, Ohio, describing it as one that gave "exact descriptions of the country the races; tribes, &c. His description of Palm trees was one of his principle topics, telling its different uses and necessities, being the principle plant which the natives of Africa honor."[41] The following month in a lecture at Wilberforce College, Hazeley, was reported to have given his audience

> many new ideas relative to African manners, customs and productions. He showed that Africa is a vast continent abounding in enormous wealth, both mineral and vegetable; that the African is susceptible to as much culture as any race enjoys, and that it is only a question of time when Africa should be one of the grandest continents on the globe in every respect.[42]

This Sierra Leonean of Nova Scotian descent might have had ties to South Carolina. A century or so after his forbearers had been enslaved and "returned" to their homeland, he brought his version of Africa to American audiences. Hazeley also encouraged his African-American audiences to consider emigration to Africa, and in 1877, along with the African-American emigrationist Chief Alfred Sam "stirred up black South Carolinians for African emigration."[43] In 1878, due to their efforts, the ship *Azor* sailed from South Carolina to Liberia with over 200 emigrants. Hazeley was an early visitor from Sierra Leone. Over the next century other Sierra Leoneans visited the USA, sharing their experiences with Americans, and connecting, as Hazeley, did with African-Americans.

It is no coincidence that as Sierra Leoneans began to travel to the USA in the late nineteenth and into the twentieth century, they sought to (re)claim their links with black populations in Diaspora. One scholar has noted that while African-Americans were searching for ties to Africa,

> the diverse peoples of Africa were also developing a growing sense of common identity in their efforts to overcome disabilities and were beginning to sense that they might gain from connections to their long-lost brothers and sisters in the Diaspora.[44]

Even today as citizens of Sierra Leone settle in the USA they have grown to appreciate their country's historical significance, appropriating parts of America's history to which they are connected. In the last twenty or so years Sierra Leoneans have been keen to (re)claim their links to the USA, and establish solid connections between the two countries. The political and economic circumstances in Sierra Leone have led to the large-scale migration of its citizens to the USA. Some of these new immigrants have articulated an increased desire to claim a relationship with America and its history. Furthermore, the growing African-American fascination with discovering their African roots (now made possible by DNA tests and other methods) has prompted African nations to reach out to their sons and daughters in the Diaspora to acknowledge them and garner their interest in aiding Africa's development.[45] A new type of exchange is taking place as solid ties are established between Sierra Leone and the USA.

The black loyalists have loomed large in these recent attempts by Sierra Leoneans to reestablish ties with African-Americans and their history. While David George, Boston King, and John Kizell are known among certain segments of Sierra Leone's population, it is the North Carolinian, Thomas Peters, who has the honor of representing the black loyalists' important historical role in the USA and their contribution to Sierra Leone. It is unclear why Peters, among the many black loyalists, is the one Sierra Leoneans have chosen to honor, but it is well known that he led the movement that would eventually result in settlement in Sierra Leone, acting as spokesman for the dissatisfied black loyalists. In December of 2011 a statue of Thomas Peters was unveiled in Freetown.[46] Sierra Leoneans all over the world, and in the country, wrote tributes to his role in the country's history. One laudatory piece captures his importance, and could also describe Boston King, David George, John Kizell, and even Edward Jones: "Thomas Peters was totally committed to freedom, and fought for it until the very last day of his life. More than anyone else, he exemplifies the spirit of hope and determination that gave birth to the city of Freetown."[47]

In 1988, the (re) discovery of historical links between the Gullah people in the USA and Sierra Leone, prompted the country's president Joseph Momoh to visit South Carolina.[48] Newspapers on both sides of the Atlantic reported the historic occasion, recording the significance of the visit. Momoh also commented on the importance of the encounter, stressing the kinship between the two groups, by observing that "we are one people, regardless of the distance that separates us," and expressing hope that the "reunion will grow stronger and stronger as the years go by." Momoh's visit was followed in 1989 by the trip of a Gullah delegation to Sierra Leone in what was described as a Homecoming.[49] In 1997 another "return" took place as Mary Moran, a black American woman who had preserved a Mende song, taught to her by her mother, Amelia Dawley, traveled to Sierra Leone. Moran visited Senehun Ngola, a Mende village, where she was "reunited" with Bendu Jabati, a woman who recognized the song as a funeral dirge. The American ethnologist Lorenzo Turner had recorded the song in the 1930s, as he sought to establish African-American roots in Africa.[50]

Finally, in 2005 in what was billed "Priscilla's Homecoming," the young girl enslaved by Elias Ball metaphorically returned home when Thomalind Polite, a young African-American woman from Charleston, South Carolina was discovered to be a descendant of the 10-year-old girl captured in the eighteenth. Like the other Americans, Polite visited Bunce Island. News outlets reported the visit, citing the strong ties between Sierra Leone and Charleston. One article reported a Sierra Leonean diplomats view:

> Many Sierra Leoneans believed she was bringing back Priscilla's spirit and establishing a new bond between Africans and African-Americans, says Sierra Leone's Ambassador at the United Nations in New York, Joe Robert Pemagbi "It's like Priscilla herself going back", he said. "It brings back to memory the sad days of slavery, and Priscilla symbolises some kind of spiritual bridge between Sierra Leone and the African-American group."[51]

Each of these visits to Sierra Leone was accompanied by a hearty welcome of the African-Americans, as they were proclaimed returned brothers and sisters.

In the years since the discovery of Gullah ties to Sierra Leone, and Momoh's visit, there has been increased interaction between Sierra Leoneans in the USA and African-Americans of Gullah heritage. In 2006 Sierra Leoneans in the USA formed the Sierra Leone Gullah Heritage, with the goal of strengthening established ties, and promoting "an understanding of the Sierra Leone Gullah Connection and to help preserve the culture on both sides." Furthermore, it declared,

> Sierra Leone has a better story than any other African country as it relates to connecting to America. Only Sierra Leone can prove with historical and empirical evidence that our people were brought to the shores of Georgia and South Carolina in the thousands. So Sierra Leone and her people should take the lead (or at least get their rightful market share amidst healthy competition) in efforts to re-connect Africa-America to Africa.[52]

In Sierra Leone a local newspaper pointed out that

> the cultural and historic links between Gullahs in the United States and Sierra Leoneans are by now common knowledge to most, if not all Sierra Leoneans. At various times interest and excitement has reached such fever pitch that even presidents were moved to action.[53]

The newspaper, commenting upon "Priscilla's Homecoming," observed that some Sierra Leoneans have found it necessary to take action into actually implementing solid ties with some of the Gullahs, on a personal and lasting basis. In the last 20 years we've had three such home comings that made national and international news; each with its own little twist in details, but all with people on both sides of the Atlantic anxious to meet and greet each other and left with wanting to know more of one another.[54]

This is certainly true in Sierra Leone as ties between the two places are also stressed. In 1994 Sierra Leoneans on the continent formed the Sierra Leone Gullah Kinship Association. The group seeks to bring awareness of the connection between Sierra Leone and the USA. The organization's founder and president, Chief Komrabai B. H. Dumbuya, noted that the Kinship Association was founded to "promote the family and historical link between Sierra Leone and the USA of America." With over 200 groups all over the country, its members give talks at schools, creating educational programs that teach students about the history. They raise money for the preservation of Bunce Island because as one member stated, it serves as the "pivot between Sierra Leone and America." Indeed Bunce Island has become representative of the relationship between Sierra Leone and the USA. The work of archeologists, historians and public history proponents, and Sierra Leone's government, has brought to light Bunce's history, making the island better known for its role as a source of enslaved African labor that ended up in the USA.[55] Scholars have recognized the historic ties between the two regions, and we know of the strong links between slave traders, operating from Bunce, and traders and planters in the Low Country region of the USA.

A recent documentary, *The African American Experience*, highlights the story of slavery and the slave trade in Sierra Leone.[56] Early in the first episode Bunce Island's role in the slave trade is addressed, as the roughly 300,000 Africans transported from Sierra Leone to the Americas are enumerated. Documentaries capturing the history of the slave trade have often focused on Cape Coast and Elmina in Ghana, or Goree Island in Senegal.[57] These coastal forts in West Africa have long been attractive to Africans in Diaspora on roots pilgrimages.[58] Sierra Leone's history has not, until recently, been highlighted in representations of the slave trade. The documentary's choice of Sierra Leone, and its role in the slave trade, is a testament to the work and public relations campaign, if you will, of many individuals who, in the last two decades, have succeeded in showing Bunce's importance to the African diaspora. While scholars have been aware of these developments, the film introduced a wider audience to this history. It also profiled Priscilla's American descendants, showing the connection between Bunce and African-Americans.[59]

In Sierra Leone Bunce stands as a symbol of that relationship. The many African-American homecomings have always included a visit to the ruins of the old slave fort. A 2011 video uploaded on YouTube titled *History of Slavery in the United States, South Carolina, Sierra Leone Kinship Campaign* lays out the efforts of the Sierra Leone Gullah Kinship Association to

use family and historical ties with the United States of America to compliment [sic] Sierra Leone's Government efforts for assistance as well as initiate the end of poverty and ignorance and to heal the wounds of slavery in our countries on both sides of the Atlantic.[60]

As the video outlines the various programs conducted by the group it is clear that a significant aim of the association is to further and maintain ties with the USA, and garner aid from the larger country on the basis of these links. Once again Bunce is central to the endeavor.

The Bra Rabbit players, a local theater group, open the video with a song chronicling the importance of Bunce Island, and the ties between Sierra Leone and the USA. They tell the history of Bunce as a "specialized market for rice planters in Georgia and South Carolina," of Thomas Knight, the islands chief agent in the eighteenth century, of slave traders like William Cleveland, the British trader who married a Sherbro woman. The constant refrain of the song stresses the veracity of the historical facts: "This na true story of our history/Come na Bunce Island/We want the world to know. This na true story of our history/All Jama for know/We want the world to know. This na evidence of our story."[61] Increasingly elements of American history have become part of Sierra Leone's as well. Sierra Leoneans, regardless of their ethnicity, have embraced the country's historical ties to the USA. Immigrants in the USA have pursued ways to create links with African-Americans. As they begin to recognize the difficulties of being of African ancestry in a country structured along racial lines Sierra Leoneans have gained an understanding of African-American history, and some have made claims on it. The Sierra Leonean government has supported these efforts and been integrally involved in attempts to resuscitate ties between Sierra Leone and the USA. South Carolina, in particular, because of its strong ties to Sierra Leone, has been a site of this reconnection.

For the African-Americans who left South Carolina to settle in Sierra Leone, this renewed interest might seem strange. Having left the USA in search of freedom and equality would it seem odd that their descendants now flock to the USA in droves, seeking the same? Would they find it ironic that the very same plantations on which they labored now draw their sons and daughters from Sierra Leone as they discover elements of their past, or would they be disappointed that the society they helped build now sends its children back to the land from which they escaped? We do not know what George, Kizell, Anderson or King would have made of this rekindled relationship between their ancestors in Sierra Leone and South Carolina. They would surely celebrate the long-standing connection between the two places.

Acknowledgements

Thanks to Ken Kelly for organizing the conference, allowing us to ruminate on this subject, as well as my mother Amelia Blyden, my husband Christopher Bickersteth, and three children, Pearl, Ayinde, and Nalo.

Disclosure statement

No potential conflict of interest was reported by the author.

Notes

1. Ball, *Slaves in the Family.*
2. Opala, "The Gullah."
3. Opala, "Priscilla's Homecoming"; Sarata, "Sierra Leone."
4. "In Motion."
5. Littlefield, *Rice and Slaves*; Fields-Black, *Deep Roots*; Gomez, *Exchanging our Country Marks.*
6. Miller, *Search for a Black Nationality*, Chap. 1. See also Shepperson, "Notes."
7. Capps et al., *Diverse Streams.* See also Capps et al., *New Streams.* These are, of course, documented immigrant numbers.
8. Fyfe, *History*; Peterson, *Province of Freedom*; Byrd, *Captives and Voyagers*; Gerzina, *Black London.*
9. Miller, *Search for a Black Nationality*; Barnes, *Journey of Hope.*
10. Gilbert, *Black Patriots*, 224.
11. Peterson, *Province of Freedom*; Wilson, *The Loyal Blacks.*
12. Pulis, *Moving On*; Pybus, *Epic Journeys*; Schama, *Rough Crossings*; Fyfe, "'*our Children*'."
13. T. Perronet Thompson to Castlereagh, November 2, 1808, Despatch 4, re: State of the Colony and its Inhabitants, CO 267/24, Public Record Office, Kew Gardens, London.
14. Alan Gilbert argues that about 23% of blacks evacuated to Nova Scotia were Charlestonians. Gilbert, *Black Patriots*, 223.
15. Brooks, "Silver Bluff Church."
16. Fyfe, *History*, 69, 101. See also Greene, "David George."
17. George and Rippon, "*An Account*," 473–484.
18. Fyfe, *History*, 55, 56.
19. Smith, "Boston King."
20. King, "Memoirs."
21. Fyfe, *History*, 55.
22. Thomas, *Paul Cuffe*, 69.
23. Ibid., 80.
24. *Extracts*, 120.
25. See Harris, *Paul Cuffe* and Thomas, *Paul Cuffe.*
26. For a comprehensive account of Kizell's life, see Lowther, *Odyssey.*
27. Kizell to Bushrod Washington, March 22, 1820, Letter 1 – No Title. The African Intelligencer, July 18200. Quoted in Lowther, *Odyssey*, 218.
28. *Extracts From the Correspondence of Mr.*, 145.
29. Anderson in Falconbridge, *Narrative*, 265.
30. Pybus, "Jubilee."
31. Clifford, *From Slavery to Freetown*, 26; Nash, "Thomas Peters."
32. "Missionary Zeal in a Negro" in Church Missionary Society, *Missionary Papers.* See also Fyfe, *History*, 133.
33. See Nicol, *Edward Jones.*
34. Powers, *Black Charlestonians*, 57. See also "Amherst College Class of 1826."
35. Hawkins, in *Black Apostles*, 244. Why Jones chose to look to Africa at this time is unclear but it has been claimed that because of laws in Carolina which prevented blacks who left the state from returning, Jones could not go back home and therefore may have chosen Africa as an alternative. Jones is believed to have gone to Liberia first and then on to Sierra Leone. This is logical given the interest of the Mission School in Liberia. Hugh Hawkins suggests that the Church Missionary Society, already established in Sierra Leone, may have enticed Jones from the American missionary establishment. Liberia was still a young colony having been in existence for only ten years or so and Jones may have believed Sierra Leone to be a more comfortable situation. Some African Americans were dissatisfied with the Liberian colony once they got there.

36. Fyfe, *History*, 199.
37. Blyden, "Edward Jones," 159–182; Hawkins, "Edward Jones"; Hawkins, "Edward Jones, Marginal Man"; Contee, "Reverend Edward Jones;" Wade, *Black Men of Amherst*; Nicol, "Jones Family"; Crowder, "Amherst to Fourah Bay"; Fyfe, *History*, 387. See also Nicol, *Edward Jones*.
38. Campbell to Secretary of State, September 5, 1836, dispatch 147, CO 267/133, Public Record Office, Kew Gardens, London.
39. Governor Stephen Hill's dispatch #57, Vol. 3, March 20, 1862, CO 267/276 1862, Public Record Office, Kew Gardens, London.
40. *Peoples Advocate*, August 5, 1876, 2. See also *Peoples Advocate*, August 12, 1876, 2 and *Peoples Advocate*, September 9, 1876, 4.
41. *Cleveland Gazette*, October 20, 1883.
42. *Cleveland Gazette*, November 3, 1883.
43. Barnes, *Journey of Hope*, 46.
44. Northrup, *Crosscurrents*, 2.
45. *Visit Sierra Leone – Blog*, "DNA Tests Bringing African." Perhaps the most striking example of this is the actor Isaiah Washington, who has traced his ancestry back to Sierra Leone. Washington was made a chief in Sierra Leone, and he subsequently established the Gondobay Manga Foundation to aid in the development of communities in Sierra Leone. Recently Washington published a memoir *A Man from Another Land*.
46. Garber, "Tribute."
47. Sesay, "Thomas Peters (ca. 1738–1792)."
48. Brooke, "Africans See Their Culture."
49. This event was chronicled in the documentary *Family Across the Sea* produced by California Newsreel. See also *The Language You Cry In*, which documents the connection between an African American family and a Mende woman.
50. "Amelia's Song."
51. Goffe, "Priscilla"; Sarata, "Sierra Leone."
52. Seibure, "Sierra Leone."
53. Ibid.
54. Ibid.
55. Opala, "The Gullah."
56. Gates, "Episode 1, The Black Atlantic."
57. In Won*ders of the African World* Gates highlighted the role of Elmina, and Goree Island was a sponsor of the most recent series.
58. Benton et al., "Find their level," 477–511.
59. My attention to Gates' choice of Bunce is to illustrate the point that his use of this particular island as a starting point meant that his viewers would be introduced to a "new" slave fort, and to another story of the slave trade. Emphasis on Bunce allowed the documentary to connect a specific African American story linking Sierra Leone to South Carolina.
60. *History of Slavery in the United States*.
61. Translation: "This is the true story of our history. Come to Bunce Island. We want the world to know. This is evidence of our story." *History of Slavery in the United States*.

References

Ball, Edward. *Slaves in the Family*. New York: Ballantine, 2001.
Barnes, Kenneth C. *Journey of Hope: The Back-to-Africa Movement in Arkansas in the Late 1800s*. Chapel Hill: University of North Carolina Press, 2004.
Benton, Adia, and Kwame Zulu Shabazz. "Find their Level: African American Roots Tourism in Sierra Leone and Ghana." *Cahiers d'Etudes Africaines* 49, nos. 1–2 (2009): 477–511.
Blyden, Nemata. "Edward Jones: An African American in Sierra Leone." In *Moving On: Black Loyalists in the Afro-Atlantic World*, edited by John W. Pulis, 159–182. New York: Garland, 1999.
Blyden, Nemata. *West Indians in West Africa, 1808–1880: The African Diaspora in Reverse*. Rochester: University of Rochester, 2000.

Brooke, James. "Africans See Their Culture Live in U.S. South", *New York Times*, October 25, 1987.
Brooks, Walter H. "The Silver Bluff Church. A History of Negro Baptist Churches in America." Washington, DC: Press of R. L. Pendleton, 1910. http://docsouth.unc.edu/church/brooks/summary.html.
Byrd, Alexander X. *Captives and Voyagers: Black Migrants across the Eighteenth-Century British Atlantic World*. Baton Rouge: Louisiana State University Press, 2008.
Capps, Randy, Kristen McCabe, and Michael Fix. *Diverse Streams: African Migration to the United States*. Washington, DC: Migration Policy Institute, 2012.
Capps, Randy, Kristen McCabe, and Michael Fix. *New Streams: Black African Migration to the United States*. Washington, DC: Migration Policy Institute, 2011.
Carrier, Tim. *Family Across the Sea*. California Newsreel: South Carolina ETV, 1991.
Church Missionary Society. *Missionary Papers*, No. XLVII (Michaelmas, 1827). books.google.com/books?id=uss7AQAAMAAJ.
Clifford, Mary Louise. *From Slavery to Freetown: Black Loyalists after the American Revolution*. Jefferson, NC: McFarland, 1999.
Contee, Clarence G. "The Reverend Edward Jones, Missionary-Educator to Sierra Leone and 'First' Afro-American College Graduate 1808? to 1865." *Negro History Bulletin* 38, no. 1 (1975): 356–357.
Crowder, Michael. *"From Amherst to Fourah Bay: Principal Edward Jones."* In *Two Hundred Years of Inter-Cultural Evolution and Perspectives for the Future: Bicentenary of Sierra Leone Symposium*. Free Town: Fourah Bay College, University of Sierra Leone, 1987.
Edward Jones. "Amherst College Class of 1826" from the *Amherst College Biographical Record, Centennial Edition (1821-1921)*. Amherst College, 1927. Also can be found at http://www3.amherst.edu/~rjyanco94/genealogy/acbiorecord/1826.html#jones-e.
Extracts from the Correspondence of Mr. John Kizell with Governor Columbine Respecting his Negotiations with the Chiefs in the River Sherbro, and Giving an Account of that River, in Report of the Committee of the African Institution, Volume 6, London, England. Google Books. books.google.com/books?id=IcAEAAAAMAAJ.
Falconbridge, Anna Maria. *Narrative of Two Voyages to the River Sierra Leone during the Years 1791-1792-1793*, edited by Christopher Fyfe. Liverpool: Liverpool University Press, 2000.
Fields-Black, Edda. *Deep Roots: Rice Farmers in West Africa and the African Diaspora*. Bloomington: Indiana University Press, 2009.
Fyfe, Christopher. *A History of Sierra Leone*. Brookfield, VT: Ashgate, 1993.
Fyfe, Christopher. *'Our Children Free and Happy': Letters from Black Settlers in Africa in the 1790's*. Edinburgh: Edinburgh University Press, 1991.
Garber, Melbourne. "A Tribute to Thomas Peters 'Black Moses' and Founding Father of Freetown." London: Krio Descendants Union. Accessed January 19, 2013. http://www.kdulondon.org.uk/a-tribute-to-thomas-peters/.
Gates, Henry Louis. "Episode 1, The Black Atlantic." In The African Americans: Many Rivers to Cross, a film by Kunhardt McGee Productions, THIRTEEN Productions LLC, Inkwell Films, in association with Ark Media, 2014.
George, David, and John Rippon. "An Account of the Life of Mr. David George, from Sierra Leone in Africa; Given by Himself in a Conversation with Brother Rippon of London, and Brother Pearce of Birmingham." *Baptist Annual Register* 1 (1790–1793): 473–484.
Gerzina, Gretchen. *Black London: Life before Emancipation*. New Brunswick, NJ: Rutgers University, 1995.
Gilbert, Alan. *Black Patriots and Loyalists: Fighting for Emancipation in the War for Independence*. Chicago: University of Chicago, 2012.
Goffe, Leslie. "Priscilla: The Story of an African slave." Accessed March 15, 2014. http://news.bbc.co.uk/2/hi/africa/4460964.stm.
Gomez, Michael Angelo. *Exchanging our Country Marks: The Transformation of African Identities in the Colonial and Antebellum South*. Chapel Hill: University of North Carolina Press, 1998.
Greene, Gael. "David George." BlackPast.org: Remembered and Reclaimed: An Online Reference Guide to African American History. Accessed January 2, 2014. http://www.blackpast.org/gah/george-david-1742-1810#sthash.IuAbPlww.dpuf.

Harris, Neck L. Trust website. "Amelia's Song: A Song Led Them Home." Accessed March 2, 2014. http://www.harrisnecklandtrust1.xbuild.com/#/amelias-song/4529751671.
Harris, Sheldon H. *Paul Cuffe: Black America and the African Return*. New York: Simon and Schuster, 1972.
Hawkins, Hugh. "Edward Jones: First American Negro College Graduate?" *School and Society*, 89 (1961): 375–378.
Hawkins, Hugh. "Edward Jones, Marginal Man." In *Black Apostles at Home and Abroad: Afro-Americans and the Christian Mission from the Revolution to Reconstruction*, edited by David W. Willis and Richard Newman, 243–253. Boston: G. K. Hall, 1982.
"*History of Slavery in the United States, South Carolina, Sierra Leone Kinship Campaign*." Part 1. Accessed March 15, 2014. http://www.youtube.com/watch?v=BrO6by8ZOp8.
King, Boston. "Memoirs of the Life of Boston King, A Black Preacher. Written by Himself, during his Residence at Kingswood School." *The Methodist Magazine*, March–June 1798. http://antislavery.eserver.org/narratives/boston_king/.
Littlefield, Daniel C. *Rice and Slaves: Ethnicity and the Slave Trade in Colonial South Carolina*. Baton Rouge: Louisiana State University Press, 1981.
Lowther, Kevin. *The African American Odyssey of John Kizell: A South Carolina Slave Returns to Fight the Slave Trade in his African Homeland*. Columbia: University of South Carolina Press, 2011.
Miller, Floyd John. *The Search for a Black Nationality: Black Emigration and Colonization, 1787-1863*. Urbana: University of Illinois, 1975.
Nash, Gary B. "Thomas Peters: Millwright and Deliverer." Accessed January 12, 2014. http://revolution.h-net.msu.edu/essays/nash.html.
"News from Sierra Leone Gullah Heritage Association." *The Sierra Leone Network,* May 30, 2006. http://groups.yahoo.com/group/SierraLeoneNetwork/message/945?threaded=1&var=1&p=1.
Nicol, Davidson. "The Jones Family of Charleston, London and Africa." In *Sierra Leone Studies at Birmingham*, edited by Adam Jones, Peter K. Mitchell, and Margaret Peil, 89–90. Birmingham: University of Birmingham, 1990.
Nicol, Davidson. The Life and Times of Edward Jones, unpublished manuscript 1994.
Northrup, David. *Crosscurrents in the Black Atlantic, 1770-1965: A Brief History with Documents.* New York: St Martins, 2008.
Opala, Joseph A. "The Gullah: Rice, Slavery and the Sierra Leone-America connection." Accessed February 23, 2014. http://www.yale.edu/glc/gullah/index.htm.
Opala, Joseph A. "Priscilla's Homecoming." Accessed March 12, 2014. http://www.yale.edu/glc/priscilla/opala.htm.
Peterson, John. *Province of Freedom; A History of Sierra Leone, 1787-1870*. Evanston: Northwestern University Press, 1969.
Powers, Bernard E. Jr. *Black Charlestonians: A Social History, 1822-1885*. Fayetteville: University of Arkansas Press, 1994.
Pulis, John W. *Moving On: Black Loyalists in the Afro-Atlantic World*. Vol. 4 of Crosscurrents in African American History. New York: Garland, 1999.
Pybus, Cassandra. "'The Day of Jubilee is Come': Isaac Anderson and Rebellion in Sierra Leone." Paper presented in the Harriet Tubman Seminar, York University, 21 March 2006.
Pybus, Cassandra. *Epic Journeys of Freedom: Runaway Slaves of the American Revolution and their Global Quest for Liberty.* Boston: Beacon, 2006.
Sarata, Phil. "Sierra Leone: A World Away: Historian Connects African Nation to Gullah Community through a Slave Girl Named Priscilla." Concord Times (Freetown), 20 November 2008. http://allafrica.com/stories/200811200963.html.
Schama, Simon. *Rough Crossings: Britain, the Slaves, and the American Revolution*. New York: Ecco, 2006.
Schomburg Center for Research in Black Culture. "In Motion: The African American Migration Experience." Accessed January 12, 2014. http://www.inmotionaame.org/migrations.
Seibure, Ibrahim. "Sierra Leone: Sierra Leone-Gullah Heritage Formed in US." Concord Times, 20 April 2006. http://allafrica.com/stories/200604200440.html.

SEM Contributor. "Martin Luther King Traces DNA to Sierra Leone." 30 September 2010. Sierra Express Media. http://www.sierraexpressmedia.com/archives/14317.

Sesay, Bhai-Dhawa. "Thomas Peters (ca. 1738-1792) True Founder of Freetown." Accessed February 12, 2014. http://sierraleonelive.com/sierra-leonean-heroes/thomas-peters-ca-1738-1792-true-founder-of-freetown/.

Shepperson, George. "Notes on Negro American Influences on the Emergence of African Nationalism." *The Journal of African History* 1, no. 2 (1960): 299–312.

Smith, Adam Christian. "Boston King." BlackPast.org: Remembered and Reclaimed: An Online Reference Guide to African American History. Accessed March 2, 2014. http://www.blackpast.org/gah/boston-king-c-1760-1802.

Thomas, Lamont D. *Paul Cuffe: Black Entrepreneur and Pan–Africanist*. Urbana: University of Illinois Press, 1988.

Toepke, Alvaro, and Angel Serrano. *The Language You Cry In*. Spain/Sierra Leone: California Newsreel, 1998.

Visit Sierra Leone – Blog. "DNA Tests Bringing African Americans to Sierra Leone." Tuesday, 29 December 2009. http://blogs.visitsierraleone.org/2009/12/dna-tests-bringing-african-americans-to.html.

Wade, Harold, Jr. *Black Men of Amherst*. Amherst, MA: Amherst College Press, 1976.

Washington, Isaiah, written with Lavaille Lavette. *A Man From Another Land: How Finding My Roots Changed My Life*. New York: Center Street/Hachette Book Group, 2011.

Williams, Walter L. *Black Americans and the Evangelization of Africa, 1877-1900*. Madison, WI: University of Wisconsin Press, 1982.

Wilson, Ellen Gibson. *The Loyal Blacks*. New York: Capricorn, 1976.

Risky business: rice and inter-colonial dependencies in the Indian and Atlantic Oceans

Kathleen D. Morrison and Mark W. Hauser

> In this paper we are concerned with some issues of inter-colonial dependency, especially in food and with a focus on rice that both directly linked the Atlantic and Indian Ocean worlds and that highlight some structural issues of colonialism, globalization, and food security more generally. This paper examines rice as a staple commodity, one that both reflected and generated inter-colonial dependencies in both ocean worlds, and how that dependency was ultimately fraught. Because the rice trade did not operate in isolation, we also of necessity include some discussion of important non-food crops such as cotton and jute. In the Caribbean, to greater or lesser extents, the colonial plantation economies relied on imported rice and other foodstuffs, needs supplied by other "knots" in the web, especially in the Carolina low country. Other British colonial possessions, too, were developed as "rice bowls" critical to the sustenance of colonized peoples and the support of commercial crops. One of these newer service colonies was British Burma, the formerly sparsely settled delta of the Irrawaddy River. No matter which ocean we center our focus on, and indeed across the "recentered" empire at large, in the Early Modern period rice was a risky business. By making this point we hope to frame a larger conversation about inter-colonial dependencies and the scales at which it is best realized.

Many oceans: the Atlantic world in the world

In our consideration of both the Atlantic and Indian Ocean worlds and their connections, we follow the example of Thomas Metcalf, who argues for "recentering empire;" not only transcending the limitations of colony-specific archives but, more critically, attending to inter-imperial linkages.[1] Between 1770 and 1830, the costs of shipping between Europe and Asia decreased by half, making it more competitive with the faster and less expensive Atlantic trade.[2] Over the course of the nineteenth and early twentieth centuries, new inter-colonial dependencies were created. Metcalf invokes the metaphor of a web to describe British inter-imperial connections in the nineteenth and early twentieth centuries; rather than colonies linked to metropoles, each "dangling separately at the end of its own string," he envisions a vast web of connections complete with "knots" or sub-imperial centers.[3] A more watery evocation of the connections that animated relations of power and production across the colonial world, connections very often crossing bodies of water, can also be envisioned. Just as a rock thrown in a pond creates ripples, so too are inter-colonial relationships linked and dependent. Here, however, we must imagine ripples emerging in an entirely different pond. These can be, in O'Gráda's evocative phrase, "ripples that drown," events or transformations of seemingly modest scale that can, nonetheless, cascade, leading to famine, death, hunger, or other problems.[4]

The Atlantic world is generally conceived as a constellation of people, polities, commercial networks, and intersecting interests whose scope is defined by the ocean rim and whose history is framed around the rise, apogee, and decline of the Atlantic trade in Africans. While the Atlantic world continues to be an important analytical anchor, there is no reason to limit our analytical gaze to the half of the globe that encompasses the Eastern Americas, Western Africa, and Europe. Recent re-appraisals of the Atlantic world have called for a shifting of analytical scale – from oceans to continents and from continents to hemisphere. According to Greene, the great potential of hemispheric approaches is comparative study.[5] In short, there is a need to place the Atlantic world in the world to draw out both comparative and interconnected histories. Following this trend, we provide an alternate definition of the Atlantic world as a densely packed set of food networks in which environmental, political, and social changes made (and still make) people's lives more precarious. Between 1700 and 1900 this very precarity became an effective form of colonial governance.[6]

A focus on commodities, such as tobacco, sugar, cotton, and indigo, has been critical in identifying the constellations of people and commercial networks that made the Atlantic world. Building on the pioneering work of Mintz, an entire genre of work has emerged which emphasizes regional and trans-regional connections as exemplified by the movements of fish, salt, chilies, chocolate, and many others.[7] While the disparate origins of such goods, often plants, animals, or disease organisms, tend to be clearly noted, generally in terms of the dominant model of the "Columbian exchange," there remain some geographical boundaries that are less often crossed, at least by scholars. One of these is that between the Atlantic and Indian Ocean worlds. In addition to more direct linkages, we point here to some parallels across the two ocean systems in the formation of inter-colonial dependency in food, dependencies constituted under conditions of structural inequality that led to heightened risk and vulnerability. Under the right (or wrong) conditions, these relationships could – and did – lead to disaster.

This article examines rice as a staple commodity, one that both reflected and generated inter-colonial dependencies in both ocean worlds, and how that dependency was ultimately fraught. Because the rice trade did not operate in isolation, we also of necessity include some discussion of important non-food crops such as cotton and jute. In the Caribbean, to greater or lesser extents, colonial plantation economies relied on imported rice and other foodstuffs, needs supplied by other "knots" in the web, especially in the Carolina low country. Barbados was one colony which relied almost exclusively on imported foodstuffs.[8] This "black rice" provided a critical prop for plantation economies in these places, making their production of sugar, coffee, and indigo by unfree labor possible.[9] Commercial crops and food crops were thus both integrated into structures of colonial power and governance, disciplining producer, and consumer alike across colonial waterscapes.

Other British colonial possessions, too, were developed as "rice bowls" critical to the sustenance of colonized peoples and the support of commercial crops. One of these newer service colonies was British Burma, the formerly sparsely settled delta of the Irrawaddy River. In the space of around 40 years, lower Burma was transformed into an intensively settled and farmed locus of wet rice agriculture. Indeed, by the early twentieth century, Burma was one of the largest exporters of rice to Europe (via London) and to British India. Southeast Asian rice had become "vital to global food security."[10] A process begun under the East India Company aegis and accelerated after 1858 with the transfer of India to direct crown rule, the demographic, political, and environmental transformation of Burma provided one "ripple" that, in 1943, threatened to drown Bengal.

No matter which ocean we center our focus on, and indeed across the "recentered" empire at large, in the Early Modern period rice was a risky business. By making this point we hope to frame a larger conversation about inter-colonial dependencies and the scales at which it is best realized. An understanding of the inter-colonial dependencies developed in one ocean – in the case of this special issue, the Atlantic Ocean – is best thought about comparatively in terms of shared colonial histories, histories whose economic arrangements and political constellations were somewhat different. Rice becomes an important lens through which to make this proposition and through the lens of rice we synthesize a body of environmental and colonial histories.

Rice in the Atlantic world: black, brown, and white

This special issue is in large part dedicated to the question of rice – its blackness, brownness, or whiteness (our paper being a singular exception). While the goal of this article is to extend the scope of analysis, there are very important themes that have emerged from the debates surrounding "black," "brown," and "white" rice. The "black rice" thesis argues that skilled rice farmers from Upper Guinea made it possible for planters to expand the cultivation of rice on plantations throughout the Georgia and Carolina low country. This scholarly project has focused on the intellectual and not just labor contributions of captive Africans in the new world. Carney is perhaps the most explicit in centering Africa and the material contributions of Africans in this new world endeavor, locating rice's cultivation in Africa, the Carolinas, Brazil, St. Domingue (Haiti), Suriname, and Jamaica.[11] Eltis, Morgan and Richards have been, perhaps, the most vocal critics of the "black rice" thesis, arguing that rice plantations could have operated in the absence of intellectual contributions of African slaves.[12] This argument is based on two observations; first that the necessary captives cited by Carney, Littlefield and Wood, were not coming from the Upper Guinea Coast, but rather from many parts of the African Atlantic and hinterland with little knowledge of rice production.[13] Second, they observe that the Upper Guinea Coast "was never uniformly committed to rice production."[14] Still others have called for a more nuanced reading, arguing for a "brown rice" hypothesis – that is, an understanding that rice only gradually entered into the eighteenth century commodity market and that its cultivation was due to many intellectual innovations, some better recorded than others.[15] Ultimately the historical development of rice cultivation in the Atlantic world has a "genome" that was multiple and difficult to disentangle.

We enter this conversation not so much to take sides in this material and metaphorical debate, but rather to reposition it. What might make rice "white" in the end, no matter whose knowledge, history and skills are exploited in its production is the way in which the asymmetries of colonial economies and knowledge regimes routinely discounted both the skills of colonized peoples and the botanical legacy of rice cultivars, indeed even species, developed by generations of farmers in both Africa and Asia. The colonial rice trade rested on exploitation of the land, labor, skills, and histories of Native Americans, Africans, and Asians. It is important to try and recuperate these contributions while also recognizing that the world in which rice was grown, traded, and consumed was one whose structures were designed to be most favorable for only a select few.

Peter Coclanis has famously argued that "a study of the rice market in the West requires that we look east, such a study provides an argument for the utility of a truly international approach to history."[16] Rice was a staple that supplied laborers in the West Indies with complex carbohydrates to supplement their meals. But by far the greatest consumer of rice in the Atlantic World was Europe, where this grain would feed the poor, be used as a starch in industrial processing, supplement animal feed, and find its byproducts used in the paper industry. Thus, like cotton, rice could also be a precursor to larger commodity chains of dietary and sumptuary goods. Also like cotton, the US Civil War had the effect of increasing demand for Asian rice on the European market. Between 1856 and 1857, approximately 700,000–800,000 acres of land were under rice cultivation in lower Burma. By 1870, that number was effectively doubled.[17] Comparison of these issues in nineteenth-century South Carolina and Burma provide an entreé for understanding an even more important similarity – the insecurity that new interdependencies brought to ordinary people in the bay of Bengal and the Caribbean Basin.

Recovering the intellectual and material contributions of colonial and colonized subjects is an important intellectual project. However, the pioneering studies of rice in the New World have rarely focused their attention beyond parts of the world that were impacted directly by events in the Atlantic World. This is a shame, since these studies offer considerable insight in their attention to different scales of analysis, their weaving of legal, economic, and social history, and most importantly, the common ground all authors in this discussion share. There are three salient points that all participants in the debate have more or less agreed to. First, that the Upper Guinea Coast was the center of rice cultivation in the Atlantic World in the beginning of the eighteenth century. Second, that by the end of the eighteenth century, the Carolina and Georgia Low Country had become the center of rice cultivation in the Atlantic World, and third, that this geographic change was accomplished through a shift to a plantation agricultural regime. This fundamental shift in the location and relationship of land and labor should not be taken as a forgone conclusion, however. Rice, as a staple to feed slaves in the West Indies, did not have to be grown in the Carolinas. The distance between South Carolina and Barbados (1967 miles) is just under two-thirds the distance between Barbados and the Upper Guinea Coast (3111 miles). Those vessels coming from West Africa would have followed prevailing winds and the transatlantic currents, reducing their transit time significantly. If one were to develop a dependable staple supply, the Guinea Coast would have been far more efficient.

The plantation form, too, was not the only or even, on a global scale, the primary mode of rice production. Across South and Southeast Asia, before, during, and after European colonialism, smallholder farming, tenant farming, and medium-scale landholdings were the primary modes of wet rice agriculture.[18] This is not, however, to suggest that exploitation and bonded or unfree labor was absent. Indeed, while there existed a range of landholding and tax situations, the correlation between regions of intensive wet rice production and hierarchies of class and caste has often been noted.[19] As discussed below, one of the primary disciplining forces over farmers in South Asia has long been debt; allied with structures of land tenure, access, and taxation, agriculturalists could become bound to the service of such debt over the course of generations.

Colonial rice plantations were sometimes attempted in Asia. For example, in 1903 in the French-held Mekong delta (Cochin China), Rémy Gressier purchased 5600 hectares of land in a colonial concession and built a checkerboard of canals equipped with pumps and electric gates. Complete with company store and a proprietary scrip with which rice-growing tenants were paid in lieu of cash, this vast rice plantation ran its own mills and boats. Enclosed within a *casier*, a "distinctively colonial, industrial construction of protective dikes and canals, mostly produced by the Department of Public Works using advanced machinery and large teams of day laborers," the Gressier estate was the most successful of these plantations, several others failing to master the complex water and land nexus of the delta with its frequent floods and shifting waterways.[20] Nor were large plantations the only agricultural regime in the Americas. Small farms, utilizing wage, bonded and unfree labor were common throughout the West Indies.[21] Their prominence in the scholarship is just overshadowed by a disciplinary focus on large estate holdings of visible and wealthy individuals. The point for us is not so much how rice plantations came to be, but rather that the plantation regime in the Low Country was used at all.

We argue here for a more expansive view of rice cultivation in the Americas that takes in both the Atlantic world as well as more distant colonial arenas. Rice production in the American south was dwarfed by cultivation in Asia, but these histories intersected (Figure 1).[22] These intersecting histories were characterized by numerous inter-colonial dependencies. The conversation centering Atlantic rice production, while acknowledging the important role of the Indian Ocean, has still not fully

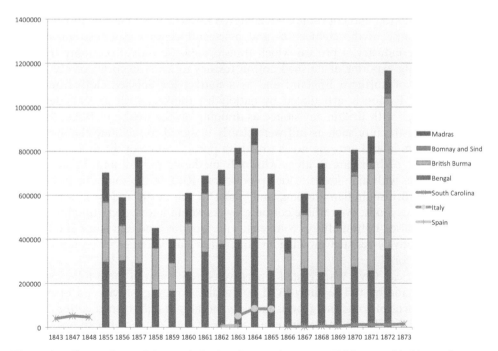

Figure 1. Comparison of rice trade in the nineteenth century. Table assembled by authors.

recognized first, the many ways in which the Atlantic and the Indian Oceans were linked and second, the parallel processes of deliberately created sub-imperial "rice bowls" servicing the production of commercial crops and capital. Parasitic upon on the labor, land, agricultural skills, and cultivars of rice and other crops, these diverse forms of extraction shared a common thread in both using and also discounting the intellectual and creative role of subjected peoples. Rather than focusing solely upon metropoles and extractive colonial enterprises, a focus on inter-territorial dependencies troubles this particular vision of the Atlantic and asks us to attend to the scope of our investigation – not just its scale.

Raised on rice: sugar, cotton, and jute

We begin our discussion of rice by first noting some of the globally circulating botanical commodities that rice made possible. While the details of these connections cannot be fully developed here, botanical commodities provide an excellent lens through which to compare Indian and Atlantic Ocean histories, as well as draw out specific histories linking them. Take the well-known case of cotton. The American Civil War had a large role in shaping global centers of cultivation and production. The shelling of Fort Sumter would have enormous implications for the commodity chains of cotton, and the machinery to process it. On the eve of the Civil War, the American Southeast commanded the largest portion of cotton's market share. According to Sven Beckert, in 1859 the South produced 77% of Britain's cotton supply.[23] By 1862, that market share dwindled and the southern states quickly realized that the embargo, put in place to force Britain to intercede on their behalf, was a failed strategy. In the intervening years mills in England, France, Germany, and Russia experienced what would come to be called the "cotton drought."

In India, cotton and cotton textiles achieved iconic status in nationalist discourse precisely because of the eighteenth- and nineteenth-century deindustrialization of India's textile industry, a process which transformed the Indian economy from the world's leading exporter of finished cotton textiles to a net exporter of raw cotton for the mills of northern England and as a market for finished cloth from those same mills.[24] Famously articulated by nationalist thinkers such as Ranade as the "drain theory," with Britain envisioned as draining off the wealth of India, forms of colonial infrastructure such as rail were clearly designed to facilitate the movement of cotton from inland growing areas to British ports.[25] Some of the most productive "cotton soils" of India are in areas with only moderate rainfall and, as such, these were not areas with high levels of rice production. Rice, in the southern and eastern parts of the British Indian Empire, and wheat in the north and west, were costly and high-status foods; even where cotton growers would have eaten drought-resistant millets and pulses, cotton always competed with food for land and labor and farmers sometimes actively resisted growing the quantities and varieties of cotton colonial rulers hoped for.[26]

The American Civil War created a massive cotton boom in India followed by an equally dramatic bust. The short-lived boom did, however, provide an opening to the development of some indigenous industry, notably Indian-owned cotton mills in Bombay. In 1856, The Bombay Spinning and Weaving Company began operation.[27] The mill contained 17,000 spindles from Manchester, and was designed and supervised by English engineers. The mill was backed, in large part, by a local Parsee merchant,

Cowasjee Nanabjoy Davar.[28] Davar would go onto to finance two more mills in Bombay. The Bombay Cotton Cleaning Company began to operate between 1856 and 1859 and the Bombay Throstle Mill Company in 1859. Davar's timing might be seen as serendipitous because of the Union's blockade of southern ports and the Confederate's hasty decision to restrict export of their cotton to Britain. Indian cotton quadrupled in price and the volume of exports changed dramatically.[29] In 1859, India contributed 15% of Britain's supply of raw cotton. By 1862 that number had risen to 75% – effectively taking over the role of the American South as the major provider of raw material for the industrial production of cloth.[30]

Other botanical commodities critical at various times to Early Modern supply chains were also raised on a diet of rice, many more so than cotton, whose growing requirements tended to locate production in drier, less rice-friendly regions. Jute, produced in quantity in British-held Bengal, especially the eastern region now part of Bangladesh, was processed in Calcutta and shipped across the colonies to make rope, gunny sacks, and other objects.[31] Indigo and opium poppies, too, were grown in Bengal, tended by rice-eating Bengali smallholders and landless laborers.[32] As in the case of Burma, discussed below, these workers, including those with title to land, were often not quite "free" in the sense that rural indebtedness could create bonds of obligation and even servitude that lasted generations. Plantation-produced sugarcane is of course the *locus classicus* of an agrarian commodity supported, in part, by rice. Cane sugar itself, along with other "drug foods" such as tea became an agent for the disciplining of Britain's own workers, a doubling-back of colonial connections that points to the critical problem emergent colonial capitalism faced vis-a-vis labor control.[33]

Of course, rice was not the only foodstuff to fuel commerce. While there exists a vast literature on the history of the wheat trade, wheat and rice were themselves linked in an international market as early as 1868, a market, as Lathman and Neal note, that linked the Atlantic and Indian Oceans: "Indian wheat exports went predominantly to England, and the correlation with English domestic wheat prices is 0.75. Indian wheat competed there with American wheat, and the correlation with American wheat [prices] in London is 0.76."[34] The rice and wheat trade were further integrated though the agency of the vast Indian market where they were substitutes, at least in part. Wheat and rice do not, however, have similar growing conditions and thus tend to be cultivated in different regions. What such talk of global trade tends to erase is the specific impact global shifts have on local farmers and consumers. As we stress, the structural inequities of colonial regimes of commerce created conditions of vulnerability, especially as the risks of food insecurity were exported across the web of empire.

The Atlantic: slaves, imports, and disaster

Food is deeply implicated in the history and historiography of the Atlantic world. It is true that interregional trade did not begin with the presence of Europeans in the sixteenth and seventeenth centuries.[35] That being said, interregional food trade and dependency only emerged through the course of the eighteenth century. Richard Dunn was perhaps the first to outline the complicated food networks of the Atlantic world.[36] By the 1660s, there was a burgeoning sugar industry in Barbados and a growing population of free whites who wished to seek their fortune on an island of limited land. In addition, the labor demands associated with sugar meant that there was an increasing population that required staple food supplies.[37] According to estimates provided in early censuses, Barbados contained 50,000 inhabitants, 30,000 of whom were "negroes" and assumed to be enslaved.[38] In 1670, King Charles granted a charter to the Lords Proprietor to establish a colony in between the English domain of Virginia and the Spanish colony of La Florida. That year, settlers from Barbados, including free and enslaved peoples, arrived at Albemarle Point between the Ashley and the Cooper rivers in what is today Charleston. The land itself was salt marshes, estuaries, and land largely comprised of sandy silt. Between 1670 and 1680, 684 whites would come to settle this colony; nearly half were from the West Indies.[39]

While the earliest settlers experimented with cultivating a variety of export-oriented commodities including sugar, lumber, tobacco, cotton, and indigo, rice would prove to be the exportable commodity through which white settlers might find their anticipated fortunes.[40] According to the US Census Bureau, between 1698 and 1774 the amount of rice exported from the 13 colonies grew enormously—from 10,407 pounds to 76,265,700 pounds (Figure 2).[41] The growth in this market was driven by demand that was not in the metropole but other colonies. According to the transatlantic database, between 1696 and 1774 just over 1,000,000 slaves disembarked in British West Indian colonies. 245,376 of those laborers disembarked in Barbados and would have been almost entirely dependent on grain supplies from North

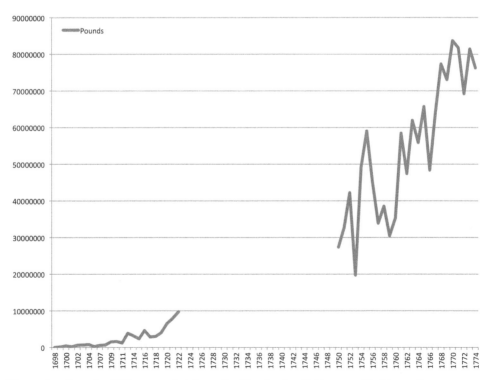

Figure 2. Pounds of Rice exported from the 13 colonies. Table assembled by authors.

America for their food.[42] What rice did engender was a degree of interregional food dependency.

When describing rice cultivation in the Americas there were, broadly speaking, two regimes. As a focus of plantation agriculture, it was either cultivated as a primary crop, as in parts of Brazil, the Georgia and Carolina Low Country, or as a secondary crop. As a primary crop, American rice cultivation grew dramatically over the course of the eighteenth century and supplied a growing demand primarily in Europe and secondarily in the Americas.[43] In Peru, Jamaica, Louisiana, Mexico, Cayenne, and the Guyanas, settlers and slaves cultivated rice as a secondary crop. Secondary crops like rice, maize, guinea corn, as well as animal domesticates, like cattle, would have been circulated between colonies through regionally organized markets, and within colonies through internal market systems. Two methods were used for supplying slave settlements in the West Indies. The first obliged planters to provide clothes, household goods and rations grown and processed for the express purpose of feeding slaves. The second method obliged planters to provide sufficient land and time for enslaved laborers to grow their own food. The enslaved would be expected to purchase household goods by selling surplus agricultural goods through legally sanctioned Sunday markets.[44] These methods were rarely mutually exclusive. For example, it was common for British planters to provide salt beef, salt fish, cornmeal, and biscuits, especially in the months immediately following hurricane season.[45] In Martinique, planters often reneged on the *ordinaire* and provided rations in places where provision grounds were common. As such, most island colonies had diverse economic interests including plantation agriculture, trade and transshipment, and provisioning.

Enforced self-reliance became colonial practice on most islands. For example in much of the British, French, and Danish West Indies, planters alloted a combination of house gardens (approximately 1/40 of an acre) and larger plots of land in areas less suited for staple commodity cultivation.[46] In Martinique, local councils passed ordinances that encouraged planters to cultivate land for slave subsistence.[47] Much of this part time food production focussed on root crops, such as manioc and taro, and fruit trees that mature relatively quickly including bananas and breadfruit. Mansucripts like Hans Sloane's description of Jamaica written between 1707 and 1725, indicates that rice became one of the crops that enslaved Africans in the Caribbean might have preferentially grown, given the right conditions.[48] Rice was grown by enslaved laborers in Martinique, Jamaica, Hispaniola, and Surinam.[49] In Jamaica, it became the third most important grain in the AfroJamaican diet after guinea corn and indian corn.[50]

Colonies, therefore, as nodes in food networks drew supplies from the internal market system, largely organized by enslaved laborers, regional networks largely organized by a host of actors, and interregional trade largely organized through merchants and planters. In the first two instances, the economic/political integrity of the plantation colony was compromised by local actors to ensure food security. On islands which lacked the kind of standing water required for growing rice, like Barbados, or the marginal land that was set aside for laborers to cultivate their own food, food had to be imported from elsewhere. The residents, enslaved and free, white and black, were far more reliant on interregional food networks than regional and local networks. There was thus a greater likelihood for them to drown from a "ripple."

By the last quarter of the eighteenth century, there was a crisis of subsistence across the Atlantic world.[51] Take, for example, the cost of food when inter colony shipping was threatened by war, hurricanes or both. Richard Sheridan has summarized the documents presented to the Jamaica Assembly between 1770 and 1782. He notes that prior to the American Revolution, the average price of rice ranged between 13 shillings 2 pence per cent weight (100 lbs) to 20 shillings per cent weight (100 lbs). During the American Revolution, this price increased by 100–200%. Between 1776 and 1782 the average price of rice per cent weight was 40–80 shillings.[52]

The rise in cost for basic foodstuffs allows us to infer a scarcity in provisions brought about by the American Revolution in Jamaica and the Eastern Caribbean. For example, in 1776, the increased unrest among slaves in Barbados, including a crushed insurrection, brought about a state of martial law. In addition to the increased numbers of troops requiring food, there was also drought at this time, making subsistence strategies even more precarious. These scarcities were intensified for ordinary people and slaves during hurricane season. Rice and guinea corn became even more important as a series of hurricanes and earthquakes reduced the amount of locally grown provisions available to enslaved laborers. This was most dramatically felt in Barbados on 10 October 1780, when a hurricane brought about the death of 2033 enslaved Africans, 6000 cattle and the destruction of over 1.3 million pounds of property. One year later, the number of deaths resulting from the hurricane was increased to 5022.[53] At one estate, Turner's Hall Plantation, net income in 1781 declined to 20% of 1779, the year before the hurricane. The cost of provisions to feed the slaves increased by 124% from 1779 leading to a net loss of 1130 pounds for its owner.[54] While it would be easy to describe such death and destruction as the result of natural disasters, disaster itself is a social construction whose ultimate outcomes relate to vulnerability and risk as well as to hazards. The severe outcomes of events such as the Barbados hurricane of 1780 followed directly upon the precarious nature of provisioning brought about by inter-colonial dependency in the Atlantic world. Such specialization made whole populations subject to the vagaries of maritime traffic and local political shifts, unevenly distributing vulnerability and risk.

Indian Ocean: peasants, exports, famine

Interregional food trade and even basic dependency upon food imports did not begin in South Asia with colonial intervention. Instead, we see a very long pre-colonial history of exchange which included a lively market in rice along well-defined circuits. By 1650, the Kanara coast of southwest India supplied rice-deficit regions further south, including Malabar – home of the "king of the spices," black pepper – and the nearby Konkan coast, including eventually Portuguese Goa, which had always to import rice. Kanara rice also went to Muscat and the Persian Gulf, where some important entrepots relied not only upon imported food, but even water. Kanara rice was not, however, shipped to the Maldives, as one might expect on geographical grounds; instead rice from far-off Bengal was brought to these islands in exchange for cargos of *cauris* (cowries). Bengal and Orissa, with their high rainfall and rich soils, exported rice to ports further south along the eastern coast of India, as far south as the Kaveri delta, also a rice-exporting area. Kaveri delta rice was used as ballast in vessels sailing to Aceh and reached Sri Lanka and the Malabar coast as well.[55]

These routes and relationships continued to be relevant even as colonial incorporation changed the political and physical landscapes of the region.

The Bengal delta was the British bridgehead in Asia, the region in which colonial intervention in landholding, taxation, and farming had its deepest roots. Here land was ideal for rice and other water-intensive crops such as sugarcane, opium, and indigo. Portuguese Goa was, as noted, consistently rice-deficit, but notwithstanding Portugese manipulation of trade, they did not fundamentally interrupt existing dependencies nor did they work to transform regional landscapes on the scale that we see in British-held Burma. Here, the East India Company came into conflict with the local Konbaung rulers of Burma, who did not allow rice exports, holding surplus paddy in granaries for disaster relief. In the mid-nineteenth century, Burma's population was concentrated in upper Burma, the drier inland part of the polity. The vast delta of lower Burma was flooded a good part of the year, its mangroves, seasonally flooded grassy plains, and scrubby forests supporting a sparse frontier population.[56]

All this would change with the annexation of lower Burma in 1852. Although the first decade of colonial rule was primarily one of military consolidation, the EIC did immediately lift the odious restriction on free trade represented by the export ban. While most rice exports initially went to the now-separate country of (upper) Burma, after the Great Uprising of 1857, known by the British as the "Sepoy Mutiny," demand in India greatly increased.[57] The rebellion of 1857, which led to the transfer of the Asian colonies to direct crown rule, also disrupted supply chains to Europe, demand met both by the newly-acquired colony of Pegu but also by expanded rice exports from Burma. Adas notes, "The outbreak of the Civil War in the United States and the subsequent decline of the Carolinas as a source of rice for Europe further enhanced Burma's position as a major supplier for London, Liverpool, and continental milling centers like Hamburg and Bremen."[58] Despite belonging to the same imperial system, import duties were not uniformly imposed. Burmese rice paid a duty in Bengal but none in London. Over the course of the late nineteenth and early twentieth centuries, the Burma delta, like the Mekong, was transformed from a watery frontier zone to an intensively settled and managed landscape overwhelmingly dedicated to rice growing. Exports surged, alongside the demographic and environmental transformation of the delta landscape (Figure 3). Like many other Asian rice-producing regions before and after European colonial expansion, the Burma delta fed both local and distant consumers. As the scale of both economic and political interconnectivity and imperial asymmetries of power grew under British rule, however, the potential of disruptions to Burma's export trade to create ripples in the pond increased.

H. B. Proctor, writing in 1882 for his fellow grain-millers in England, made a passionate case for the expansion of rice consumption in the UK (most rice coming in to London was, as noted, used industrially or exported to other parts of Europe), noting that rice made excellent animal feed, bread additive, and could be used as a substitute for potatoes. His work illustrates the low cost and ubiquity of Burmese rice in England (Figure 4). While Burmese production was not organized into plantations, in some sense we can picture the entire delta as a newly constructed zone of industrial, commercial agriculture. Proctor notes:

> The rice trade of England continued in extremely small compass, and was limited to the varieties produced in Carolina, Bengal, and Madras, until the year 1852, when the most

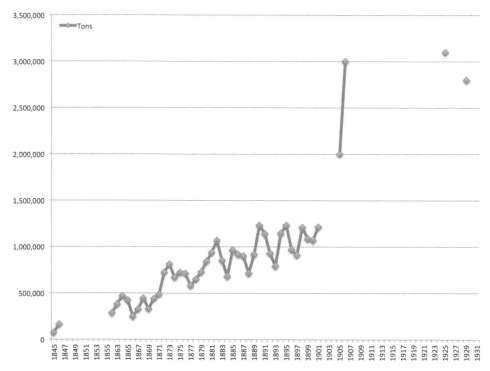

Figure 3. Rice exports from lower Burma, 1845–1929. Table assembled by authors.

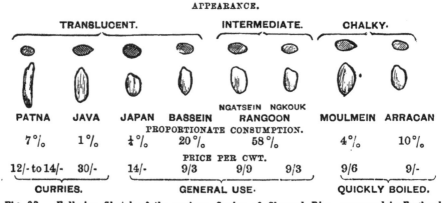

Figure 4. Image from *Rice: its history, culture, manufacture, and food value,* 35. Varieties of rice consumed in England and their prices. Note that the five varieties on the right are all from Burma, making a total of 78%. Only 7% come from India (Patna) though this type is noted to be best for curries. Image in public domain.

fertile provinces of Burma were conquered and annexed to the British Empire. Of all countries in the world, Burma is the best adapted for the cheap cultivation of rice; all that was wanted was a just and strong Government, able to put down petty internal warfare, and willing to protect the cultivators from excessive taxation, violence, and oppression.[59]

But *Pax Britannia* and "good government" were the perhaps least of the changes wrought by colonial rule in Burma. Massive flood embankments to hold back salt water and channel river water were built in both Bengal and British Burma, transforming regional hydrologies, vegetation, and agricultural possibilities.[60]

The intensive farming of lower Burma relied on the rice-growing skills of indigenous Burmese and, increasingly, Indian farmers. Smallholders and tenants, often using hired migrant labor from southern India – where rice production had already been established for nearly two thousand years – drew on the staggering agrobiodiversity of rice varieties (landraces) developed to suit all forms of production and taste.[61] Deftly controlling the flow of water through channels and across paddies, wet rice in the delta included both bunded (bordered) paddy fields and large expanses of land planted with "floating" rice, cultivars with extremely long stems adapted to deep water. Successful paddy rice production depends on maintaining a constant, slow flow of water through the fields, something quite difficult to engineer across a level landscape. Near harvest, fields must be drained at just the right time. Despite colonial denigration of the skill and labor involved – Proctor notes for example that rice was not manured, adding in almost the next breath that crop stubble was burned to promote fertility – wet rice farming in fact relied on detailed local knowledge and skills as well as a botanical legacy of diverse cultivars.[62] Nursery paddies, where seedlings are grown before being transplanted, are typically heavily fertilized and tended. In lower Burma, seed was either broadcast directly into plowed and flooded paddies (in which case no transplantation would occur), or else broadcast thickly into nurseries (Figure 5) for later transplantation.

Crop processing, too, was initially carried out using traditional technologies (Figure 6), but increasingly European-owned mills came to dominate. Adas notes that by 1898 there were 47 rice mills in lower Burma, of which 64% (and all of the largest mills) were owned by Europeans. European capitalists also "owned the companies which provided rail and steamboat transportation within the Delta and steamship communication with India, the Far East, and Europe."[63] The mode of industrial production was thus different, but in some ways comparable to the plantation, with control over labor and technology, as well as coercive force, key elements of control.

Across the British empires, inter-colonial migration was significant, not just for the supply of poor agrarian laborers, but also for the ranks of the military and mid-level administrators, mostly supplied from the Indian colony.[64] For Burmese farmers, perhaps the most significant Indian migrants were Indian moneylenders, especially the Nattukottai Chettiars of Madras, who operated as primary lenders to networks of Burmese moneylenders. As debt was a major impediment to mobility, land ownership, and freedom of productive decision-making, these inter-imperial links loomed large in rural lives.

Across the Bay of Bengal from the Burma delta, the long-colonized Presidency of Bengal was itself a rice-exporting region and a producive agricultural zone where, as noted, commodities such as jute, sugarcane, indigo, and opium poppies had all been grown and sent out to support imperial enterprises. Bengal did, however, experience periods of scarcity, none worse than the great Bengal famine of 1943. This famine was made famous by the work of economist Amartya Sen, who argues that this was a "boom" famine, one in which there was no shortage of food overall, but rather a failure of exchange entitlements consequential to colonial rule. O'Grada makes a

Figure 5. (a)–(d) Burmese woodblock images reproduced from Proctor 1888. Upper left, man plowing the flooded paddy field with bullocks, upper right, man broadcasting rice seed; lower left, man and woman transplanting rice; lower right, woman and men harvesting rice. In images 5(c) and 5(d), a woman is shown bringing lunch to the field. Images from *Rice: its history, culture, manufacture, and food value,* 15, 16, 17, 18. Images in public domain.

compelling case that there was, in fact, some shortfall of food in Bengal leading up to the famine, though this does not challenge Sen's basic insight – and our point here – linking insecurity, risk, and the potential for crisis with structures of power as much as conditions of nature. Some scholars have argued that Bengal's rice crop was struck by a disease known as "brown spot of rice," a new twist on the "color" of rice in colonial contexts.[65]

In the context of both war and colonial subjugation, Bengal's difficulties proved deadly. With the Japanese occupation of lower Burma (1942–1945), and the increased military demand for food in Bengal, the British made a series of disastrous decisions, including destroying rice stocks in order to deny them to the enemy (who never made it further west) and commandeering all boats, even the small ones used by Bengali fishermen, who would suffer the most during the famine. Too, the diversion of crop land to the production of commercial commodity crops, a fundamental condition leading to the development of sub-imperial "rice bowls" in the first place, played a special role in

Figure 6. (a)–(e) Images from *Rice: its history, culture, manufacture, and food value,* Burmese woodblock images reproduced from Proctor 1888. Upper left, men with bullocks threshing paddy, 19; upper right, winnowing apparatus, 20; middle left hulling and decorticating devices, 26; middle right, 28, "paying the cultivators." Note that the figure with the desk, presumably the moneylender, has an armed guard. Three Burmese men and one woman sit in attitudes of supplication, one man holding up a piece of paper, perhaps with the record of his credit or debt. Bottom, measuring the rice, 25. Images in public domain.

war with commodities such as jute constituting essential *matériel*. Mortality estimates from this disaster range widely, from a low of 1.5 million to a high of 4 million, with the death of perhaps 2 out of Bengal's 60 million residents a realistic figure.[66]

Discussion

In this article, we have attempted to locate the Atlantic World in the world by comparing rice as a staple commodity in global trade. In both the Atlantic and Indian Ocean areas, colonial extraction required deep knowledge, skilled farmers, labor, and finance. As a staple commodity, rice supported the cultivation of other staple commodities, facilitating industrialization and capital accumulation. These insights have been discussed and debated by others. In this paper we add to the conversation by focussing on the role of this global structure in reflecting and materializing inter-colonial dependency. By comparing two "rice bowls" from two different centuries – South Carolina and its links to the Atlantic World, and Burma and its links to the Indian Ocean – we can see how, as Roy puts it, famine (and other disasters) both "constitute a rupture in the existing moral economy" and also, even more so, "bring into scandalous relief everyday forms of poverty and inequality." Rice becomes an important lens through which to make this proposition and through the lens of rice we synthesize a body of environmental and colonial histories.[67]

The comparison between rice bowls, we admit, is not perfect. Interregional food networks emerged in the Atlantic in part through European engagement with the Americas and Africa. In the Indian Ocean, interregional food networks have a deep and complicated history. In addition, rice exports from South Carolina were relatively small in comparison with global exports from ports in India and Burma both before and after the American Civil War. That said, we can make some initial claims that are very important. First, in the case of both regions, Europe's colonial engagement brought about an increased diversity of food networks, spinning new webs across colonized landscapes and in many cases, dramatically reshaping those landscapes themselves as well as the composition of their human inhabitants. As such, colonial engagement was a project of forcible translation whereby existing commercial and intellectual networks were appropriated and expanded, as the contributions of colonized peoples were simultaneously discounted. Second, and following the first point, these networks were aggregated into far fewer nodes, with new imperial and sub-imperial centers developing. The scale of these network expanded, too, with some "spiders" able to tug on webs stretched across the entire world. At work, then, was also a process of transformation.

Combined, these processes lead us to posit reduced food security for all involved; in the Atlantic a more wholesale reorganization, but in both cases, sharply reduced autonomy, flexibility, and choice on the part of producers critically dependent upon botanical commodity prices, imported food, and coercive regimes of power. This utter lack of food security led directly to food crisis. Colonized peoples were not, however, passive in the face of such connections. In some cases, such as the locally organized internal economies of the Caribbean, subsistence production, or rice trade operating outside of company demands, represented a form of agency over food security reasserted by local actors. On the small farms of South and Southeast Asia, those who could often voted with their feet, moving to new regions, to cities, rejecting or, in most cases, exchanging one form of insecurity for another. These cases did not undermine the coeval projects of translation and transformation, however. They in fact made them work. The "Columbian exchange," with its novel world landscape of organisms, was not the beginning of interregional dependencies or inequities, but it ushered in new juxtapositions of power, hunger, and risk, including new insecurities built on older botanical and intellectual legacies. Rice – black, brown, and white – was (and is) one of those legacies.

Acknowledgements
The authors would like to thank Gayatri A. Menon, Kenneth G. Kelly, Timothy K. Earle, and the anonymous reviewers for their comments on earlier drafts of this article.

Disclosure statement
No potential conflict of interest was reported by the authors.

Notes
1. Metcalf, *Imperial Connections*, 1.
2. Solar, "Opening to the East."
3. Metcalf, *Imperial Connections*, 7–8.
4. O'Gráda, "Ripple that Drowns?"
5. Greene, *Hemispheric History*.
6. For a discussion of how food security was closely linked with the American Revolution, its casualties and possibilities, see Smith, "Food rioters and the American Revolution." Similarly see, Mukerjee, *Churchill's Secret War*.
7. Kurlansky, *Salt*; Kurlansky, *Cod*; Mintz, *Sweetness and Power*; Moss and Badenoch, *Chocolate*.
8. Littlefield, *Rice and Slaves*, 75.
9. Carney, *Black Rice*.
10. Smith, "Lord Killearn," 1.

11. Carney, "Rice and Memory"; Carney, "African Rice and Slaves"; Carney, "'With Grains in Her Hair'"; Carney and Voeks, "Landscape Legacies."
12. Eltis et al., "Black, Brown, or White?"
13. Eltis et al., "Agency and Diaspora in Atlantic History," 1334.
14. Ibid., 1345.
15. Hawthorne, "From 'Black Rice'," 152.
16. Coclanis, "Distant Thunder," 1051.
17. Adas, *Burma Delta*, 22.
18. "Hill rice" or "dry rice" is typically sown in more humid upland regions and integrated into systems of swidden agriculture. This form of production is almost exclusively organized by households, as its labor and scheduling requirements are significant different from those of "wet" or paddy rice. This is not to say that "dry" rice was never commercially produced, however. Entirely different cultivars are typically used for different modes of farming. See Morrison, *Rice*.
19. For recent periods, see Mencher, *Agriculture and Social Structure*. This same point is made for pre-colonial contexts by Stein, *Peasant State*. Both are discussed in Morrison, "Daroji Valley."
20. Biggs, *Aerial Photography*; Biggs, *Quagmire*.
21. Higman, *Slave Populations*; Higman, *Plantation Maps*.
22. Although both India and Burma were part of the British Empire, they had distinct administrative apparatus.
23. Beckert, "Emancipation and Empire," 1409–1410.
24. Tarlo, *Clothing Matters*.
25. Still the best discussion of the economic critique of colonialism in South Asia is found in Chandra, *India's Struggle for Independence*. For a similar discussion on the impacts of rail see Goswami, *Producing India*.
26. Morrison, *Great Transformations*; Hazareesingh, "Cotton, Climate and Colonialism."
27. In 1855 a firm located in Bharuch (Broach), Gujarat was the first industrial mill to spin cotton in India, although certainly cotton-spinning had long been a significant cottage industry. See Metha, *Cotton Mills*.
28. Chaloner, *Industry and Innovation*, 113.
29. Charlesworth, *Peasants and Imperial Rule*, 135.
30. Beckert, "Emancipation and Empire," 1413.
31. Ray, "Struggling against Dundee."
32. South Carolina's indigo trade in mid-1740s boomed because of the depression in Carolina rice at the same time, the Carolina plantation system producing an elastic supply of the two crops. See Nash, "South Carolina Indigo." Starting in the seventeenth century, in Bengal indigo was grown on European-owned plantations staffed by "servile labor in various forms." See Kumar, *Indigo Plantations*.
33. Mintz, *Sweetness and Power*; Thompson, "Time, Work-Discipline, and Industrial Capitalism."
34. Latham and Neal, "The International Market," 272.
35. Hauser and Curet, *Islands at the Crossroads*.
36. Dunn, "English Sugar Islands." Dunn, *Sugar and Slaves*.
37. Dunn, *Sugar and Slaves*.
38. Dunn, "English Sugar Islands," 82.
39. Baldwin, *First Settlers of South Carolina*.
40. Dethloff, "Colonial Rice Trade," 234, figure 2.
41. Littlefield, *Rice and Slaves*, 75.
42. Database, *Voyages*.
43. Dethloff, "Colonial Rice Trade," 234.
44. Berlin and Morgan, *Cultivation and Culture*; Debien, *Esclaves*; Handler and Wallman, "Production Activities"; Hauser, *Black Markets*; Marshall, "Provision Ground"; Mintz and Douglas, *Jamaican Internal Marketing System*; Moitt, *Women and Slavery*; Tomich, *Petite Guinée*.
45. Britain, *Papers Presented to the House of Commons*; Britain, *Respecting the Slave Trade*; Dirks, *Resource Fluctuations*.
46. Marshall, "Provision Ground."

47. Debien, *Esclaves*; Moitt, *Women and Slavery*. For a recent review of domestic economy of slaves in Martinique, see Handler and Wallman, "Production Activities."
48. Sloane, *A voyage to the islands Madera*.
49. Carney, *Black Rice*, 75–77.
50. Long, *History of Jamaica*.
51. Sheridan, "Crisis of Slave Subsistence"; Mulcahy, *Hurricanes and Society*, 77–86; Sheridan, "Domestic Economy," 629.
52. Sheridan, "Domestic Economy," 629.
53. Ibid., 632.
54. Mulcahy, *Hurricanes and Society*, 80.
55. Subrahmanyam, *Political Economy of Commerce*, 50–57. Ifran Habib among others describes some of the interregional connections of Bengal under the Mughals, just prior to the establishment of British control. See Habib, *Atlas of the Mughal Empire*.
56. The primary source for the colonial history of Burma is Adas, *Burma Delta*.
57. Ibid., 30–31. On 1857 see Bhattacharya, *Rethinking 1857*.
58. Adas, *Burma Delta*, 31; Adas, *Colonization, Commercial Agriculture*, 1.
59. Proctor, *Rice*, 1.
60. Adas, *Burma Delta*; D'Souza, "Drowned and Damned"; Adas, *Colonization, Commercial Agriculture*.
61. Indian migrants to British Burma constituted 2% of the population in 1872 and 7% by 1901. See Adas, *Burma Delta*, 85.
62. Proctor, *Rice*, 37. Most nutrients in wet rice come from water rather than soil, so in places with silty, nutrient-rich soil there may be no need for fertilization.
63. Adas, *Burma Delta*, 109–110.
64. The flow of Indian laborers to Burma was large-scale and sustained, increasingly dramatically after the introduction of steamships. Note, too, that many of the British officers were themselves from subjugated places such as Ireland and Scotland. See Ibid., 96.
65. Sen, "Ingredients of famine analysis"; O'Grâda, "Ripple that drowns?"; Dasgupta, "Bengal famine."
66. O'Grâda, "Ripple that drowns?," Collingham further explores the role of food supply in the operation of World War II, See Collingham, *Taste of War*.
67. Roy, *Alimentary Tracts*.

References

Adas, Michael. *The Burma Delta: Economic Development and Social Change on an Asian Rice Frontier, 1852–1941*. Madison: University of Wisconsin, 1974.

Adas, Michael. "Colonization, Commercial Agriculture, and the Destruction of the Deltaic Rainforests of British Burma in the Late Nineteenth Century." In *Global Deforestation and the Nineteenth Century World Economy*, edited by Richard Tucker and J. F. Richards, 95–110. Durham, NC: Duke University, 1983.

Baldwin, Agnes Leland. *First Settlers of South Carolina, 1670–1680*. Columbia, SC: South Carolina Tricentennial Commission, 1969.

Beckert, Sven. "Emancipation and Empire: Reconstructing the Worldwide Web of Cotton Production in the Age of the American Civil War." *The American Historical Review* 109, no. 5 (2004): 1405–1438.

Berlin, Ira, and Philip D. Morgan. *Cultivation and Culture: Labor and the Shaping of Slave Life in the Americas*. Charlottesville: University of Virginia, 1993.

Bhattacharya, Sabyasachi. *Rethinking 1857*. Delhi: Orient Longman, 2008.

Biggs, David. "Aerial Photography and Colonial Discourse on the Agricultural Crisis in Late-Colonial Indochina, 1930–1945." In *Cultivating the Colonies: Colonial States and Their Environmental Legacies*, edited by Christina Folke Ax, 109–132. Columbus: Ohio University, 2011.

Biggs, David. *Quagmire: Nation-Building and Nature in the Mekong Delta*. Seattle: University of Washington Press, 2012.

Carney, Judith A. "The Role of African Rice and Slaves in the History of Rice Cultivation in the Americas." *Human Ecology* 26, no. 4 (1998): 525–545.

Carney, Judith A. *Black Rice: The African Origins of Rice Cultivation in the Americas.* Cambridge, MA: Harvard University Press, 2001.

Carney, Judith A. "'With Grains in Her Hair': Rice in Colonial Brazil." *Slavery and Abolition* 25, no. 1 (2004): 1–27.

Carney, Judith A. "Rice and Memory in the Age of Enslavement: Atlantic Passages to Suriname." *Slavery and Abolition* 26, no. 3 (2005): 325–348.

Carney, Judith A. and Robert A. Voeks. "Landscape Legacies of the African Diaspora in Brazil." *Progress in Human Geography* 27, no. 2 (2003): 139–152.

Chaloner, William H. *Industry and Innovation: Selected Essays.* London: Cass, 1990.

Chandra, Bipan. *India's Struggle for Independence, 1857–1947.* New Delhi: Penguin Books India, 1989.

Charlesworth, Neil. *Peasants and Imperial Rule Agriculture and Agrarian Society in the Bombay Presidency 1850–1935.* Cambridge: Cambridge University Press, 1985.

Coclanis, Peter A. "Distant Thunder: The Creation of a World Market in Rice and the Transformations It Wrought." *The American Historical Review* 98, no. 4 (1993): 1050–1078.

Collingham, Lizzie. *Taste of War: World War II and the Battle for Food.* New York: Penguin, 2012.

Dasgupta, M. K. "The Bengal Famine, 1943 and the Brown Spot of Rice – An Inquiry into Their Relations." *History of Agriculture* 2, no. 3 (1983): 1–18.

Debien, Gabriel. *Les Esclaves Aux Antilles Françaises, Xviie–Xviiie Siècles.* Basse-Terre: Société d'Histoire de la Guadeloupe, 1974.

Dethloff, Henry C. "The Colonial Rice Trade." *Agricultural History* (1982): 231–243.

Dirks, Robert. "Resource Fluctuations and Competitive Transformations in West Indian Slave Societies." In *Survival in Human Populations*, edited by Charles D. Laughlin Jr. and Ivan A. Brady, 122–180. New York: Columbia University Press, 1978.

D'Souza, Rohan. *Drowned and Damned: Colonial Capitalism and Flood Control in Eastern India.* New York: Oxford University Press, 2006.

Dunn, Richard S. "The English Sugar Islands and the Founding of South Carolina." *The South Carolina Historical Magazine* 72, no. 2 (1971): 81–93.

Dunn, Richard S. *Sugar and Slaves; the Rise of the Planter Class in the English West Indies, 1624–1713.* Chapel Hill: University of North Carolina, 1972.

Eltis, David, Philip Morgan, and David Richardson. "Agency and Diaspora in Atlantic History: Reassessing the African Contribution to Rice Cultivation in the Americas." *The American Historical Review* 112, no. 5 (2007): 1329–1358.

Eltis, David, Philip Morgan, and David Richardson. "Black, Brown, or White? Color-Coding American Commercial Rice Cultivation with Slave Labor." *The American Historical Review* 115, no. 1 (2010): 164–171.

Estimates Database. "Voyages: The Trans-Atlantic Slave Trade Database." Accessed March 10, 2014. http://www.slavevoyages.org/tast/assessment/estimates.faces

Giménez, Eric Holt, and Annie Shattuck. "Food Crises, Food Regimes and Food Movements: Rumblings of Reform or Tides of Transformation?" *The Journal of Peasant Studies* 38, no. 1 (2011): 109–144.

Goswami, Manu. *Producing India: From Colonial Economy to National Space.* Chicago, IL: University of Chicago Press, 2010.

Great Britain. *Papers Presented to the House of Commons.* London: House of Parliament, 1798.

Great Britain. *Papers Presented to the House of Commons on the 7th May 1804, Respecting the Slave Trade.* London: House of Parliament, 1804.

Greene, Jack P. "Hemispheric History and Atlantic History." In *Atlantic History: A Critical Appraisal*, edited by Jack P. Greene and Philip D. Morgan, 299–316. New York: Oxford University Press, 2009.

Habib, Irfan. *An Atlas of the Mughal Empire: Political and Economic Maps with Detailed Notes, Bibliography and Index.* Aligarh: Centre of Advanced Study in History, Aligarh Muslim University, 1982.

Handler, Jerome S., and Diane Wallman. "Production Activities in the Household Economies of Plantation Slaves: Barbados and Martinique, Mid-1600s to Mid-1800s." *International Journal of Historical Archaeology* (2014): 441–466.

Hauser, Mark W. *An Archaeology of Black Markets: Local Ceramics and Economies in Eighteenth-Century Jamaica.* Gainesville: University Press of Florida, 2008.

Hauser, Mark W., and L. Antonio Curet. "Islands at the Crossroads." In *Islands at the Crossroads: Migration, Seafaring, and Interaction in the Caribbean*, edited by L. Antonio Curet and Mark W. Hauser, 201–219. Tuscaloosa: University of Alabama Press, 2011.

Hawthorne, Walter. "From 'Black Rice' to 'Brown': Rethinking the History of Risiculture in the Seventeenth- and Eighteenth-Century Atlantic." *The American Historical Review* 115, no. 1 (2010): 151–163.

Hazareesingh, Sandip. "Cotton, Climate and Colonialism in Dharwar, Western India, 1840–1880." *Journal of Historical Geography* 38, no. 1 (2012): 1–17.

Higman, Barry W. *Slave Populations of the British Caribbean, 1807–1834.* Baltimore, MD: Johns Hopkins University Press, 1984.

Higman, Barry W. "Plantation Maps as Sources for the Study of West Indian Ethnohistory." In *Ethnohistory: A Researcher's Guide*, edited by Wiedman Dennis, 107–136. Williamsburg, VA: Department of Anthropology, College of William and Mary. Studies in Third World Societies Publication Number 35, 1986.

Kumar, Prakash. *Indigo Plantations and Science in Colonial India.* Cambridge: Cambridge University Press, 2012.

Kurlansky, Mark. *Cod: A Biography of the Fish That Changed the World.* New York: Penguin, 1997.

Kurlansky, Mark. *Salt: A World History.* New York: Penguin, 2002.

Latham, A. J. H., and Larry Neal. "The International Market in Rice and Wheat, 1868–1914." *The Economic History Review* 36 (1983): 206–280.

Littlefield, Daniel C. *Rice and Slaves: Ethnicity and the Slave Trade in Colonial South Carolina.* Urbana: University of Illinois Press, 1991.

Long, Edward. *The History of Jamaica Reflections on its Situation, Settlements, Inhabitants, Climate, Products, Commerce, Laws and Government.* Montreal: McGill-Queen's University Press, 2002.

Marshall, Woodville K. "Provision Ground and Plantation Labour in Four Windward Islands." In *The Slaves' Economy: Independent Production by Slaves in the Americas*, edited by Ira Berlin and Philip Morgan, 48–67. London: Frank Cass, 1991a.

Marshall, Woodville K. "Provision Ground and Plantation Labour in Four Windward Islands: Competition for Resources during Slavery." *Slavery and Abolition* 12, no. 1 (1991b): 48–67.

McDonald, Bryan L. *Food Security, Dimensions of Security.* Cambridge: Polity Press, 2010.

McMichael, Philip. *The Global Restructuring of Agro-Food Systems.* Ithaca, NY: Cornell University Press, 1994.

Mehta, S. D. *The Cotton Mills of India 1854 to 1954.* Bombay: The Textile Association, 1954.

Mencher, Joan P. *Agriculture and Social Structure in Tamil Nadu: Past Origins, Present Transformations, and Future Prospects.* Durham, NC: Carolina Academic Press, 1978.

Metcalf, Thomas R. *Imperial Connections: India in the Indian Ocean Arena*, 1860–1920, vol. 4. Berkeley: University of California Press, 2007.

Mintz, Sidney W. *Sweetness and Power: The Place of Sugar in Modern History.* New York: Viking, 1985.

Mintz, Sidney W., and Douglas Hall. *The Origins of the Jamaican Internal Marketing System.* New Haven, CT: Yale University Press, 1960.

Moitt, Bernard. *Women and Slavery in the French Antilles: 1635–1848.* Bloomington: Indiana University Press, 2001.

Morrison, Kathleen D. *Daroji Valley: Landscape History, Place and the Making of a Dryland Reservoir System.* New Delhi: Manohar, 2009.

Morrison, Kathleen D. "Great Transformations: On the Archaeology of Cooking." In *The Menial Art of Cooking: Archaeological Studies of Cooking and Food Preparation*, edited by Sarah R. Graff and Enrique Rodríguez-Alegría, 231–244. Denver: University Press of Colorado, 2012.

Morrison, Kathleen D. "Rice." In *The Archaeology of Food: An Encyclopedia*, edited by Karen Bescherer Metheny and Mary C. Beaudry, 436–438. New York: Alta Mira Press, 2014.

Moss, Sarah, and Alexander Badenoch. *Chocolate: A Global History.* London: Reaktion Books, 2009.

Mukerjee, Madhusree. *Churchill's Secret War: The British Empire and the Ravaging of India during World War II*. New York: Basic Books, 2011.

Mulcahy, Matthew. *Hurricanes and Society in the British Greater Caribbean, 1624–1783*. Baltimore, MD: Johns Hopkins University Press, 2006.

Nash, Robert C. "South Carolina Indigo, European Textiles, and the British Atlantic Economy in the Eighteenth Century." *The Economic History Review* 63, no. 2 (2010): 362–392.

O'Gráda, Cormac. "The Ripple That Drowns? Twentieth-century Famines in China and India as Economic History." *The Economic History Review* 61, no. s1 (2008): 5–37.

Proctor, H. B. *Rice: Its History, Culture, Manufacture, and Food Value*. London: William Dunham, 1882.

Ray, Indrajit.: "Struggling against Dundee: Bengal Jute Industry during the Nineteenth Century." *Indian Economic and Social History Review* 49, no. 1 (2012): 105–146.

Roy, Parama. *Alimentary Tracts: Appetites, Aversions, and the Postcolonial*. Durham, NC: Duke University Press, 2010.

Schanbacher, William D. *The Politics of Food : The Global Conflict between Food Security and Food Sovereignty*. Santa Barbara, CA: Praeger Security International, 2010.

Sen, Amartya. "Ingredients of Famine Analysis: Availability and Entitlements." *The Quarterly Journal of Economics* 96, no. 3 (1981): 433–464.

Sheridan, Richard B. "The Crisis of Slave Subsistence in the British West Indies During and after the American Revolution." *The William and Mary Quarterly* 33, no. 4 (1976): 615–641.

Sheridan, Richard B. "The Domestic Economy." In *Colonial British America: Essays in the New History of the Early Modern Era*, edited by Jack P. Greene and J. R. Pole, 43–85. Baltimore, MD: Johns Hopkins University Press, 1984.

Siok-Hwa, Cheng. *The Rice Industry of Burma, 1852–1940*. Singapore: Institute of Southeast Asian Studies, 1968 (first reprinted 2012).

Sloane, Hans. *A Voyage to the Islands Madera, Barbados, Nieves, S. Christophers and Jamaica, with the Natural History of the Herbs and Trees, Four-Footed Beasts, Fishes, Birds, Insects, Reptiles, &C. Of the Last of Those Islands; to Which Is Prefix'd an Introduction, Wherein Is an Account of the Inhabitants, Air, Waters, Diseases, Trade, &C. Of That Place, with Some Relations Concerning the Neighbouring Continent, and Islands of America. Illustrated with the Figures of the Things Describ'd, Which Have Not Been Heretofore Engraved; in Large Copper-Plates as Big as the Life. By Hans Sloane, M. D. Fellow of the College of Physicians and Secretary of the Royal-Society. In Two Volumes. Vol. I*. London: printed by B. M. for the author, 1707–1725.

Smith, Barbara Clark. "Food Rioters and the American Revolution." *The William and Mary Quarterly* 51, No. 1 (1994): 3–38.

Smith, T. O. "Lord Killearn and British Diplomacy Regarding French Indo-Chinese Rice Supplies, 1946–1948." *History* 96, no. 324 (2011): 477–489.

Solar, Peter M. "Opening to the East: Shipping between Europe and Asia, 1770–1830." *The Journal of Economic History* 73, no. 3 (2013): 625–661.

Stein, Burton. *Peasant State and Society in Medieval South India*. Oxford: Oxford University Press, 1980.

Subrahmanyam, Sanjay. *The Political Economy of Commerce: Southern India 1500–1650*, vol. 45. Cambridge: Cambridge University Press, 2002.

Tarlo, Emma. *Clothing Matters: Dress and Identity in India*. Chicago, IL: University of Chicago Press, 1996.

Thompson, Edward P. "Time, Work-Discipline, and Industrial Capitalism." *Past and Present* 38 (1967): 56–97.

Tomich, Dale. "Une Petite Guinée: Provision Ground and Plantation in Martinique, 1830–1870." In *The Slaves' Economy. Independent Production by Slaves in the Americas*, edited by Ira Berlin and Philip D. Morgan, 68–91. London: Frank Cass, 1991.

Index

Note: **Bold** page numbers refer to tables; *italic* page numbers refer to figures and page numbers followed by "n" denote endnotes.

ACS *see* American Colonization Society (ACS)
Adas, Michael 111
Africa 84–89
African agency in Atlantic rice 7
The African American Experience 92
African-Americans 84; emigration movements 85; settle in Sierra Leone 93; in South Carolina 83–84
African Diaspora 35, 37n13, 37n14; archaeologies of 24–27
Africans: in Atlantic world 24–25; commercial rice economies 4, 7; enslavement of 83; handiwork of 70; "heel–toe" sowing techniques 7; indigenous rice knowledge system 6; labor 66, 69, 101; mosquito-borne illnesses 16; rice cultivation technology evolution 17; slave trading enterprises 45; on Upper Guinea coast 2, 6; *vs.* commercial agricultural system 10
"Agency and Diaspora" (Eltis and Morgan) 6
Agha, Andrew 2
agricultural intensification 15
"Agroecology" 5
AISLE *see* Archaeological Initiative for the Sierra Leone Estuary (AISLE)
d'Almada, Andre Alvares 10–12
Amazonia rice plantations 6
America 89–93; *see also* USA
American Civil War: cotton boom in India 104; shaping cultivation 104
American Colonization Society (ACS) 87
American Revolution 108
American rice cultivation 107
American War of Independence 84, 85
Angelou, Maya 27
archaeological implications: of slave trade 2
Archaeological Initiative for the Sierra Leone Estuary (AISLE) 27
archaeological resources: Bangalan 48–51; Farenya 52–56; Rio Pongo 46–47; Sanya Paulia 56–60

archaeology: of agriculture 69–72; of Atlantic Africa 24
artifact: soil an 66, 67–69
"Atlantic Creoles" 45–47, 51–53, 55, 60
Atlantic Ocean 2, 99–101; black, brown, and white rice in 101–104; definition of 100; inter-colonial dependencies in 99–101; rice cultivation in 102; rice in 101–104; slaves, imports, and disaster 105–108
Atlantic period 24, 25, 33–35
Atlantic rice farmers: dry season bias 16; heel–toe sowing methods 6; irrigation technology 11; mangrove rice nurseries 12; rice species, introduction of 12; settlement patterns 17
Atlantic Slave trade 45
Atlantic trade 99; in Africans 100
Atlantic world 2; Africa and Africans 24–25; history and conceptual frame 36n2; Sierra Leone hinterland in 32–35
Avicennia africana 7, **9**

Babson, David 75
Bakoro 59
Balanta 11, 13; in pre-colonial Guinea-Bissau 12
Baldé, Maladho Siddy 53
Ball, Elias 83, 91
Bangalan, archaeological resources: excavation 49; mound complex mapping *48*, 48–49; pedestrian survey 50; trading lodge 49–51; two story structures 49
"baracoons" 60
Baum, Robert 17
Beckert, Sven 104
Bengal: rice crop 112
Bengal famine of 1943 111–112
Betia 55, 56
Black Majority (Wood) 4
"Black majority": South Carolina 15
The Black Poor 84, 85
Black Rice (Carney) 5

"black rice" 100, 101
"Black Rice Hypothesis" 1
Bluehouse Swamp 72, 74, 75, 77
Blyden, Nemata 2
Bolton-on-the-Stono Plantation 69
Bolton project 70
The Bombay Spinning and Weaving Company 104–105, 116n27
botanical commodities: cotton 104–105; jute 105; sugar 105
The Bra Rabbit 93
British Burma 100–101
British Crown colony 85
British humanitarians 85
British settlers: experimented with crops 4
British West Africa Squadron 32
"brown rice" 101
Bunce Island 28, 28–31, 38n53, 83, 92, 93, 95n59; business and political connection 29, 30
"Bunce Island: A Cultural Resource Assessment" (DeCorse) 38n49
Burma: colonial rule in 110, 111; cultivation of rice 110; Indian laborers to 111, 117n64; rice cultivation in 102; rice exports 109, *110*; rice exports from 109, *110*, 111
Burmese woodblock *112, 113*
Bush, George Walker 30

Cabo Verde 25, 27
Campbell, William 87, 89
cane sugar 105
Canot, Theodore 48–50, 58
Cape Coast Castle 38n46
Caribbean: colonial plantation 100, 114; planters in 14; rise in 108
Carney, Judith 1, 2, 5, 27
Carney, Judith A. 101
Carolina: economic production 4–5; rice agriculture in 1
Carolina Lowcountry 27
Carolina planters 5, 6–7
Carr, Edward 2
Carson, William 70
Charleston 64, 65; enslavement in 86–88; rice cultivation in 75; road project for 72–75
Charleston County Soil Survey 74
Chinsman, J. B. 38
Church Missionary Society 94n35
City Council of Freetown 38
Cleveland Gazette 89
Cleveland, William 93
Coastal languages 9, **9, 10**
coastal rice farmers 17
coastal topography 15
Coclanis, Peter 102
Coker, Daniel 88, 89
colonial engagement: Europe 114

colonialism: in South Asia 116n25
colonial plantation: Caribbean 100
colonial rice plantations 103
colonoware 77
"Columbian exchange" 100, 115
commercial rice industry: in Georgia Lowcountry 5, 6; in South Carolina 4, 5, 14–16
Company of Gambia Adventurers 29
Company of John & Alexander Anderson 29, 32
Conté, Henrietta 52
Conté, Lansana 52
cotton 104; production in India 104–105
"cotton drought" 104
Creighton, James 88
Crowfield Plantation 75
Cullum, George W. 70

Davar, Cowasjee Nanabjoy 105
Dean Hall 70; drainage systems at 70; embankment at *71*; rice plantation 77
DeCorse, Christopher R. 2, 38n49, 39n71
defensive architecture 13
"de-natured" intensive agricultural systems 16, 18
"ditch digging" 72
Donnan, Elizabeth 5
"drain theory" 104
"drug foods" 105
"dry season bias" 16
Dumbuya, Komrabai B. H. 92
Dusinberre, William 16

Edelson, S. Max 6
Eltis, David 6, 101
embankment 65–66, 69–70; excavation in *67*; roots in West Africa 76; shovel test in 67; at Stobo plantation *67*
enslaved Africans 5–7, 18, 32, 65, 69, 70; in Bunce Island 28; provision grounds 14–17
enslaved laborers: in Lowcountry 15, 18; in South Carolina 5, 7
Europe: colonial engagement 114
European economies 24–25
Europeans: on Guinea Coast 27–32
European traders 10, 11, 29, 46–47

Faber, Paul 57, 58
Fall, ElHadj Ibrahima 2, 46, 48
Family Across the Sea 95n49
Farenya, archaeological resources: excavation 54, 55; palace area of 52–54, 56; renovation construction 52–53; ruins of the church 54, 55; site complex map *53*
farmers: primary disciplining forces 102–103
Farnsworth, Paul 37n13
Ferguson, Leland 2, 75, 76
"field kitchen" 76
Fields-Black, Edda L. 2, 27

Fitzjames, Alexander 89
food: in Atlantic world 105; in Bengal 112; cost of 108; inter-colonial dependency in 100; for land, labor and farmers 104; networks 100, 105, 107, 114; production on root crops 107; security 107, 114, 115n6
"Fortified Towns of theKoinadugu Plateau" (DeCorse) 39n71
Fraser, John 48
Freetown 84, 85
From Africa to Brazil (Hawthorne) 6
Fyle, C. 39n73

Gambia 5, 12, 13, 59; trade settlement of 60
George, David 86–88, 90
Georgia Lowcountry: commercial rice industry in 5, 6; enslaved laborers in 15, 18; rice plantations 16
Gilbert, Alan 94n14
Glaze-Poppenheim Plantation 69
Global Positioning System (GPS) 59, 69, 75
Gowerie plantation 16
GPS *see* Global Positioning System (GPS)
Grant, Oswald & Company 29
Greene, Jack P. 100
grumetoes 31
Guinea Coast: Europeans on 27–32
Gullah 84, 90, 91; language 27

Haitian revolution 46
Hampton Plantation 76–77
Hauser, Mark W. 2
Hawkins, Hugh 94n35
Hawthorne, Walter 6
Hazeley, Jacob 89, 90
heel–toe sowing methods 6, 7
Herskovits, Melville 26
Highlands languages 8, 9, **10**
"hill rice" or "dry rice" 116n18
Hill, Stephen 89
historical archaeologist 65
History of Slavery in the United States, South Carolina, Sierra Leone Kinship Campaign 92–93
"huge hydraulic machines" 15

illegal slave trade: on Rio Pongo 2, 45, 46, *47* (*see also* Rio Pongo)
India: cotton production in 104–105
Indian Ocean 2, 103–105, 108–114; interregional food networks 114
"indigenous knowledge system" 5
indigenous languages 7
inland embankments 76
inland rice field: complexity of 75; Glaze-Poppenheim Plantation 69; hydrological principle and technology 68

Inland rice production 15
intensive agricultural systems 16
inter-colonial dependencies: in Atlantic ocean 99–101, 103
interregional food networks 107, 114
interregional food trade 105, 108, 114
irrigation 15

Jackson, Jesse 27
Jones, Edward 88, 89, 94n35
Joseph, Edward 59
Joyner, Charles 78

Kanara rice 108
Kaveri delta rice 108
Kelly, Kenneth 46, 52, 54
Kelly, Kenneth G. 2
King, Boston 86–88, 90
Kizell, John 86–88, 90
Knight, Thomas 93

Laguncularia racemosa 7
Laing, Alexander Gordon 33
lalas 12
landlord–stranger relationship 45
"landscape gradient" 5
Laurens, Henry 30, 83
Lawson, John 14
Liberia 87, 94n35
Lightbourn, Elizabeth Baily Gomez 51–56
Limerick Plantation 14
linguistic evidence 7–9
Littlefield, Daniel C. 1, 5, 27, 101
Low Country state: experiences in 86

A Man from Another Land (Washington) 95
mangrove ecosystems: biological and botanical studies of 8, 9
mangrove rice-growing techniques 7, 16
Mark, Peter 51
Mboteni-speakers 8, 9
Memoire de Farenya project 46
"*-Mer*"/"salt" 7
Metcalf, Thomas 99
Middleton, Thomas 69
Mintz, Sidney W. 100
Momoh, Joseph 90, 91
Morgan, Philip 6, 101
Morrison, Kathleen 2
Mouser, Bruce 2
"Mungo Paul" 48, 51
Myrick, Matthew 70

National Register of Historic Places (NRHP) 72, 75
"Negro fields" 14
Nesbitt, Alexander 70
non-food crops 100

Nova Scotia 85–87
Nova Scotians 85, 88
NRHP *see* National Register of Historic Places (NRHP)
Nyara Beli 52–56

O. glaberrima 12
O'Gráda, Cormac 99–100, 111–112
Ormand, John 48, 59
Oryza sativa 12
Oswald, Richard 30, 83

paddy rice production 111
Peters, Thomas 87, 90
Philips, Charlie 69, 72, 75
plantation agriculture 107
Plantation Enterprise in Colonial South Carolina (Edelson) 6
Portuguese Goa 109
Portuguese traders 10–13, 19n15, 27, 46
pottery production 77–78
poudrière 53
pre-Atlantic African past 25, 35, 36n5
"Priscilla's Homecoming" 91–92
Proctor, H. B. 109, 110
Proto-Coastal language 7, 8
"The Province of Freedom" 13
The Province of Freedom 84
Pulsipher, Lydia Mihelic 14, 20n34

Raban, John Rev. 88
"recentering empire" 99
Registers of Liberated Africans 37n15
Rhizophora racemosa 8
rice 114; in Atlantic Ocean 101–104; Atlantic ocean world 102; black, brown, and white 101–104; consumption in UK 109; cultivation in Atlantic world 102; exports 108, 109, *110*, 111, 114; exports in Burma 109, *110*; in Indian Ocean 108–114; Kanara rice 108; Kaveri delta rice 108; production in South Carolina 75; production in West Indies 102; sowing techniques 6; as staple commodity 100, 102, 114
Rice and Slaves (Littlefield) 5
Rice Coast 84
rice farmers 9, 11; Upper Guinea Coast 17, 18, 19n24, 101; West African 5, 7, 12, 18
Richardson, David 6
Rio Nunez region 7–11, 45, 46
Rio Pongo Archaeological Project 46
Rio Pongo, illegal slave trade on 45, 46, *47*; Anglican Church at 54; archaeological work on 46–47; Bangalan 48–51; Farenya 52–56; Sanya Paulia 56–60

"salt"/"*-Mer" 7, **8**
Sam, Alfred 90

Sanya Paulia, archaeological resources 56–60; excavation 58; mound's construction 57, 58; pedestrian survey at 58, 59; presbytery structure 59; site complex map 57, *57*
Savannah River rice plantations 16
savonnerie 53
Sen, Amartya 111, 112
settlement patterns 25, 34; in South Carolina 15; in Upper Guinea Coast 12, 16–18
Sharp, Granville 84
Sheridan, Richard 108
shovel test in embankment 67
Sierra Leone: archaeological, ethnographic, and historical data 33, 39n72; black loyalists 86; British Crown colony 85; Bunce Island 83, 92, 93, 95n59; Bunce Island's role in 29; Christianity in 88; connection to the USA 84, 90, 92; Gullah ties to 91, 92; hinterland in Atlantic world 32–35; migration of citizens 90; Nova Scotian migration to 87; rice field in 76; slavery in 32, 33, 38n54; slave trade on 2; ties to South Carolina 83, 86, 89, 93
Sierra Leoneans: with African-Americans 83, 90; migration to the USA 84, 89–91; slave factory in 83
Sierra Leone Company 85, 87
Sierra Leone Estuary 24, 27–29, 32, 38n54
Sierra Leone Gullah Kinship Association 92
Sierra Leone Protectorate 32
Sitem-speakers 8, 9
slave settlements: in west Indies 107
slave trade 46, 47; archaeological implications of 2; economic importance of 25; on Sierra Leone 2; in South Carolina 83, 84, 87, 88; on Upper Guinea coast 2; on West African Coast 28
Sloane, Hans 107
soil: an artifact 66, 67–69
South Asia: colonialism in 116n25
South Carolina: African American archaeology in 2; African-Americans in 2, 83; "Black majority" 15; colonoware 77; commercial rice industry in 4, 5, 14–16; enslaved Africans in 75; enslaved laborers in 5; floodgates in tidal rice fields 15–16; inland rice fields 76; Inland rice production 15; Rice Coast 84; rice cultivation 64; rice growing plantation 1; slave trade in 83, 84, 87, 88; ties to Sierra Leone 83, 86, 89, 93
Stobo, James 65–66, 68, 69
Stobo Plantation 65, *66*, *67*, 69, 72
story of Priscilla 29, *31*, 32
Susu-speakers 9, **11**
swamp cultivation 15
Syracuse University AISLE 27, 28

tidal rice 15, 17, 68, 70, 75
Tomich, Dale 36n5
Treaty of Paris 30

"trunk minder" 76
Turner, Lorenzo 91
Turner, Lorenzo Dow 26, 27, 37n23

UK: rice consumption in 109
upland embankment 66, 70, 72, 74, 75
Upper Guinea coast: Africans on 2; mangrove rice farmers in 19n24; slave trade on 2
Upper Guinea Coast: enslaved Africans in 6; dry season bias 16; health effects in 16–18; historical sources 16, 17; mangrove rice farmers 12, 19n24; microenvironments 7–14; rice farmers 17, 18, 19n24, 101; rice species in 12; settlement patterns in 16–18
USA 89–93; black loyalists in 90; immigrants in 93; Sierra Leone connection to 2, 84

Walker, George Herbert 30
Walker InstituteWorkshop 26
WalkerWorkshop 2–3
Washington, Isaiah 27, 95
West Africa: embankment roots in 76; peasants in 13–14; pottery and clay architecture 77; rice production 14, 17, 18
West African: food production system 5; rice farmers 5, 7, 12, 18
West African Rice Coast region 5
West Africans 76; rice crops production 64–65
West Indies: rice production in 102; slave settlements in 107
Wilkie, Laurie A. 37n13
Wood, Peter 4, 5, 101
Woodstock Plantation 69, 72, 74

Yalunka settlements 33, 39n73
Yenia 55
"*-*Yop*" 7